FORCE OF IMAGINATION

FORCE OF IMAGINATION

The Sense of the Elemental

John Sallis

INDIANA UNIVERSITY PRESS   BLOOMINGTON AND INDIANAPOLIS

THIS BOOK IS A PUBLICATION OF

INDIANA UNIVERSITY PRESS
601 NORTH MORTON STREET
BLOOMINGTON, IN 47404-3797 USA

HTTP://WWW.INDIANA.EDU/~IUPRESS

Telephone orders   800-842-6796
Fax orders   812-855-7931
Orders by e-mail   IUPORDER@INDIANA.EDU

THE PAPER USED IN THIS PUBLICATION MEETS THE MINIMUM REQUIREMENTS OF AMERICAN NATIONAL STANDARD FOR INFORMATION SCIENCES — PERMANENCE OF PAPER FOR PRINTED LIBRARY MATERIALS, ANSI Z39.48-1984.

MANUFACTURED IN THE UNITED STATES OF AMERICA

LIBRARY OF CONGRESS CATALOGING-IN-PUBLICATION DATA
SALLIS, JOHN, DATE
FORCE OF IMAGINATION : THE SENSE OF THE ELEMENTAL / JOHN SALLIS.
P.   CM. — (STUDIES IN CONTINENTAL THOUGHT)
INCLUDES BIBLIOGRAPHICAL REFERENCES AND INDEX.
ISBN 0-253-33772-0 (CLOTH : ALK. PAPER) — ISBN 0-253-21403-3 (PBK. : ALK. PAPER)
1. IMAGINATION (PHILOSOPHY)   I. TITLE.   II. SERIES.
BH301.I53 S25 2000
128'.3 — DC21
00-027604
1   2   3   4   5   05   04   03   02   01   00

TO JERRY

AGAIN, AND ALWAYS

... das einzige, wodurch wir fähig sind,
auch das Widersprechende zu denken, und
zusammenzufassen,—die Einbildungskraft.

—F. W. J. SCHELLING, *System des transzendentalen
Idealismus*

The Imagination is not a State: it is
the Human Existence itself.

—WILLIAM BLAKE, *Milton*

In every landscape the point of astonishment
is the meeting of the sky and the earth. . . .

—RALPH WALDO EMERSON, "Nature"

CONTENTS

6. THE ELEMENTAL

7. TEMPORALITIES

8. PROPRIETIES

9. POETIC IMAGINATION

ACKNOWLEDGMENTS

It is as if this book has always been already under way, never simply begun. Even if measured from the datings of the earliest sketches, its genesis has been protracted, drawn out quite beyond what was envisaged. The book has required, in several senses—including that to which Nietzsche alludes in the Preface to *The Dawn*—slow writing.

The earliest sketches go back to a time, just after the completion of *Being and Logos,* when a fellowship from the Alexander von Humboldt-Stiftung afforded me the leisure needed for such a project to begin to take shape. A very preliminary draft was composed during a stay in Paris in the early 1980s, made possible by support from the American Council of Learned Societies. I continued developing and reshaping the project as I worked, simultaneously, on several other, more textually oriented studies (*Delimitations, Spacings, Echoes, Crossings*); these, as well as my other, later books, have left indelible traces in the present discourse. A more definitive draft of the initial chapters was composed during stays in Brussels and in Bochum, again with generous support from the Alexander von Humboldt-Stiftung. The final draft was written in Boalsburg in the years 1996–99. Very able assistance with production was provided by Nancy Fedrow and Robert Metcalf, to whom I am grateful. I am grateful also to my editor and friend Janet Rabinowitch for her generous efforts in behalf of this book.

Because of the complex genesis of this project, I have ventured only a few presentations directly related to it: my inaugural lectures at Loyola University of Chicago, Vanderbilt University, and The Pennsylvania State University, respectively; a research session at the Collegium Phaenomenologicum in 1994; and, as the book came to completion, papers entitled "Monstrous Imagination" and "The Elemental Earth," presented to the British Society for Phenomenology and the International Association for Environmental Philosophy, respectively.

It goes perhaps without saying that much of what was eventually drawn into this discourse was first sketched on singular occasions in places distinctively evocative: a deep Alpine valley, certain islands in the Aegean, the scene of a snowstorm in Pennsylvania, the sun-baked summer landscape of Umbria, the mountains around Soglio and Sils Maria, the canyons and desert of Utah, the sites of the temples at Sounion and at Agregento. On certain occasions in such places there comes an appeal that enlivens imagination and attests to the elemental.

BOALSBURG
JANUARY 2000

FORCE OF IMAGINATION

PROLUSIONS

I. ECHOING —

Imagine being there.

Imagine both sensing and sensed. Imagine them together. Enact the sensing imaginally with such force as to bring forth what would—if it were an instance of sensing and not of imagining—be sensed, what would be sensed while also, decisively, exceeding sense.

Let each sense share in what is wondrous and monstrous there. Yoking each to what would be sensed, double this double across the entire range of human sensibility. And beyond.

Imagine, then, being there, listening in silence as the swift mountain stream bursts and raves over the rocks. Imagine being there in the valley over whose pines, crags, and caverns the fast cloud-shadows and sunbeams sail. Imagine hearing the chainless winds as they come to drink the odors of the giant brood of pines and to hear the old and solemn harmony of their mighty swinging. Imagine then training one's eyes on the towering summit as it rises above what cannot but seem the scene of some ancient devastation, now strewn with unearthly forms of ice and rock. Imagine be-

1

ing there where its lofty peak commands every view, opening one's vision to its remoteness and serenity, feeling the intensity of the sun's rays and at the same time the coolness of the mountain air, sensing with—and beyond—all one's senses the elemental conflict between fire and ice that rages there on high.

One could, then, perhaps also imagine having heard the song before hearing it sung to the words to which the poet set it. It is a song of the mountains, a song that celebrates what the primaeval mountains announce, their teaching.

The song was written in the valley of Chamonix in 1816. Shelley gave it the name of the mountain of which it sings: *Mont Blanc.*[1] Yet the poet's design is not just to sing of the mountain but to let the song of the mountain itself and of all that is gathered around it sound forth in the poetic song. The poet would echo a wild sound, like that of the roaring stream, itself echoing in the caverns of the ravine—

A loud, lone sound no other sound can tame[.]

(l. 20)

---

1. In *The Complete Poetical Works of Percy Bysshe Shelley,* ed. Neville Rogers (Oxford: Oxford University Press, 1975), 2:75–80. In the citation of lines 80–83, 94–100, 139–41, Shelley's original punctuation has been restored.

The poem *Mont Blanc,* dated 23 July 1816, is supplemented by Shelley's second letter to Peacock, in which he gives a diary account (with entries dated 22, 24, 25, and 28 July) of his trip to Chamonix, of what he observed there, and of his extraordinary response. For example, in the entry of 22 July, "I never knew—I never imagined—what mountains were before. The immensity of these aerial summits excited, when they suddenly burst upon the sight, a sentiment of ecstatic wonder, not unallied to madness. And remember this was all one scene; it all pressed home to our regard and our imagination.... Nature was the poet, whose harmony held our spirits more breathless than that of the divinest.... We were travelling along the valley [of Chamonix], when suddenly we heard a sound as of the burst of smothered thunder rolling above; yet there was something in the sound, that told us it could not be thunder. Our guide hastily pointed out to us a part of the mountain opposite, from whence the sound came. It was an avalanche. We saw the smoke of its path among the rocks, and continued to hear at intervals the bursting of its fall.... There is more in all these scenes than mere magnitude of proportion: there is a majesty of outline; there is an awful grace in the very colours which invest these wonderful shapes—a charm which is peculiar to them, quite distinct even from the reality of their unutterable greatness." In the entry of 24 July: "The verge of a glacier, like that of Bossons, presents the most vivid image of desolation that it is possible to conceive. No one dares to approach it; for the enormous pinnacles of ice which perpetually fall, are perpetually reproduced." In the entry of 25 July: "We have returned from visiting the glacier of Montanvert, or as it is called, the Sea of Ice, a scene in truth of dizzying wonder.... The summits are sharp and naked pinnacles, whose overhanging steepness will not even permit snow to rest upon them. Lines of dazzling ice occupy here and there their perpendicular rifts, and shine through the driving vapours with inexpressible brilliance: they pierce the clouds like things not belonging to this earth" (*Essays, Letters from Abroad, Translations and Fragments,* ed. Mrs. Shelley [London: Edward Moxon, 1852], 2:62–75).

Attentive, yet

> . . . as in a trance sublime and strange[,]
>
> (l. 35)

letting be called into play his

> . . . own separate fantasy,
>
> (l. 36)

the poet would put into song what arises from the darkness of the ravine:

> One legion of wild thoughts, whose wandering wings
> Now float above thy darkness, and now rest
> Where that or thou art no unbidden guest,
> In the still cave of the witch Poesy—
>
> (ll. 41–44)

The poet offers his song as an echo of what he has heard sung in the mysterious tongue of the mountain wilderness. For, indeed,

> The wilderness has a mysterious tongue[.]
>
> (l. 76)

The mountain has its voice, though not all have ears with which to hear it:

> Thou hast a voice, great Mountain, to repeal
> Large codes of fraud and woe; not understood
> By all, but which the wise, and great, and good
> Interpret, or make felt, or deeply feel.
>
> (ll. 80–83)

Of what does the mountain sing? It sings of all living things and of itself. Echoed in the poem, its song proclaims:

> All things that move and breathe with toil and sound
> Are born and die; revolve, subside, and swell.
> Power dwells apart in its tranquillity,
> Remote, serene, and inaccessible:
> And *this*, the naked countenance of earth,
> On which I gaze, even these primaeval mountains
> Teach the adverting mind.
>
> (ll. 94–100)

The song of the mountain conveys a teaching. It is a teaching concerning the power of the earth, the secret strength of things, and the force of imagination.

3

When the silent and solitary earth displays its naked countenance towering into the heaven,

> Far, far above, piercing the infinite sky,

> (l. 60)

the silence is in a sense—to a certain kind of sense—broken and the solitude breached. Then the earth's remoteness and power become all the more manifest, displayed precisely there in the towering peak. The power is not just that supposed once to have lifted earth itself into the heaven, once long ago, in a past so remote that, if one asks about it,

> None can reply—all seems eternal now.

> (l. 75)

There is no more than a hint of the ancient power, a mere trace of it borne by the countenance displayed there above:

> Mont Blanc yet gleams on high:—the power is there,
> The still and solemn power of many sights,
> And many sounds, and much of life and death.

> (ll. 127–29)

Its power is held in reserve, not as if it were merely potential, but in the sense of remaining withheld from view, remote from those who, nestled in the valley below, gaze up at the lofty peak. The power there above goes unseen; it is withdrawn from all the senses and, while indeed attested, yields only to imagination. The power is there, the power of sights unseen and sounds unheard, the power of driving snow, of howling winds, of deafening thunder and the blinding flash of lightning, all withdrawn there above where none can behold them. Yet while

> . . . none beholds them there,

> (l. 132)

all who gaze upon the lofty peak will be drawn to imagine the sights and sounds that go unseen and unheard there.

Resounding in song, the poet directs his words back to the mountain:

> The secret Strength of things
> . . . , inhabits thee!

> (ll. 139, 141)

Its power is a strength reserved, held in secret, withheld from view, *in its very display of its countenance.* Yet such power, more manifest than ever in the towering peak, is the secret strength that belongs to all things, their power to keep themselves in reserve, unseen, in their very display of their countenance. It is this secret strength that allows them to remain always withdrawn to some extent from the gift of heaven, that lets them be sheltered from its excess of light, that articulates their very coming to light. If thought would attentively follow things as they come to light, it must be governed by this articulation, by the secret strength of things:

> The secret Strength of things
> Which governs thought, and to the infinite dome
> Of Heaven is as a law, inhabits thee!

(ll. 139–41)

It is of this secret strength that mountain and earth, stars and sea, the most elemental things of nature, sing. Yet the secret is told only to imagination, capable, as it is, of celebrating what goes nonetheless unseen and unheard. Indeed the secret will always have been entrusted to those imaginings that can fill with song even those things that, like earth itself, remain silent and solitary. Thus the poem concludes:

> And what were thou, and earth, and stars, and sea,
> If to the human mind's imaginings
> Silence and solitude were vacancy?

(ll. 142–44)

II. BEING THERE —

Things come to pass.
All and each.
The ancient temple of Zeus as well as its very stones, more ancient still, yet worn away by the unabated persistence of the elements, crumbling away into grains of sand. The deer in the forest as well as the trace of a scent so slight as to be noticed only by such a creature. Humans living distractedly in the city they have built, secure up to the moment when even the earth begins to tremble or the approaching storm threatens with winds that can carry everything away and with lightning that, in the instant of its monstrous flash, can reduce to ashes any thing that earth and the other gifts of heaven have raised and ennobled.
Things come to pass.
They come into the light of day. They come into the open, receiving in their exposure not only the gift of light but all else given from above. Endowed with these gifts, receptive of them, things prosper and flourish.
As when, after the gladdening rains have come, the trees of the grove glisten in the sunlight.
As when, seeing something for the first time, a young child is touched by wonder.

And yet, exposed to the elements, things are allotted their time. They pass finally back into darkness, not a darkness like that of the nocturnal sky but another kind, a darkness that holds no promise of light, a night that portends no coming of day. Then things are relieved of themselves, and their mere remains return to the earth, to its closure.

As when, struck down by the violence of a long-forgotten storm, the trunk of a great oak lies on the forest floor, still sheltering and nourishing other living things while itself being slowly reclaimed by the earth.

As when, amidst the grief of those who live on, the earthly remains of a loved one are interred.

Thus things come to pass.

In thus coming to pass, things can become manifest. Being there in the interval between coming and passing, being there as such, things are offered to sense. They offer themselves to sense, not by means of some action but in an offering that is occurrent by their very being there—so thoroughly so as to preclude sequential ordering and to put in suspension the otherwise ready assumption that things first come to pass and then offer themselves in a manifestation. Their very entry into openness and light exposes them to the possibility of showing themselves to one capable of vision. Yet, precisely by virtue of being there where things come to pass, a thing never shows itself alone. Neither does anything ever show itself fully, exhaustively—such is the secret strength of things, that they hold themselves back. Whatever becomes manifest shines forth from within its surroundings and, in offering itself to vision, holds itself in reserve. Its surroundings and its allusion to its virtual aspects are, in turn, set within an expanse delimited in its outer reach by the elements and finally by what is most elemental, earth and sky.

As when, toward evening, one glances across the valley and discerns the trees of the grove standing out, not without reserve, against the distant mountain, which in turn is silhouetted against the darkening sky.

Yet the capacity for vision of things (most generally, sensibility as such) does not suffice to guarantee their self-showing. The one to whom something can come to be shown must be capable not merely of directing vision to the expanse in which the thing comes to pass but also of gathering around it the various moments and elements that pertain to its self-showing, setting it, as it were, within its surroundings, granting it its place in the open expanse between earth and sky. It is attested that we ourselves have this double capacity, that we are ourselves such a one as can sustain the self-showing of things. Not that such a one can force things to show themselves. Nor that such a one can justly shift the site of manifestation into itself, appropriating the event in such a way that it would be set within, the very conditions of its possibility being determined by its interior locus. Rather, it is only that such a one, presented with the image, can gather around that image all that belongs to the thing's self-showing.

As when, letting one's gaze come to rest on the trees of the grove glistening in the sunlight, they stand out against mountain and sky while silently alluding to all the other views that one could imagine them offering to vision.

Self-showing requires that one be there where the requisite moments and elements are to be gathered, that one come to let them be gathered. Yet the gathering is neither the production of a unified presence nor the result of an action one would in some capacity perform. Rather, coming about by force of imagination, this gathering preconditions all production, dislocates all presence, and founds the very possibility of action. If one is engaged with the image and takes up toward the elemental a bearing that draws the elements around the expanse of things, then force of imagination can bring about the spacing of this expanse: it is there that things show themselves.

III. SPIRALING —

There is no saying in advance how manifestation is to be enticed to double back upon itself in such a way that the constitution of its expanse can be analyzed. No organon prescribes the traces—not even the *kind* of traces—in which an enticing glimpse of that doubling would be offered. And though, in the case of imagination, the doubling back upon itself may be more apparent, its initial appearance serves for the most part only to set in relief the obliqueness of imagination with respect to the axes of the classical philosophical schema. For one could not venture simply to understand imagination, to form a concept of it, without the risk—or at least the suspicion—that in submitting it to understanding rather than to itself one would do violence to it. One might, then, keep imagination at a distance from the concept and resolve to develop its intrinsic capacity to double back upon itself, venturing to imagine imagination by forming an image of it, even if not without a certain circulation through language. Thus in Bachelard's texts one finds various highly enticing traces of such circulations—for example:

> Imagination is a tree. It has the integrating virtues of a tree. It is roots and branches. It lives between earth and sky. It lives in the earth and in the wind.[2]

And yet, beyond enticement, beyond provocation, it cannot remain a matter simply of siding with the image rather than the concept; for the classical schema will continue to operate with an inexorability that will require one again and again to revalorize the image and that will reduce the circulation through language to an incoherent move—a move toward the concept—

2. Gaston Bachelard, *La Terre et les Rêveries du Repos* (Paris: Librairie José Corti, 1948), 300.

that tacitly confirms precisely what the revalorization of the image would deny.

There is also no saying in advance how disruptive the deconstruction of the classical schema will prove to be. But if this operation is to be sustained beyond mere redefinition and inversion, if it is to reopen the expanse of manifestation beyond the obstructions generated in the wake of the classical schema, then the demand for rigorous determination cannot be evaded; neither can it be dissolved into mere insistence on the image. It is precisely this requirement that makes phenomenology indispensable, even if phenomenology cannot itself remain untouched by the disruption released by the deconstruction of the classical schema, even if in that wake phenomenology cannot but undergo mutation. For the very sense of rigor prescribes that rigorous determination of the expanse proceed from manifestation itself, from the way in which things themselves show themselves; and even if there should prove to be a self-withholding intrinsically operative in manifestation, it could be marked as such only by adherence to the self-showing of things. But, above all, it would be a matter of pairing the oblique counterforce of imagination (which philosophy has never succeeded in stabilizing and domesticating)[3] with the deconstruction of the classical schema and of letting this double force induce a rigorous redetermination of imagination.

Yet heretofore the phenomenology of imagination has given only the slightest intimation of the destabilizing counterforce of imagination and indeed has done so almost inadvertently, by way of certain aporias that are hardly even addressed as such. For the most part and certainly in its primary intent, the phenomenology of imagination has been confining and, in some respects and some instances, reductive. Specifically, it has undertaken to realign and stabilize imagination by submitting it to the basic schema of intentionality. What is decisive in this regard is the expulsion of the image from consciousness. Such an expulsion is required, most unambiguously, in the case of perception: from the *Logical Investigations* on, Husserl never ceased to stress that in perception there is no image within that would serve to represent a thing outside. Perception is thus irreducible to consciousness of an internal image; on the contrary, as Husserl attempts to demonstrate, the consciousness of an image presupposes perception and therefore cannot itself provide the basis for perception.[4] Yet even in the case of imagining, the schema of intentionality remains intact: when one imagines something, what one intends is that thing itself.

Sartre is even more unequivocal regarding the fundamental error that

---

3. See *Delimitations: Phenomenology and the End of Metaphysics,* 2nd ed. (Bloomington: Indiana University Press, 1995), chap. 1.

4. See especially Edmund Husserl, *Logische Untersuchungen* (Tübingen: Max Niemeyer, 1968), II/1:421–24.

8

phenomenology is to correct by aligning all modes of consciousness with the schema of intentionality. The error, he says, lay in supposing that the image was *in* consciousness and that as such it was a likeness of the things outside that were to be represented either perceptually or imaginally by means of the image. Sartre draws an image of this erroneously conceived consciousness of images: "We pictured consciousness as a place peopled with small likenesses [*simulacres*] and these likenesses were the images."[5] Sartre is convinced that the source of the error lies in the habit of thinking in space and in terms of space. Yet Sartre's assertion that when one perceives or imagines a particular object it remains *outside* consciousness merely reverses what it opposes without breaking at all with the alleged source of error: for this assertion is itself no less determined by a thinking in space and in terms of space. One wonders: in order to conceive properly the consciousness of images, is it required that one think without reference to space, or is it not perhaps that one needs to think more rigorously the spacing of the image?

In any case imagining would be, like perception, a way in which consciousness relates to an object. If a sense is still to be given to *image*, the word can signify nothing but this mode of relation, and one would need to say, with Sartre, that "an image is nothing else than a relationship."[6] But there would be less likelihood of reverting to the erroneous conception if one simply dispensed with the word *image*, or rather, reserved it for that particular type of imaginal consciousness in which, as with a photograph, a perceptual object functions as an image of something else that one intends through the image. Such a mode could be properly termed consciousness of an image. It is as such (as *Bildbewusstsein*) that Husserl distinguishes this type of imaginal consciousness from *Phantasie*, in which there is no perceptual object functioning as an image or analogue through which one intends something else. Thus Husserl, as well as Sartre, distinguishes two basic types of imaginal consciousness: image-consciousness, in which a perceived object is intended as an image of something else (as with a photograph of a person), and phantasy, in which one imagines an object directly, without anything perceptual serving as support for the imaginal intention.[7]

---

5. Jean-Paul Sartre, *L'Imaginaire* (Paris: Gallimard, 1940), 15.

6. Ibid., 20. In his earlier book on imagination, Sartre draws the same conclusion: "There are not, and never could be, images *in* consciousness. Rather, an image *is a certain type of consciousness*. An image is an act and not a thing. An image is a consciousness *of* something" (*L'Imagination* [Paris: Presses Universitaires de France, 1936], 162).

7. In his initial analyses Husserl regards the structure of phantasy as twofold, in distinction from the threefold structure of image-consciousness. Whereas the latter involves (1) a perceived object intended (2) as image (3) of something, phantasy lacks the first moment, the perceptual thing, involving only (1) a mental image and (2) that which is imaged by (intended through) it. However, as Husserl develops his analyses, he comes more and more to call into question the alleged mental image in phantasy (see *Phantasie, Bildbewusstsein, Erinnerung: Zur Phänomenologie der Anschaulichen Vergegenwärtigungen*, Husserliana 23, ed. Eduard Marbach

9

Sartre stresses the poverty of the image, that is, of the object as imagined in phantasy. Whereas the perceived object constantly overflows one's consciousness of it, the imagined object is, according to Sartre, "never anything more than the consciousness one has of it." He says even that "the world of images is a world where nothing *happens*."[8] While one may well agree that the *flesh* of the object, as Sartre calls it, is not the same in something imagined as in something perceived, is it certain that what is imagined can have no recoil whatsoever on the imaginal consciousness, that there is no secret strength of things imagined? Is it manifest that, as Sartre concludes, the only depth of the imagined object is the ambiguity corresponding to its meagerness, to its "*essential poverty*"?[9] Is it manifest that imagination offers nothing, that in and through imagining nothing can come to be revealed beyond what was already explicit in and to the imaginal consciousness? Or is one not rather more inclined by manifest experience to grant a disclosive power to imagination? Does imagination inevitably fall short of the secret strength of things, touching only their surface and never apprehending them in the flesh in the way that perception seems to do? Or is it rather only to imagination that the secret strength of things is disclosed?

The reductive consequences of such impoverishment of imagination become unmistakable in Casey's phenomenology of imagining, amplified precisely as a result of the concreteness and precision of the analyses. In these analyses the impoverishment of imagination appears in what Casey calls the irrevocable frontal character of the imagined; as imagined, the object is given all at once and thus completely without reserve, without any concealed aspects that might be disclosed in a subsequent recoil upon the imagining consciousness.[10] Thus, imagining things will never reveal anything whatsoever about those things, about the truth of those things. Instead, Casey links imagining to possibility, to the entertaining of pure possibilities that are posited and contemplated for their own sake. It is this route that leads, then, to the reductive conception finally proposed: "In this respect, imagining may be regarded as a special form of *self-entertainment* in which the imaginer amuses himself with what he conjures and contem-

---

[The Hague: Martinus Nijhoff, 1980], 16–30, 55, 150, 276; I have discussed these analyses and their development in *Double Truth* [Albany: State University of New York Press, 1995], chap. 7). Sartre, too, refers to a mental image that functions in imaginal consciousness in the absence of any analogue such as a portrait, caricature, etc. But he refers to the "great difficulty" involved here: it lies in the fact that reflection reveals nothing about such a mental image, that, even though it is necessary to assume that there is such a mental image functioning as an analogue—analogously to the analogue of image-consciousness—one cannot gain reflective or introspective access to it, and so, with regard to its nature and components, one is reduced to conjectures (*L'Imaginaire,* 110f.).

8. *L'Imaginaire,* 25f.

9. Ibid., 255.

10. Edward S. Casey, *Imagining: A Phenomenological Study* (Bloomington: Indiana University Press, 1976), 91f.

plates by and for himself alone. . . . *Imagining is entertaining oneself with what is purely possible.*"[11]

Thus is imagining reduced to self-entertainment, to conjuring up pure possibilities. As if possibilities and the bringing forth of the possible had no bearing on truth. As if in the formula—entertaining oneself with what is purely possible—every word did not begin to slide away into an abyss of questions from the moment a more expansive and differentiating discourse is put in play and opened to the enormous legacy philosophy has bequeathed concerning the extent of imagination and attesting to its force.

Even without yet venturing such a discourse, it is possible to circumscribe three areas in the phenomenology of imagination that remain highly exposed to critique, to expose three connections that reflect unmistakably the confining tendency, connections that a freer analysis will break for the sake of release into a more differentiated, if less stable, field.

The first connection, that of the image to essential poverty, is the other side of a nonconnection, that of imagination to disclosure and truth. What is at issue in this connection and nonconnection is the disclosive force of imagination; it is a question of whether the imagined is no more than a flat surface incapable of reflecting anything not already explicit to the imagining consciousness or whether through imagining, through engagement with the imagined, something other can come to light, whether, from the play of the imagined, something can be disclosed that would otherwise have escaped consciousness, something that in a sense will have escaped consciousness by coming from elsewhere, by arising otherwise than through the explicit intention operative in the imagining.

In Sartre's analysis there is virtually no trace of any such force of imagination. Imagined objects he compares to mere silhouettes; void of any unseen depth, they are incapable of offering anything that could surprise the imaginer. There is nothing compelling about the imagined: "The imagined object [*l'objet en image*] is an unreality. . . . But then none of these objects call upon me to act, to do something. They are neither weighty, insistent, nor compelling: they are pure passivity, they wait. The faint breath of life we breathe into them comes from us, from our spontaneity."[12] Although Sartre grants that the imagined object can appear "with a certain coefficient of generality,"[13] such appearance grants no insight into what something truly is in general; the generality of the imaginal is nothing but its impoverishment, its lack of determination, its mere abstractness. From such a quasi-object nothing is disclosed, nothing is to be learned.

Casey is no less insistent on the poverty of the imagined. His analysis is intent on showing that the imagined object is mere surface, that it lacks

---

11. Ibid., 119.
12. Sartre, *L'Imaginaire*, 240.
13. Ibid., 178.

both the exterior depth that perceptual objects have by being positioned in a spatial field at a determinate distance from the observer and the interior depth that gives perceptual objects their palpability and plenitude.[14] On the other hand, Casey does note, referring to Husserl, that imagination figures constitutively in phenomenological method itself, especially in the method of free variation. To this extent the phenomenology of imagination cannot but bring imagination to bear on imagination: "we must *use* imagination in order to give an adequate descriptive account of imagination."[15]

Husserl, too, insists on the distinction: in perception the object itself appears, whereas in imagination it appears merely in an image. Yet, in the analyses developed in the *Logical Investigations,* he avoids overly impoverishing the imagined, granting, instead, extensive parallels between the imagined and the perceived. Thus he does not take the imagined to be merely frontal: "To the synthesis of manifold perceptions, in which the same object always presents itself, there corresponds the parallel synthesis of manifold imaginations in which the same object appears *imaginally* [*zur bildlichen Darstellung kommt*]."[16] In the more detailed analyses in the manuscripts collected in *Phantasie, Bildbewusstsein, Erinnerung,* lack of depth and of concrete determinateness does not figure at all in Husserl's way of contrasting the imaginary with the perceptual. The difference is constituted, rather, by a certain global modification: in phantasy everything remains as in the corresponding perception, except that "everything is modified into the *quasi,* i.e., the imaginary."[17] Even in much later texts Husserl does not hesitate to refer in this regard to the quasi-time of the imaginary ("*What is imagined in phantasy* [das Phantasierte] *is always* something *temporal . . . ,* but its time is a *quasi-time*"); neither does he hesitate to say that "in all phantasies . . . there is constituted a single quasi-world."[18]

Yet even more decisive is the way Husserl comes in *Ideas I* to focus on imagination, not just as a theme of phenomenology, but as empowering

---

14. Casey, *Imagining,* 92. In this regard Casey cites Merleau-Ponty: "The imaginary has no depth; it does not respond to our efforts to vary our point of view [upon it]." Merleau-Ponty's text adds: "it does not lend itself to our observation." At that point there is a note referring to Sartre's *L'Imaginaire* (*Phénoménologie de la Perception* [Paris: Gallimard, 1945], 374).

In general Merleau-Ponty is himself remarkably reticent about imagination. Yet in the discussion following his presentation of the text "The Primacy of Perception and Its Philosophical Consequences," in resisting those who would construe this primacy as confinement to the perceptual, Merleau-Ponty remarks that man does not live only in the realm of the real, that "we also live in the imaginary." He adds: "The same creative capacity which is at work in imagination . . . is present, in germ, in the first human perception (and I have obviously been incomplete on this point)" (*The Primacy of Perception,* ed. James M. Edie [Evanston: Northwestern University Press, 1964], 40).

15. Casey, *Imagining,* 225.

16. Husserl, *Logische Untersuchungen,* II/2:58.

17. Husserl, *Phantasie, Bildbewusstsein, Erinnerung,* 214.

18. Husserl, *Erfahrung und Urteil: Untersuchungen zur Genealogie der Logik,* ed. Ludwig Landgrebe (Hamburg: Claassen Verlag, 1964), 196, 200.

phenomenological analysis as such, whatever the theme. Husserl does not conceal how paradoxical it must seem for phenomenology, enjoined to return to the things themselves, to employ phantasy and its fictions. Yet, however paradoxical it may seem, one can, according to Husserl, "say in strict truth, if one well understands the ambiguous sense, that *'fiction' constitutes the vital element of phenomenology as of all eidetic science,* that fiction is the source from which the knowledge of 'eternal truths' draws its sustenance."[19] In effect, Husserl poses—yet without quite posing—the double genitive that sets the designation *phenomenology of imagination* turning upon itself, that sets imagination turning back upon itself in a way that is more rigorously mediated than that which merely appeals to images. And yet, it is precisely this turn that Husserl seems never really to have ventured. The question, it seems, remained unasked: how, in view of the analysis of imagination, can imagination function with such force at the very center of phenomenological analysis (for instance, in the use of free variation)? One can only wonder whether, if Husserl had confronted this question, he would not have been led to call into question the secondariness that, despite the parallels, he always took imagination to have over against the primacy of perception.

This is, then, the second of the three connections, that between imagination and perception. For Sartre this connection is one of complete mutual exclusion. Imagination and perception he takes to constitute "the two main irreducible attitudes of consciousness," and from this he takes it to follow that "they exclude each other."[20] The inception of imagining is the annihilation of perception, and conversely.

Though also stressing the discontinuity between imagination and perception, Casey loosens the exclusivity, grants a certain secondary, nonessential overlap. Specifically, he allows that imagining can sometimes supplement perception: for instance, as one is looking at an object from the front, one can also imagine what its unseen sides look like by summoning up a series of imaginative presentations of those sides hidden from one's frontal view. In this case imagining would thus serve to fill out what in perception alone would remain a series of empty intentions. Although Casey acknowledges that it is tempting to install imagining within perception in a more constitutive, and not merely supplementary, mode, assigning to imagination the function of adumbrating the unseen aspects or at least of effecting their concordance with the seen, he refuses this move for the allegedly simple reason that one must make an effort to summon up imaginative presentations, whereas the unseen aspects of a perceptual object are intended without any explicit effort being required.[21] And yet, that certain

---

19. Husserl, *Ideen zu einer reinen Phänomenologie und phänomenologischen Philosophie,* Erstes Buch, Husserliana 3, ed. Walter Biemel (The Hague: Martinus Nijhoff, 1950), 163. See my analysis in *Double Truth,* 124–35.

20. Sartre, *L'Imaginaire,* 231.

21. Casey, *Imagining,* 138f.

imaginative presentations require effort by no means excludes the possibility that at another level imagining may already have been effective spontaneously in adumbrating the unseen aspects or in setting them in concordance with the seen, especially considering the stress that, in another phase of his analysis, Casey puts on the possibility of spontaneous imagining, one characteristic of which he takes to be effortlessness.[22]

But all these analyses merely circle around and reaffirm the connection that Husserl puts into effect from the *Logical Investigations* on: though imagination may supplement perception in various ways, and though, in a certain global or structural sense, it arises through modification of the perceptual attitude, imagination is nonetheless fundamentally distinct from and inferior to perception. Whereas phantasy, for instance, renders somehow present (in Husserl's terms: quasi-present) something that is not present, perception presents the thing itself in its bodily presence (*leibhafter Gegenwart*).[23] Husserl fixes this distinction as that between *Vergegenwärtigung* and *Gegenwärtigung*. He terms it "the fundamental distinction," indeed "an ultimate and felt distinction."[24] Yet it is less than evident how the status of the distinction as most fundamental, as ultimate, could be certified by feeling, by its being felt. One cannot but wonder whether this curious—indeed, for Husserl, anomalous—appeal to feeling serves only to leave undisturbed— that is, unquestioned—the continued operation of the distinction and the subordination of imagination it effects. Insulating perception from the encroachment of imagination, protecting the bodily presence of the perceived from imaginal contamination, this distinction remains axiomatic in the phenomenology of imagination; in the very opening of the field it is already assumed.

This axiomatic distinction points to the third of the problematic connections. For what it seems necessary to exclude from playing any essential, constitutive role in perception is imagining, and this amounts to an exclusion of imagination as such only on the assumption that imagination deploys its force solely in and as imagining. To imagine, whether in the form of phantasy or of image-consciousness, is to apprehend an image in such a way as to intend something in or through the image. In the case of phantasy the image will be brought forth by consciousness, whether spontaneously or otherwise, whereas in the case of image-consciousness the image will be pregiven perceptually, borne by a perceptual object. The question is whether imagination can deploy its force only in these ways, only in apprehension in or through an image. Is it certain that imagination—that what has been called by the diverse names that we gather in *imagination*—comes about only as imagining, only in the specific comportment to images that

---

22. Ibid., 67–69.
23. Husserl, *Ideen I*, 99.
24. Husserl, *Phantasie, Bildbewusstsein, Erinnerung*, 106.

this name designates and that the phenomenology of imagination—or rather, of imagining—takes as the exclusive theme of its analyses? Is it certain even that imagining is the primary mode in which the force of imagination is deployed, that it is the most anterior operation? What if there were a more anterior operation of imagination, an operation quite other than imagining, and what if this more anterior operation were constitutive even for perception? If such a deployment of the force of imagination should prove already in effect in the very event in which things come to show themselves, then perhaps one could begin to understand how, at another level, imagination could issue in a disclosure pertinent to things themselves.

As a scene depicted in a painting or pictured as one reads a novel can be disclosive of things themselves.

IV. REPEATING HERE AFTER —

A methodological reason is sometimes cited in defense of the reduction of imagination to imagining: bound by the demand for evidence, phenomenology is obliged to analyze experiences or acts rather than powers or faculties.[25] Yet this reason is binding only if one assumes a concept of the subject by which terms such as *imagination* would name a nonmanifest power that somehow produces a specific type of manifest act such as imagining. From the moment such a concept of subject—to say nothing of *the* concept of subject as such—is called into question, the alleged reason for the reduction disappears.

Yet the reduction of imagination is not only a matter of phenomenological theory and the rigor it demands. On the contrary, one might well suppose that the theoretical concept of imagination as no more than the self-entertainment of conjuring up images of the purely possible only translates into a more disciplined and quasi-descriptive form the guise in which imagination most commonly appears today. The theoretical concept would, then, merely inscribe a seeming; it would say how imagination seems today and how we, submitted to this seeming, take it to be. In this guise imagination not only is reduced to the mere entertaining of images for their own sake, but also precisely thereby—because these images have lost all bearing on things themselves—it undergoes such extreme contraction that it is no longer thought capable even of opening onto the space of decision. Decisions come ever more to be based, not on what would once have been called imaginative foresight, but merely on calculation and prediction. It becomes inconceivable that imagination could sustain any essential relation to the future, and foresight is accordingly reduced to little more than extrapolation from the present. Yet from the present and its extrapolation one can perhaps never experience the absolute resourcefulness and the

25. Ibid., 3; Casey, *Imagining*, 3.

absolute danger of the future, the absolute resourcefulness and danger that one could be tempted to identify precisely as the future. The very relation of imagination to time comes to border on the inconceivable.

And yet, the guise in which imagination appears today is not merely an incipient concept that philosophical theory would then fully articulate. For this guise involves not only a representation of imagination (as reduced to imagining) but also an extreme, if virtually empty, valorization. Each moment, representation and valorization, can momentarily disguise or expel the other. Thus, the guise in which imagination appears today is such as to harbor an inner dynamism by which each moment turns repeatedly yet indecisively into a disguise of the other. The intrinsic instability of this guise has nowhere been so provocatively and compactly formulated as in a short piece by Beckett called "Imagination Dead Imagine," indeed in its very opening: "No trace anywhere of life, you say, pah, no difficulty there, imagination not dead yet, yes, dead, good, imagination dead imagine."[26] One can also read the piece itself, beyond this opening, as inscriptively enacting the very destabilizing said in the opening.

The valorization, virtually empty yet practically effective, keeps in play a trace, a mere trace, of a legacy, in place of that legacy. One will say that the legacy is that of Romanticism, perhaps even, for Anglophones, English Romanticism. Yet if ever there was an era, the thought and poetry of an era, that utterly resisted generalizations and syntheses, it is precisely this epoch of almost unprecedented inceptiveness and intensity. This is perhaps why the legacy has proved so elusive and, as regards imagination in particular, endures as little more than the empty trace of valorization. If one would begin to recover the legacy, one needs to suspend the all-too-well-known generalizations about so-called Romanticism and set about rereading, slowly and carefully, these almost singular texts, exercising the patience required in order to let their provocative force come into play.

For instance, the letter that Keats wrote to his friend Benjamin Bailey on 22 November 1817.[27] In the letter Keats writes of "the authenticity of the Imagination" and of "the truth of Imagination." His intent is not simply to state a truth—or even the truth—about imagination but rather to say how there belongs to imagination a comportment—indeed a privileged comportment—to truth as such. To say what is decisive in this comportment to truth, he requires less than a single sentence: "What the imagination seizes as Beauty must be truth—whether it existed before or not—." Here the intrinsic connection between imagination and beauty needs to be kept in mind: it is not as though, along with various other comportments, imagination sometimes comports itself to beauty. Rather imagination is as such en-

---

26. Samuel Beckett, *Collected Shorter Prose 1945–1980* (London: John Calder, 1986), 145.

27. *The Letters of John Keats 1814–1821,* ed. Hyder Edward Rollins (Cambridge, Mass.: Harvard University Press, 1958), 1:183–87.

gaged in comportment to beauty, and, in whatever it relates to, it is always directed to beauty. Beauty is what, in Keats' word, imagination *seizes*. This seizing can take two forms: imagination may apprehend the beauty of things that are, or it may envisage the beauty of those that are to be but are not yet. In Keats' saying of the truth of imagination everything depends on this twofoldness, on its peculiar configuration.

The connection to which Keats' saying is addressed is not, however, that between imagination and beauty, which, rather, is assumed by the saying. The connection addressed is that of imagination's seizing of beauty, on the one hand, to truth, on the other—that is, to the establishing of truth. Keats' saying declares that imagination's seizing of beauty is an establishing of truth: "What the imagination seizes as Beauty must be truth—."

There are resources on which one could draw (the critical philosophy, for instance) in order to interpret Keats' saying, in order to elaborate the specific sense in which beauty and truth are to be understood here and in order thereby to determine specifically how Keats comes around to declaring this sameness, which philosophy has both repeatedly posited and yet seldom ceased to contest. One could also put the letter to Bailey aside and turn at this point to the celebrated poem that the letter appears to prefigure, focusing then on the final lines of *Ode on a Grecian Urn*:

> When old age shall this generation waste,
> Thou shalt remain, in midst of other woe
> Than ours, a friend to man, to whom thou say'st,
> "Beauty is truth, truth beauty,"—that is all
> Ye know on earth, and all ye need to know.[28]

> (ll. 46–50)

And yet, if one yielded to either of these ventures, one would have missed precisely what is most decisive in the saying that Keats undertakes in the letter. Indeed one would have missed the most forceful indication of something so singular in Keats' saying of the truth of imagination that it will undermine every effort to integrate what Keats says into some alleged general Romantic view of imagination.

The relevant indication lies, not in Keats' declaration that imagination's seizing of beauty is an establishing of truth, but in what he immediately adds: "What the Imagination seizes as Beauty must be truth—*whether it existed before or not*" (emphasis added). Presumably one is to conclude that there are two connections in which the establishing of truth can occur: the truth may have existed before the establishing, in which case the establishing would consist in recalling it, remembering it; or the truth may not have existed before the establishing, in which case the establishing would consist

---

28. John Keats, *Complete Poems*, ed. Jack Stillinger (Cambridge, Mass.: Harvard University Press, 1982), 282–83.

in bringing it about, instituting it for the first time, originating the truth or, in Keats' idiom, creating it.

And yet, to come to the most decisive point, these are not two different ways, not two distinct connections, in which the establishing of truth occurs. Rather, they are two moments that belong to every such establishing of truth, two moments that, within the establishing of truth, belong together in their opposition. In imagination's seizing of beauty, truth is established by being both originarily brought about and remembered. Truth is established by being both created and repeated. The establishment of truth is, at once, both originary and memorial.

Everything depends on thinking this paradoxical togetherness, or rather, in Keats' idiom, on seizing it in such a way that it might be established as the very truth of truth. It is precisely to this end that, in the letter to Bailey, Keats proposes a comparison with Adam's dream: "The Imagination may be compared to Adam's dream—he awoke and found it truth." The reference is to the creation of Eve as presented in Book 8 of *Paradise Lost*.[29] Having promised to bring

> Thy likeness, thy fit help, thy other self,
>
> (l. 450)

God brings sleep to fall on Adam, to close his eyes:

> Mine eyes he closed, but open left the cell
> Of fancy my internal sight, by which
> Abstract as in a trance methought I saw,
> Though sleeping, where I lay, and saw the shape
> Still glorious before whom awake I stood, . . .
>
> (ll. 460–64)

Once Eve has been formed, Adam wakes to

> . . . behold her, not far off,
> Such as I saw her in my dream, . . .
>
> (ll. 481–82)

On the one hand, the creation of Eve occurs and is beheld in a dream; it comes about in fancy, in internal sight, to a sight to which nothing external is presented, so that what is presented, even if as if external, can only have been brought forth by fancy. Thus, imagination—for *fancy* is of course another name for what is called *imagination*—brings about the creation of Eve, that is, brings forth Eve herself, indeed originarily, creatively. Yet, on the other hand, when Adam wakes, he beholds her as he saw her in the

---

29. *The Poems of John Milton*, ed. John Carey and Alastair Fowler (London: Longman, 1968), 837–40.

dream—that is, he discovers that she has (also) been brought forth outside the dream, that, while brought forth in imagination, she proves (also) to exist—to have been brought into existence—outside. Yet the discovery of her as existing outside the dream is precisely a remembering, recognizing her to be such as was seen in the dream. Thus, Adam both brings her forth in fancy and remembers her, recognizes the existing Eve, as being the same as the Eve produced in fancy. In his imagination Adam both creates Eve and yet repeats in fancy what comes about outside it; he brings her forth originarily and yet only repeats the production that takes place outside the dream.

The consequences of this twofoldness, of this configuration of imagination as, at once, originative and memorial, are virtually without limit. Keats intimates this in the letter to Bailey when, having just referred to "those who delight in sensation," he writes: "Adam's dream will do here and seems to be a conviction that Imagination and its empyreal reflection is the same as human Life and its spiritual repetition." He leaves it unsaid whether the empyreal reflection belonging to imagination is applied to the heavenly abode of the divine or, following the ancients, to the upper region of pure fire, the starry heaven; he leaves it unsaid, too, whether the spiritual repetition of life occurs after life or within it. But the implication of the link to "those who delight in sensation" is unmistakable.

Keats' saying of the truth of imagination—"What the Imagination seizes as Beauty must be truth—whether it existed before or not—" is followed, or rather, extended, by the following: "for I have the same Idea of all our Passions as of Love they are all in their sublime, creative of essential Beauty—." But if imagination in its passions is creative of essential beauty, then such beauty, precisely by virtue of being created, is not essential in the classical sense. Neither, then, is the truth (established by imagination) to be regarded as essential, that is, as belonging to an essential order, that is, as intelligible over against the sensible. If the beauty and truth brought forth by imagination are essential, then they can only be so in a sense that diverges from the classical sense, in a sense of essence that is drawn back to sense. As when, surprised by an old melody sung by one pictured as more beautiful than is possible, one is "mounted on the Wings of Imagination so high—that the Prototype [i.e., what would otherwise be the idea or essence] must be here after—that delicious face you will see—."

Keats refers at this point to his "favorite Speculation," which, he says, may be known by his "first Book." This reference to Book 1 of *Endymion* (the work that he was engaged in finishing at the time of the letter to Bailey) is meant to explain why he has "the same Idea of all our Passions as of Love." For, toward the end of Book 1 of *Endymion*,[30] Keats draws a sharp contrast

---

30. Keats, *Complete Poems*, 83f.

between what he calls "fellowship with essence" and, on the other hand, love. Here, briefly, is how he presents the former:

> Wherein lies happiness? In that which becks
> Our ready minds to fellowship divine,
> A fellowship with essence; till we shine,
> Full alchemiz'd, and free of space. Behold
> The clear religion of heaven!

(ll. 777–81)

But then, once this presentation has been drawn out, there is an abrupt turn:

> But there are
> Richer entanglements, enthralments far
> More self-destroying, leading, by degrees,
> To the chief intensity: the crown of these
> Is made of love and friendship, and sits high
> Upon the forehead of humanity.
> All its more ponderous and bulky worth
> Is friendship, whence there ever issues forth
> A steady splendour; but at the tip-top,
> There hangs by unseen film, an orbed drop
> Of light, and that is love: its influence,
> Thrown in our eyes, genders a novel sense,
> At which we start and fret; till in the end,
> Melting into its radiance, we blend,
> Mingle, and so become a part of it,—
> Nor with aught else can our souls interknit
> So wingedly: when we combine therewith,
> Life's self is nourish'd by its proper pith,
> And we are nurtured like a pelican brood.

(ll. 797–814)

Little wonder, then, that, in the letter to Bailey, Keats goes on to exclaim: "O for a Life of Sensations rather than of Thoughts." In the starkest contrast to denigration of the sensible for the sake of the intelligible, Keats ironically proposes (as "another favorite Speculation") that enjoyment in the hereafter will consist in repetition of earthly joys—"that we shall enjoy ourselves here after by having what we called happiness on Earth repeated in a finer tone and so repeated—." This is the point at which Keats refers to "those who delight in sensation," differentiating them from his friend Bailey, who at this time was at Oxford reading for holy orders: "And yet such a fate can only befall those who delight in sensation rather than hunger as you do after Truth—." In the entire letter this is the only occurrence of the word *truth* that is capitalized.

The repetition ironically projected into the afterlife belongs integrally to this life: "the simple imaginative Mind may have its rewards in the repeti[ti]on of its own silent Working coming *continually* on the spirit with a fine *suddenness*" (emphasis added). For repetition, the memorial moment in the twofoldness of imagination, comes continually to interrupt creation, to suspend it as at the moment when Adam "awoke and found it truth." In its establishing of truth imagination is not only creation but also, at once, passion,[31] that is, in Keats' idiom, "delicious diligent Indolence."[32]

Its passion is in a sense unlimited—that is, the very condition of the highest creativity, in men of genius, is that they be receptive without limit, that they be capable of becoming anything. But—like the Timaean χώρα— this requires that "they have not any individuality, any determined Character." In a letter to Richard Woodhouse written nearly a year after the letter to Bailey, Keats refers to such expropriation of self in still more radical terms, saying of "the poetical Character itself" that "it is not itself—it has no self—it is everything and nothing."[33] In its proper pith—in the genius, in the poet—imagination is no longer a power of the subject. It exceeds individuality and determinate character. It is in excess of the self.

V. TURNING —

Already there is inversion, reversal.

It is an inversion that one would call fundamental, even absolute, were it not such as to deprive fundament of any governing status, thus disturbing the very order of fundamentality and withdrawing from every would-be absolute its privileging absolution. It is a reversal of ground and grounded, of origin and originated, of original and image—that is, of all the values, of all the hierarchical oppositions, linked to the superordination of intelligible over sensible.

Already there is such inversion. Already with Keats, in what he says of those who delight in sensations as well as in his own exclamation "O for a Life of Sensations rather than of Thoughts." Already such inversion is broached in his ironic proposal that enjoyment in the hereafter or, as he writes it, the here after—which, in either inscription, can of course signify

---

31. "This is a movement of the passions as the Greeks understood it. Pathos, like its Latin equivalent, *passio*, implies an imposition from without which happens to a man who remains passive. These passions 'are in their sublime creative of essential Beauty.' . . . Imagination is a 'silent working' which repeats what is already there, and this repetition 'comes continually on the spirit with a fine suddenness' which surprises as original" (David Pollard, *The Poetry of Keats: Language and Experience* [Sussex: Harvester Press, 1984], 26).

32. Letter to J. H. Reynolds (19 February 1818), *Letters of John Keats*, 1:231.

33. Letter to Richard Woodhouse (27 October 1818), ibid., 1:387.

either life after death or a later period of life—will consist in repetition of earthly joys.

With Keats inversion is broached, announced, even poetized, as near the beginning of *Endymion:*[34]

> Therefore, on every morrow, are we wreathing
> A flowery band to bind us to the earth,
> Spite of despondence, of the inhuman dearth
> Of noble natures, of the gloomy days,
> Of all the unhealthy and o'er-darkened ways
> Made for our searching: yes, in spite of all,
> Some shape of beauty moves away the pall
> From our dark spirits. Such the sun, the moon,
> Trees old, and young sprouting a shady boon
> For simple sheep; and such are daffodils
> With the green world they live in; . . .

(ll. 6–16)

Poetized as a move of binding us to the earth—over against the prospect of fellowship with essence, of the clear religion of heaven, heretofore taken to offer, in the here after, flight and refuge from our o'er-darkening ways here now—the inversion is none other than that announced by Nietzsche, in the voice of Zarathustra: "I beseech you, my brothers, *remain true* [treu] *to the earth,* and do not believe those who speak to you of unearthly [*überirdischen*] hopes! Poison-mixers are they, whether they know it or not. Despisers of life are they, dying ones [*Absterbende*] and themselves poisoned, of whom the earth is weary: so let them go!"[35] Whereas the poet, poetizing also his own work, attests that he is weaving a flowery band by which to bind us to the earth, letting some shape of beauty appear in the sun, the moon, trees, daffodils, Zarathustra denounces those who poison life and issues an imperative: remain true to the earth. And: let those go, let go of those, who project a true world beyond the earthly. The sense of the imperative is: the earth is the true to which now one is to remain true.

Since Nietzsche this inversion has imposed itself ever more imperatively. Nietzsche's story of "How the 'True World' Finally Became a Fable" has been told and retold, repetition layered upon repetition, subtly inclining this fabular narrative in one way or another. A certain responsiveness to this imperative remains nonetheless itself imperative.

The inversion demanded is that of the superordination of intelligible (νοητόν) over sensible (αἰσθητόν). One readily takes this distinction and this ordering of its terms to have been posited in the Platonic dialogues,

---

34. Keats, *Complete Poems,* 65.

35. Nietzsche, *Also Sprach Zarathustra,* in vol. VI 1 of *Werke: Kritische Gesamtausgabe,* ed. Giorgio Colli and Mazzino Montinari (Berlin: Walter de Gruyter, 1968), 9.

though it has all too seldom been considered just how this distinction enters into and functions within those discourses. Even less has it been considered to what extent this distinction and everything that hinges on it serve in the Platonic texts to mark something problematic, even enigmatic or aporetic, rather than constituting an established axiom, even the very axiom of fundament that would be the fundamental axiom on which philosophy, metaphorized as an edifice, could be built.

In any case the imperative—in force at least since Nietzsche—is that this superordination be inverted: that what previously occupied the superior position, the intelligible with its character as ground, ἀρχή, truth, now be subordinated to the sensible with its character as appearance and as an image remote from truth. Today it is hardly any longer necessary to say that such an inversion, simply as such, is impossible—or rather, that it must be paired with a displacement or reinscription that erodes the very schema of the ordering, or that it produces such incoherence as to release and invite a range of shifts and transformations that will not have been determinable by the inversion alone. Nietzsche recognized that the subordination of the intelligible brings in effect the abolition of this allegedly true world and that with this abolition there will also be abolished the very world to which it now would—but cannot—be subordinated. The apparent world will have been abolished almost as unconditionally as the "true world"; for once the sensible is no longer governed by the superordinate intelligible, its very character as appearance, as a remote shining of truth, is effaced. Thus, what results is not just an inversion of the Platonic schema but rather a reorientation to the sensible newly interpreted outside the schematic opposition between true and apparent. Whatever configuration unfolds will now need to be traced as an opening from and within the sensible.

Yet there are also certain determining limits that need to be marked in this radical reconfiguration of the Platonic superordination of intelligible over sensible. In this regard it is of the utmost significance that the Platonic move that eventually produces the distinction and ordering between intelligible and sensible is characterized as a turn to λόγοι. In the pivotal passage in the *Phaedo* Socrates speaks of his fear that, like those who look at the sun during an eclipse, he would be blinded if he looked directly at things and tried to grasp them by vision or other senses. He continues: "So, it seemed to me to be necessary to have recourse [or: to flee for refuge—καταφεύγω] to λόγοι and investigate [or: see—σκοπεῖν] in them the truth of beings [τῶν ὄντων τὴν ἀλήθειαν]."[36] Now, in the reconfiguration around the sensible, what is to be relinquished is neither the Socratic turn to λόγος nor the power of speech that motivates this turn, its power to outdistance sense; what is to be relinquished is the subordination of speech to an order of signification absolutely anterior to it. Rather than assuming speech to be

---

36. Plato, *Phaedo* 99e.

expression of preconstituted meaning, it is to be construed as it opens from within the sensible, even if also doubling the sensible.

As with the very words *sensible* and *sense,* which would need to be reinscribed outside the opposition to the intelligible, and indeed through a reinscription that would not be—and would not take itself to be—controlled by preconstituted significations that the words would only express. The word *sense* has peculiar resources pertinent to such reinscription by virtue of harboring in itself the very distinction at issue, harboring it as a differentiation between two senses of *sense,* an abysmal differentiation presupposing the very distinction it would mark.

Still more decisive here after—following these mere prolusions—is a reorientation of the sensible to the elemental. This reorientation is a turn to which nothing in the Socratic turn to λόγοι directly corresponds, though it does renew another Platonic move, the Timaean turn back to those mere traces of such things as fire and earth as they were before the cosmos itself was made. This reorientation to the elemental is to be primarily a turn to earth and sky, each of which in its distinctive way eludes (and thus breaches) the distinction between intelligible and sensible. Or, to risk—in hopes of renewing—one of the most ambiguous and abused words bequeathed by philosophy, a word nonetheless so forceful that ever again it returns to say something decisive, the turn has to do with *nature.* It is a turn to *nature* as a name for the sensible at large, yet also, more specifically, to nature in what Emerson calls the common sense: things relatively "unchanged by man: space, the air, the river, the leaf"—that is, nature in distinction from art in the sense of τέχνη.[37] Finally and most decisively, as a reorientation to the elemental, it is a turn toward that in nature which exceeds nature, toward that which, itself of nature, is nonetheless beyond the things of nature to such an extent as to constitute the encompassing elements within which, coming to pass, things show themselves. It is a turn that passes through nature toward the hypernature in nature.

There is another remote effect of the Nietzschean inversion, one that today has come to be reinforced by suspicions arising from the most disparate sources, suspicions of certain pervasive forms of anthropocentrism. In reference to philosophy, the suspicion is that for too long—indeed from the beginning—it has made man the measure of all things, even—and perhaps most powerfully—when it has set itself in opposition to the Protagorean maxim. For the Socratic turn from natural things to λόγοι involves also, in Cicero's phrase, bringing philosophy down from the heavens and turning it to the investigation of human life and morals and things good and bad.[38] The Socratic turn was also—even if not without a certain recoil—a

---

37. Ralph Waldo Emerson, "Nature," in *Selected Writings,* ed. Brooke Atkinson (New York: Random House, 1950), 4.

38. Cicero, *Tusculan Disputations* V.10.

turn from wild nature and the elemental to human life and the city. In the dialogues Socrates constantly enacts this adherence to the city, and on the rare occasion, dramatized in the *Phaedrus,* when he does leave the city and discovers in the countryside along the Ilissus the fragrantly blooming trees, the charming breeze, the summer music of the cicadas, and the soft grass on which to recline, Socrates asks Phaedrus to excuse him for being such a stranger to this kind of place: "I am fond of learning. Now the country places and the trees will not teach me anything, but the people in the city will."[39] Partly, no doubt, because people speak and trees do not. But also because that about which he would be taught is not nature but people and their institutions, their cities. Even when, at the furthest extreme, Plato has Timaeus present (while Socrates listens in silence) an extended discourse on nature, that entire discourse is framed by the political discourses it would ultimately serve.[40]

The turn to wild nature and the elemental would remove the frame. It would contest the hegemony of (at least a certain) ethics and politics, venturing to become, as it were, more Presocratic. The turn would reinstall the human in wild nature and in its bearing on the earth and beneath the sky, returning human nature to nature. It would grant provocations that exceed the question of how humans are best to be ordered in the city and to comport themselves to one another, opening to the provocations that can arise in experiencing the uncanny look in the eyes of an animal or in witnessing its strength and ferocity, in feeling the gentle breeze against one's face or in taking refuge from the howling storm, in setting one's feet upon the earth or in burying a loved one beneath it, in gazing bedazzled at the starry heaven or in shuddering at its austere remoteness.

One may thus be provoked to set about wreathing a flowery band to bind us to the earth.

Or to think how the things of nature—and what things are not finally somehow of nature?—come to show themselves upon the earth and beneath the sky, entrusting their secret to imagination alone.

---

39. Plato, *Phaedrus* 230d.
40. I have discussed this political frame in *Chorology: On Beginning in Plato's "Timaeus"* (Bloomington: Indiana University Press, 1999), chap. 4.

1

ON (NOT SIMPLY) BEGINNING

A. SENSE

Beginning, then, with sense—

Marking, thus, a beginning—

Even though, in philosophy or at its limit, one will never simply have begun.

Never will it quite suffice to detour—to have detoured—through the question of beginning. As though the question and the way through it could be made simply to vanish in the moment of beginning, into the moment of beginning. Leaving not a trace.

None (therefore) will simply have begun.

Not even Hegel, who most rigorously of all undertakes to determine the point with which philosophy is to begin. The beginning is to be "the simplest of all," requiring only the "simple exposition" entitled by the question: "With What Must the Science Begin?" It is intended, not to lead up to the beginning, but rather to eliminate everything preliminary, everything that would precede—and thereby displace—the beginning: "This insight [into the beginning] is itself so simple that this beginning as such requires no

preparation or further introduction; and, indeed, these preliminary, external reflections about it were not so much intended to lead up to it as rather
to remove [or: cross out, cancel—*entfernen*] all preliminaries."[1] But what
the simple exposition shows is that the preparation, the mediation that supplies the beginning, is self-superseding (*Aufheben ihrer selbst*), that is, that the
mediation that leads to the beginning supersedes itself in the emergence of
a beginning that is immediate. The presentation of philosophy's coming
upon the scene (its coming to its beginning as such) is thus shown to dissolve in the immediate answer that its very mediation supplies to the question of beginning. And yet, this presentation, the *Phenomenology of Spirit,* was
written; even if it may be crossed out, erased, even burned, reduced to ashes,
one cannot but wonder whether it will simply have been dissolved into the
immediacy of the beginning, leaving not a trace.

In marking the beginning Hegel will not simply have begun. For, rather
than simply moving on from the beginning, advancing from it and leaving
it behind, the advance proves to be a retreat to its ground, a circling back
to the beginning. Hegel sketches the course of this advancing retreat in
one of the remarks that he adds to the simple exposition, despite this exposition's being "complete in itself [*für sich fertig*]": "The advance is a retreat
[*Rückgang*] into the ground, to the originary and true, on which depends
and, indeed, from which is brought forth, that with which the beginning is
made. . . . This last, the ground, is then that from which the first proceeds,
that which at first appeared as an immediacy."[2] In the end what the beginning proves to require is the final result, with which the circle closes upon
itself and returns to the beginning. This is what Hegel writes in a text designated as the Introduction (*Einleitung*) to the presentation of the entire system of *Wissenschaft,* that is, to the *Encyclopaedia:* "The standpoint which thus
appears to be *immediate* must within the science be converted into result,
the ultimate result in which science reaches again its beginning and returns
into itself. In this manner philosophy shows itself to be a circle that returns
upon itself, that has no beginning in the way that other sciences do."[3] In
the end there proves to have been no beginning; that is, everything to
which the beginning leads reflects back upon it, compounding it again and

---

1. G. W. F. Hegel, *Wissenschaft der Logik I (1832),* vol. 21 of *Gesammelte Werke* (Hamburg:
Felix Meiner Verlag, 1985), 65.

2. Ibid., 57.

3. Hegel, *Enzyklopädie der philosophischen Wissenschaften im Grundrisse (1827),* vol. 19 of *Gesammelte Werke* (Hamburg: Felix Meiner Verlag, 1989), §17. The passage remains unchanged
in the 1830 edition. A corresponding discussion is found in the *Logic:* "What is essential for
the science is not so much that the beginning be a pure immediacy, but rather that the whole
of the science be in itself a circle in which the first is also the last and the last is also the
first. . . . Through this progress, then, the beginning loses the one-sidedness that it has as
something simply immediate and abstract; it becomes something mediated, and hence the
line of the scientific advance becomes a *circle*" (Hegel, *Wissenschaft der Logik I [1832],* 57f.).

again until finally it becomes the result with which *Wissenschaft*—philosophy as such—turns back into itself.

And yet, though he will never simply have begun, Hegel declares a beginning: "The beginning is therefore *pure being.*"[4] The italics, marking the beginning, could also occasion a question, a kind of repetition of the question "With what must the science begin?" One may ask whether the beginning thus marked is being or just the word *being?* What would be required in order, inscribing *being,* to begin with being? There would be required the very movement of signification, the advance from the word to its sense. But this advance would be a retreat in advance of the beginning: to begin with being would require acceding, in advance, to the sense of *being.* To begin with being would require already having begun with sense, even with the sense of *sense.* To begin with being, marking this beginning as such, is not simply to have begun.

None will ever simply have begun.

Least of all, Plato.

The beginning is marked by the word λύσις: the *release* of the prisoners previously chained in the underground cave. Also by περιαγωγή: the *turning-around* by which the release is fulfilled. Yet the release will already have been prepared: the question is what such release would be like if something of this sort *were by nature to happen* to them (or: were to be suited to them—συμβαίνω). Nature will already have prepared their release and turning-around by giving them sight (τὸ ὁρᾶν).[5] Before the beginning they will already have been endowed with sense, will already have begun with sense.

Indeed with a sense of the beginning. In beginning, at the moment of their release and turning-around, they will already have a sense of the beginning that would also be the end, the beginning toward which the philosophical advance is directed. They will already have returned from the beginning of all things (ἡ τοῦ παντὸς ἀρχή),[6] doubling back in such a way that, gifted with sense, they can come, in their release, to redouble the beginning. To begin is always to begin again.

Can one wonder that the beginning is marked only at the center of the *Republic,* that at the beginning there is only the mythic allusion to it?

As the beginning—the release—is displaced by a precedent sense that it can only redouble, so too does the beginning that is sensed in advance progressively withdraw. The withdrawal is conspicuous in the very structure of the philosophical advance, in the reiteration of the passage from image to original: what seems an original proves to be only an image behind which the original has retreated. Moreover, at the center of the *Republic* one is—at the very least—left wondering whether the beginning that would be

---

4. Hegel, *Wissenschaft der Logik I (1832),* 56.
5. Plato, *Republic* 515c, 518d.
6. See Plato, *Republic* 511b.

the final original will not always have withdrawn into its own veiled image-making, into fathering and sending images of itself without ever imparting itself as such.[7]

In the *Timaeus* the withdrawal is indisputable, though most directly it is a withdrawal of that other beginning called, among its many names, the third kind or the χώρα. This other beginning is one that would have preceded the beginning of all things; what, above all, is both said and enacted in the discourse on the χώρα—the chorology, this bastard discourse, as Timaeus calls it—is the elusiveness of this beginning. Yet the effects of this fugitive kind cannot simply be isolated and contained; on the contrary, they spread throughout the entire discourse of the *Timaeus*, which is accordingly marked by false starts, disorder, and interruptions followed by new—that is, redoubled—beginnings. It is thus most remarkable that the *Timaeus* issues the injunction that one begin at the beginning: "With regard to everything it is most important to begin at the natural beginning."[8] The explicitness of the injunction only points up all the more conspicuously how utterly the *Timaeus* cannot but fail to begin at the beginning. Of necessity (ἀνάγκη).

None will ever simply have begun.

And yet, aside from the history of philosophy and its texts, one could venture to imagine simply beginning. Such a beginning would seem to be offered by sense, to sense. It would be the simplest of all beginnings: merely beholding, in silence, what presents itself to sense. One would begin by casting one's glance as if for the first time, by turning one's ear and extending one's hand, so as to submit to the spell of sense, hardly yet distinguishing even between seeing and seen, hearing and heard, touching and touched.

One would, then, have imagined a beginning that, perhaps most radically, would carry out the appeal to experience on which philosophy has rarely ceased to insist. One would in deed—in the imagined deed—have affirmed what Hegel calls the principle of experience (*das Prinzip der Erfahrung*): "The principle of *experience* contains the infinitely important determination that, for a content to be accepted and held to be true, man must himself *be there with it* [*der Mensch selbst* dabei sein *müsse*]."[9] Even though in affirming a principle (even by imagining) one would already have posed a threat to the alleged simplicity of the beginning. Especially, remembering that *principle* is a not so remote translation of ἀρχή.

Yet, even if, keeping all such doubling reflection at bay, one persists in the mute beholding of sense—or rather, in imagining it—this very persis-

---

7. See Plato, *Republic* 506e, together with my discussion in *Being and Logos: Reading the Platonic Dialogues*, 3rd ed. (Bloomington: Indiana University Press, 1996), 405.

8. Plato, *Timaeus* 29b.

9. Hegel, *Enzyklopädie (1827)*, §7. Unchanged in the 1830 edition.

tence will only make it all the more manifest that such beholding is drawn out of itself, that it is submitted to bonds that both exceed it and, as it were, make it exceed itself. For beholding is responsive. It follows upon the promptings of what is to be beheld, responds to these promptings; it is precisely such response. It will always have been solicited and will have followed upon a prior receptiveness to that solicitation. Seeing is always having seen. Yet this anterior seeing is not so much a seeing *of something* as rather an opening of vision to the visible. It is a kind of prospection that is not yet a beholding of anything but that will always have opened beholding to a beyond, drawn sense out into the distance, constituting a beginning before the beginning, redoubling the beginning. It is a protractive prospection binding apprehension to manifestness.

As soon as one turns to behold mutely what presents itself to sense, a double affirmation will already have come into play. One will have received the solicitation to behold, welcoming it, and will have opened oneself to what is there to behold, exposing oneself to it. One will have awakened to the light. One will have heard what resounds in all things. One will have said, if still mutely: yes, yes.

The simplicity of the beginning will be violated not only because something proves to be anterior to it but also, more decisively, because this anteriority is a matter of free arrival rather than mere insistence, because it is a gift coming as if from nowhere.

One could indeed not even imagine simply beginning. Not even on the assumption that philosophy could begin without speech coming to double sense and thus, from the beginning, to compound the beginning with another beginning, a δεύτερος πλοῦς.

Giving way, then. Forgoing the pretense of simply beginning.

And yet, beginning with sense. Marking, thus, a beginning.

Already it is conspicuously double. For what the marking of the beginning inscribes is the word *sense*. And yet, one would not begin merely with the isolated word; in fact to the extent that the word is isolated from others and especially from its signification, it ceases even to be a word, becoming a mere shell, a visible mark that no longer marks anything and with which one could begin nothing. At the very least one would begin with the word as signifying, with *sense* as giving way to sense in the movement of signification—thus with *sense* and sense and the transition from one to the other. Yet this transition, the movement of signification as such, is precisely the movement from signifier to signified, from word to sense. Thus, in setting out to signify sense, one will already have broached sense as belonging, as it were, to the very sense of signification. From the moment one sets out to effect the transition from *sense* to sense, one will already be oriented to sense. Before signifying any specific sense, one will always have been open to sense as such. The very opening of speech is an openness to sense, a mute affirmation of sense anterior to every sense.

To begin with sense is thus not, as one might have supposed, to begin with what is over against speech (in one regard or another); it is to begin with the very opening of speech, at its threshold.

But it is to begin also with the word. *Sense* derives from the Latin *sensus, sentire,* which in turn translate the Greek αἴσθησις and αἰσθάνομαι. In Greek philosophy from Plato on, αἴσθησις signifies the apprehension of things (or of the condition of one's own body) by sight, hearing, taste, smell, or touch and by way of the particular bodily organs ordained for each of these senses. As such, αἴσθησις is set in opposition to another kind of apprehension, νόησις, apprehension carried out not by any of the five senses but by what the Greeks call νοῦς. In the history of philosophy νοῦς and the constellation of words around it never cease being retranslated and redetermined in response to varying philosophical and nonphilosophical provocations. If through all these transformations anything remains, it is that what is thus apprehended, what is (called) noetic or intelligible (τὸ νοητόν), is something inaccessible to αἴσθησις, at least to αἴσθησις alone. It is such as cannot be seen, heard, or otherwise sensed. And yet, it can be such as in some manner to accompany things seen or heard: as when, reading or hearing a word, one apprehends its sense.

Thus, as soon as one draws out the opposition between τὸ νοητόν and τὸ αἰσθητόν, one notices how *sense* erodes this opposition. Nothing could be more remarkable, considering that, from Plato on, this opposition remains the most fundamental of all, establishing the very sense of fundament and fundamental and holding within its orbit the other oppositions and determinations that philosophy sets up as fundamental, as constituting first principles. Throughout all the translations, mutations, appropriations, even through the philosophical revolutions that put it utterly in question in its classical form, the opposition remains both intact and determinative—to such an extent that even Kant, in a very late work, could write: "This ultimate end toward which all of metaphysics aims is easy to discover and can provide the basis for its definition: metaphysics is the science of advancing by reason from knowledge of the sensible to knowledge of the supersensible."[10]

Sense erodes this opposition because its sense is, in a sense, unlimited.[11] It houses within itself the most gigantic ambivalence, the scene, as it were,

---

10. I. Kant, *Preisschrift über die Fortschritte der Metaphysik,* ed. F. T. Rink, in vol. 20 of *Kant's Gesammelte Schriften* (Berlin: Walter de Gruyter, 1942), 260. This work, which Kant left unpublished, dates from 1804.

11. "Thus—and this is the example of examples—the sense of the word *sense* traverses the five senses, the sense of direction, common sense, semantic sense, divinatory sense, sentiment, moral sense, practical sense, aesthetic sense, all the way to that which makes possible all these senses and all these senses of *sense,* their community and their disparity, which is not sense in any of these senses, but in the sense of that which comes to sense" (Jean-Luc Nancy, *Le Sens du Monde* [Paris: Galilée, 1993], 30).

of the original γιγαντομαχία περὶ τῆς οὐσίας. It indifferently couples what is called the sensible, the things of sense, *and* signification, signified sense, sense of a sort that can only be apprehended noetically. It will of course be said that these are two senses of *sense,* and yet in this very phrase one will have marked the abysmal character of the distinction: to distinguish between the two senses of *sense* presupposes the very distinction that it would draw. The ambivalence is further compounded by the indifference of *sense* with respect to the difference between apprehending and apprehended: to sense something or to have a sense of it is to apprehend its sense.

If one were to picture a vertical line cut by a horizontal into two unequal segments, and if the four quadrants thus formed were taken to represent the alternatives generated by combination of the two sets of opposed terms (intelligible/sensible, apprehension/apprehended), then the word *sense* could be used for each of the four quadrants. One could say that to begin with sense is to begin with everything, with the entire field of which philosophy would take the measure. Not even the directionality belonging to that field, its verticality, would be omitted, provided one kept in play that rare sense of *sense,* akin to French *sens,* in which it signifies the direction of a motion. *Sense* will be extendable even to what resists being located in this field: it can signify also that at which one aims in seeking to decipher something cryptic or to interpret a dream. The sense of *sense* can even be transferred back to discourse itself: one can write nonsense, and one can talk good sense.

Even at the limit of philosophy it is with sense that one would begin again. Proposing to rekindle the γιγαντομαχία περὶ τῆς οὐσίας, Heidegger sets out to raise anew the question of the sense of being (*Sinn von Sein*). And Nietzsche, twisting free of the distinction between the intelligible and the sensible, would inaugurate a new interpretation of the sensible, that is, a new determination of the sense of the sensible.[12]

B. IDIOM

The inversion that has imposed itself at least since Nietzsche produces both a restriction and a release of sense. The imperative is to abandon the "true world" that has finally become a fable, to turn away from the intelligible (τὸ νοητόν) so as now to restrict sense to the sensible (τὸ αἰσθητόν). By cancelling the subordination of the sensible to the intelligible, this turn also abolishes the character of the sensible as appearance: "With the true

---

12. See Martin Heidegger, *Nietzsche* (Pfullingen: Günther Neske, 1961), 1:231–54. The incisive translation of *Herausdrehung* as *twisting free* is taken from David Krell's translation of this text.

world we have also abolished the apparent one!"[13] By abolishing the apparent, by releasing the sensible from the very schema of truth and appearance, the turn twists the sensible free and releases it to itself. What results is a turn to the sensible, a turn back to the sensible now released from the compulsion of being the mere locus where a remote truth appears. This turn outlines the limit, determines philosophy at the limit, philosophy in this time in which the very name lags behind what it is imperative to venture. At the limit this venture will be limited to the sensible, to what belongs within, or at least opens from, the sensible. Its limit will be the limit of sense in this sense.

And yet, in restricting sense, this limit also excludes. In releasing sense to itself, the turn releases sense in another sense from itself. For the imperative is to turn from the intelligible, to let it go now that it has been abolished, now that the true world has finally become a fable. Yet even the fable that remains and turns back into its own telling must, as such, as a story to be told, have sense. Even the fable that Nietzsche tells about how the true world finally became a fable must still signify. But the shift, the replacement, is decisive: in place of the true world of signified intelligibles there remain only the signifiers that constitute the fable, even though—and everything depends on this condition—they must somehow signify something as the very condition of remaining signifiers rather than becoming the mere husks of words.

This effect needs to be precisely gauged. With the abolition of the intelligible, it cannot be merely a matter of then abandoning the intelligible so as to turn to the sensible. For the turn is not itself simply locatable within the sensible or sensibility, but rather, responsive to an imperative, it takes place primarily in the form of speech. At the limit outlined by the turn to the sensible, the venture that becomes imperative is that of giving a new interpretation of the sensible. Yet what is required is not just to interpret the sensible differently, to take it to have a different sense (or a different configuration of senses) from that which it was previously taken to have. Rather, what is now required is a discourse that would double the sensible—interpret it, as it were—without recourse to the intelligible. What is required is a discourse that would endure the loss of the intelligible, a discourse of signifiers no longer taken to correspond to, and to be guaranteed as such by, signified intelligibles.[14] If there is no realm of established signi-

---

13. Nietzsche, *Götzen-Dämmerung*, vol. VI 3 of *Werke: Kritische Gesamtausgabe* (Berlin: Walter de Gruyter, 1969), 75.

14. The subordination of language to an anterior order of signification is often designated, following Derrida, by the term *logocentrism*. Without disputing that this term may in some contexts be effective, there is, on the other hand, a danger of its producing a certain foreclosure. For, in order to be suitable, it requires that λόγος be taken in a late, Hellenistic sense, whereas in the Platonic dialogues—to say nothing of the earlier Greek thinkers—its sense is

fications that would be anterior to language, that would control it by requiring that speech always only express these antecedent senses, then speech will be unsettled. Once the signifiers with which the sensible would be doubled are no longer secured by connection to intelligible signifieds, their sense is no longer guaranteed. Nonsense is no longer merely the external opposite of significant speech but rather a threat that haunts all speech. At the limit where philosophy becomes discourse on the sensible, it becomes insecure. Once the sense of its words is no longer preestablished and thus guaranteed, once discourse is released from the bond to anterior sense, then other ways must be found by which to lend it the capacity to say something. Or rather, since, short of simply collapsing back into themselves, the signifiers of discourse will say something, even if nonsense, ways must be found by which to let the discourse engender sense in and through the very movement in which it comes to double the sensible. As the style of a writer can engender a sense that could never be arrived at merely by combining the significations of the particular words, phrases, or sentences employed.[15]

It is in this connection that one speaks of a particular writer's idiom, but also of the idiom or dialect belonging to a limited region and especially of the idiom of a particular language, the genius, as it were, of the language that endows it with its singular capacity to say things in a sense that could never simply be duplicated in other languages. The same effect is exhibited by idioms in a language, by the divergence of their sense from what is called the literal sense. In idiom (in all these senses) it is a matter of certain linguistic operations that are not simply controlled by invariant bonds joining signifiers to preestablished signifieds. It is precisely such operations that become imperative when those bonds are broken. As discourse on the sensible, philosophy at the limit cannot but become idiomatic.

In May 1805, as he was writing the *Phenomenology of Spirit,* Hegel penned a letter to the classicist J. H. Voss, the translator of Homer into German. In the letter Hegel draws a parallel between Voss' accomplishment and Luther's: "Luther made the Bible speak German, and you have done the same for Homer—the greatest gift that can be made to a people. For a people remains barbarian and does not view what is excellent within the range of its acquaintance as its own true property so long as it does not come to know it in its own language." Then, with the requisite moderation, Hegel writes of his own intent: "If you will kindly forget these two examples, I

---

not detached from that of speech. Furthermore, there are passages in the dialogues where the word λόγος functions in ways that work precisely against what one would call logocentrism.

15. "This [contemporary philosophical labor] presupposes a different relation of philosophy to its own presentation. Once the possibility of signifying truth is a thing of the past, another style is necessary. The end of philosophy is, without a doubt, first of all a question of style in this sense. It is not a matter of stylistic effects or ornaments of discourse, but of what sense does to discourse if sense exceeds significations" (Nancy, *Le Sens du Monde,* 37).

may say of my endeavor that I wish to try to teach philosophy to speak German."[16]

Though moderation might prescribe virtual silence in this regard and in any case interminable hesitation, it would not be entirely inappropriate today to wish to try to teach philosophy to speak English. This wish might indeed be nourished by an eccentric image of philosophy at the limit, an image of its spinning off from the German center or even from the German/French or Germanic/Latinate axis, off toward the philosophical outskirts of Europe, emigrating to a land—even Hegel called it the land of the future—where one might pretend, even in speaking this language, to have left Europe behind. A fanciful image, no doubt. Not to say simply parochial.

For Hegel, as for Schelling, the task remained primarily one of translation. In order that the German people might come into possession of the most excellent of works, especially those of antiquity, it was required that the wealth of significations informing these works be taken up into the German language. In its classical determination (itself established by antiquity), to translate is to bear something across an interval. The interval is that between two languages, and what is borne across this interval is the sense of the word. As a movement from a word, phrase, etc. in one language to the corresponding word, phrase, etc. in another language, translation proceeds by way of—or rather, circulates through—the signification, which is invariant with respect to different languages and which, in particular, is shared by the two words, phrases, etc. between which translation moves. One could represent translation in this classical sense as a task of envisioning the signification of a unit in one language so as then to discover in the other language a unit having the same signification; it would thus be a matter of movement from a signifier to its signified to a signifier that in the other language has precisely this same signified. What Hegel, in his letter to Voss, adds to this classical determination is the moment of appropriation: by discovering the configuration of signifiers in German that are capable of signifying the wealth of significations in, for instance, Classical Greek and by yoking those significations to those signifiers by means of such exemplary products as Voss' translation of Homer, those significations and the works they inform can come to be appropriated by the German people as their own. Indeed, once these bonds are in place, it is as if the externality of the signifiers could, in a sufficiently rigorous discourse, be cancelled and the difference so thoroughly effaced that the result would be a discourse of the signifieds themselves, a pure presentation. There is perhaps no more succinct indication of such a prospect than that found in Schelling's *Presentation of My System of Philosophy*. Schelling begins with a brief Introduction (entitled *Vorerinnerung*), in which he sets about explaining the intent and the method of the work and then, as the final sen-

---

16. *Briefe von und an Hegel*, ed. J. Hoffmeister (Hamburg: Felix Meiner, 1952), 1:99f. (#55).

tence of the Introduction, writes: "From this point on, only the thing itself is to speak [*Von jetzt an spreche nur die Sache selbst*]."[17]

But with philosophy at the limit, it cannot be only a matter of translation or of a translational appropriation of—and ultimately to—the order of significations. Yoking the native signifiers to the established significations of, for instance, Hegel's German—teaching philosophy to speak English— cannot suffice for a discourse that at the limit must endure the loss of anterior signification. Indeed, with this loss, the classical determination of translation is put into question, as is the very possibility—the limit of the possibility—of translation. Without signified intelligibles to secure it, philosophical discourse will no longer be translational in the classical sense; it will no longer consist in the movement from signified to signifier, from insight to expression (with or without reference to another order of signifiers, to another language). If, becoming idiomatic, it remains translational at all, it will be so only in an unheard-of sense.

What ways are open to philosophy at the limit? What ways offer for its discourse the possibility of engendering sense? What are the ways of shaping its idiom so as to lend it the capacity not only to say something sensible (in both senses) but also to do so in a manner that can be binding? Not that such discourse would simply begin *ex nihilo*; on the contrary, it will always assume a certain sense. It will resume signs belonging to a language yet now lacking the guarantee of making sense. In such discourse one will necessarily speak a language (philosophy at the limit speaking English, German, etc.), and yet one will need to do so without giving in to what Nancy calls a kind of somnambulistic Platonism that consists in taking words as if they were immediately to be equated with things, or, more precisely, with the sense or essence of things.[18] It would be a matter of resuming the words of one's language without taking the security of their sense for granted, without failing to heed the possibility—the threat—of nonsense. Or, positively, it is a matter of resuming them in such a way as to engender sense anew and thereby to endow the discourse with an appropriate binding power.

Three ways may be sketched, leaving open the question whether they are fully formalizable and hence capable of presentation in advance. Leaving aside also all totalizing claims, as one must when it is a question of idiom. And acknowledging from the outset that the three ways are not entirely distinct, not wholly independent.

---

17. F. W. J. Schelling, *Darstellung meines System der Philosophie*, in *Schriften von 1801–04* (Darmstadt: Wissenschaftliche Buchgesellschaft, 1968), 10.

18. "If there is an illusion from which one must protect oneself today more than ever, it is the illusion that consists in getting hung up on *words* (history, philosophy, politics, art . . .) as if they were immediately [to be equated] with *things*. Those who insist obstinately on this illusion—that is, basically on the realism of the idea—reveal by this type of somnambulistic Platonism that they have not yet joined our time or its end" (Nancy, *Le Sens du Monde,* 14).

Leaving this very discourse itself suspended, exposed to the very possibilities that it would begin to counter.

One of the ways relies on a kind of remembrance. Specifically, it involves a remembrance of an old—even ancient—word and of a sense of that word that resists being excluded by the turn that philosophy carries out at the limit. The remembrance is such as to bring back a significant word that remains at the limit—that is, that perdures even after the Nietzschean turn and that does so precisely because, in its original context, it already broaches suspension and interruption that are akin, if from afar, to those effected by that turn. Such remembrance cannot but proceed by way of an old text, by an operation that translates the text back to itself (for instance, translating the Platonic text back, as it were, into Greek). By means of this operation, one not only would clear away what the text has subsequently been made to say but, above all, would expose what it has been made not to say. Or rather, one would bring its retreat of sense to show itself, no doubt putting into play not only remembrance but also—in a perhaps unheard-of sense—imagination.

The word that imposes itself in this regard as the example of examples is the Platonic word χώρα. Yet the remembrance not only brings back such an old word but comes to hear it in a native word, lending the native word a capacity to say something (of the) sensible, letting it engender sense anew through the infusion of remembrance effected by such complex, idiomatic translation. As in a discourse on what is called *spacing*.

A second way moves through phenomenology. Yet it does so in such a manner as to submit phenomenology to a mutation and in both regards links up with a particular remembrance. The text by way of which the remembrance proceeds is Plato's *Seventh Letter*, and the significant word that it brings back is τὸ πρᾶγμα αὐτό. The passage is well-known. Its author writes that there are no writings of his that deal with what he seriously pursues in his studies. For there is no saying it as with other things learned; rather, from being often with τὸ πρᾶγμα αὐτό, it is brought to birth in the soul instantaneously (ἐξαίφνης), as light is kindled by a leaping spark.[19]

It would be difficult to enumerate all the decisive junctures in the history of philosophy and beyond where appeal has been made to τὸ πρᾶγμα αὐτό—which is to be heard now in *die Sache selbst* and in *the thing itself*—and where that move has been paired with a distancing from texts and often from speech as such. When Descartes turns from the books of the tradition to the great book of the world, he comes, as he says, "to reflect on the things that present themselves [*à faire telle réflexion sur les choses qui se présentaient*]."[20] In this regard Hegel draws the sharpest of contrasts between the

---

19. Plato, *Seventh Letter* 341c.

20. R. Descartes, *Discours de la Méthode* (Paris: Hatier, n.d.), 18. See *Oeuvres de Descartes*, ed. Charles Adam and Paul Tannery (Paris: Vrin, 1996), 6:9.

writing (or reading) of prefaces and the need to tarry with and lose oneself in the thing (*Sache*), to be preoccupied with it, to surrender to it.[21] And Husserl, launching the very project of phenomenology, proposes to proceed by "being guided by the things themselves [*Sachen selbst*], getting away from talk and opinion back to the things themselves, questioning them in their self-givenness."[22]

Phenomenology radicalizes, and at the same time orients in a certain direction, both the Platonic disclaimer regarding writing and speech and the appeal to the (now pluralized) things themselves. Its injunction is that one put aside all talk and opinion and turn to things themselves as they give themselves, as they present themselves. It may therefore seem paradoxical that phenomenology is also precisely the prospect onto which the turn of philosophy at the limit opens. For what comes to be required is that sensible things be envisaged not by referral to the intelligible but rather *from themselves*. Yet they can be envisaged from themselves only by being taken in their self-givenness, as they present themselves. It could be said even that one would need to continue taking them as appearances, though now in a different sense, not as appearances *of* something that would exceed the field of appearances, merely appearing there from afar, but as they themselves appear in their self-giving. What sets phenomenology apart—even if historically phenomenology has not always adhered to this motif—is its insistence on the identity of the things themselves, its insistence that appearing things are themselves the things themselves, that they are not the mere appearances of things themselves that, remote from appearances, would shine in and through them. To the extent that phenomenology adheres to this motif, insisting on this insistence, it can appropriately be called pragmatology.

Putting aside all talk and opinion, suspending even the entire legacy that philosophy has bequeathed through its texts, phenomenology as pragmatology would turn rigorously to the things themselves. Indeed this turn, this insistence on being bound by the things themselves, determines the very sense of rigor; to proceed rigorously is precisely to let every step be determined by and from the things themselves. Yet to proceed at all is to carry out a return to discourse, to come back to speech and, most likely, to writing. Even if, layering suspension upon suspension, pragmatology could simply begin, the simplicity of the beginning would be violated by the return to—the return of—discourse that would come into play from the beginning. Setting discourse aside in order to be bound by the things themselves, pragmatology could not but come back around to discourse in order to double in discourse the things themselves as they present themselves.

---

21. See Hegel, *Phänomenologie des Geistes*, vol. 9 of *Gesammelte Werke* (Hamburg: Felix Meiner, 1980), 9–11.

22. Husserl, *Ideen I*, 42.

Indeed what is enjoined in the appeal to the things themselves is that this discourse be bound by the self-presentation of the things themselves. By being bound to the things themselves as they present themselves from themselves, the discourse becomes rigorous; by being thus bound, it acquires its binding power. By the same stroke, it is endowed with a certain resistance to the insecurity and the nonsense that threatens the discourse of philosophy at the limit. By being bound to the things themselves, by drawing what is said from the things themselves as they present themselves, pragmatological discourse engenders sense from the things themselves.

What Husserl calls the principle of all principles merely elaborates what is already enjoined in the appeal to the things themselves. Again, everything begins with a suspension of talk and opinion, with distance being taken from mere theories: "Yet enough of such inverted, perverted theories [*Doch genug der verkehrten Theorien*]." Husserl literally, textually, suspends his statement of the principle of all principles within his statement of its distancing from such theories. Here, in translation, is what he writes exactly as he writes it, straining the syntactical possibilities of English even more than those of German: "In regard to the *principle of all principles*: that *every originarily donative intuition* [jede originär gebende Anschauung] is *a legitimizing source of knowledge*, that *everything originarily* (so to speak, in its bodily actuality) *offered* to us in *'intuition'* ['Intuition'] *is to be accepted simply as what it presents itself* [*gives itself*—sich gibt] *as being*, but also *only within the limits in which it there presents itself*, no conceivable theory can mislead us."[23] Husserl declares that any statement that does nothing further than lend expression to such givens (*Gegebenheiten*) through mere explication and precisely measured significations (*genau sich anmessende Bedeutungen*) is an *absolute beginning* (*ein absoluter Anfang*).[24]

And yet, one cannot but suspect that any such allegedly absolute beginning—simply beginning—will prove to have been compromised by some anteriority. Especially now, with philosophy at the limit, the question is whether one can assume that secure significations are at hand for simply

---

23. Ibid., 52. This principle remains completely intact in the *Cartesian Meditations*. Calling it "*a first methodological principle*" and connecting it more explicitly with the question of beginning, Husserl writes: "It is plain that I, as one who is beginning philosophically, since I am striving toward the presumptive end, genuine science, must neither make nor continue to accept any judgment as scientific that I have not derived from evidence, from *experiences* [*aus Erfahrungen*] in which the things and complexes of things [*Sachen und Sachverhalte*] in question are present [*gegenwärtig*] to me as *they themselves*" (Husserl, *Cartesianische Meditationen und Pariser Vorträge*, vol. 1 of *Husserliana*, ed. S. Strasser [The Hague: Martinus Nijhoff, 1950], 54).

24. Husserl, *Ideen I*, 52. Much the same declaration occurs in the *Cartesian Meditations* in conjunction with the statement of the first methodological principle: "All that has been developed as beginnings of philosophy we must first acquire by ourselves" (Husserl, *Cartesianische Meditationen*, 53). In his English translation Cairns substitutes the following variant: "Everything that makes a philosophical beginning possible we must first acquire by ourselves" (Husserl, *Cartesian Meditations*, trans. Dorion Cairns [The Hague: Martinus Nijhoff, 1960], 13).

explicating, simply doubling in the order of discourse and signification, the givens to which they would be rigorously bound. Are established significations simply available that can be measured and ascertained to measure up exactly to the givens? Is there a measure capable of governing such mere explication, capable of assuring that what is said neither exceeds, falls short of, nor deviates from what is given to originary intuition? Is there a store of secure significations from which one would have only to choose those that fit? Or, now, with philosophy at the limit, does the transition from the intuited things themselves to discourse not become more unforeseeable, something quite other than mere explication? Can it be only an operation of fitting statements to things intuited, even assuming that it is self-evident what such fittingness, this measure, would consist in? Is there not required instead an operation that, in binding the discourse to the things themselves, begins to secure the discourse itself against the threat of nonsense, against the nonsense that can surreptitiously have invaded in advance any signification that one would merely employ naively in an explication?

These questions link up not only with the critique of the phenomenological principle of all principles that has determined the most decisive subsequent developments (by Heidegger, Levinas, Derrida, and others); especially where the questions touch on that of an absolute beginning, they are pertinent also to the question of presuppositionlessness (*Voraussetzungslosigkeit*).[25] This is the question that deconstruction, as one calls it, poses most directly to classical, Husserlian phenomenology. Yet the question whether phenomenology contains a presupposition, indeed a metaphysical presupposition, does not orient a search merely for an assumption that has managed somehow to escape the scrutiny of the phenomenologist, an assumption that, once detected, could be either expelled or justified so as in either case to leave phenomenology intact. On the contrary, the question is that of a presupposition that would belong to the very constitution of phenomenology, a presupposition that could not be called into question without exposing phenomenology as such to the possibility of undergoing a mutation.

In this regard Derrida's accomplishment is to have shown that the very vigilance of the phenomenologist, governed by the requirement of rigor, is already controlled by a massive metaphysical presupposition. This pre-

---

25. In his Preface to Boyce Gibson's 1931 translation of *Ideen I*, Husserl draws a connection between the orientation to beginning and an "absolute freedom from all presuppositions." Curiously, however, he goes on to characterize himself as only a beginner: "The author's convictions on such lines have become increasingly self-evident as his work progressed. If he has been obliged, on practical grounds, to lower the ideal of the philosopher to that of a downright beginner, he has at least in his old age reached for himself the complete certainty that he should thus call himself a beginner." But to accept being a beginner and nothing more for one's entire life—even if still dreaming of "the 'promised land' on which he himself will never set foot"—comes very close to admitting finally that one will never simply have begun.

supposition, constituting classical phenomenology from within, is most transparently expressed precisely in the principle of all principles, in the all-determining role that it assigns to "originary self-giving evidence, the *present* or *presence* of sense to a full and originary intuition."[26] For it is not as though presence to intuition is first made all-determining with the advent of phenomenology; on the contrary, such recourse to presence is—as Heidegger showed already in the 1920s[27]—ever again repeated in the history of philosophy. Thus it is that Derrida aims at "beginning to confirm that the recourse to phenomenological critique is the metaphysical project itself in its historical achievement and in the purity, yet now restored, of its origin."[28] To have recourse to the principle of all principles, to its assignment of an all-determining role to presence to intuition, would not be, then, to broach an absolute beginning at all but rather would be only to begin again, to redouble—even if in the purity of its origin—the beginning ventured ever again from Plato to Hegel.

The deconstructive or double reading of Husserl's text undertakes to show how, despite all its classical coordinates (the priority of intuition, the stigmatic *now*, the priority of expression over indication), Husserl's work instigates also a certain countermovement that disturbs all these coordinates. In each direction in which such a reading is ventured (temporalization, intersubjectivity, etc.), it is a matter of recognizing an irreducible nonpresence as having constitutive value. It is a matter of recognizing that when things come to show themselves there are always constitutive moments that are withheld from presence, that are not given to intuition. To a discourse rigorously governed by the principle of all principles, such moments will remain inaccessible and unmarked as such, even though they bear on the very constitution of things themselves as they show themselves, even though Husserl's own concrete work on the things themselves, instigating a countermovement, serves to disclose the operation of precisely such moments.

In this manner phenomenology as pragmatology undergoes a mutation. Its defining orientation can no longer be toward presence alone but rather

---

26. Jacques Derrida, *La Voix et le Phénomène* (Paris: Presses Universitaires de France, 1967), 3.

27. In his 1925–26 lecture course *Logik,* Heidegger writes: "By radically comprehending the concept of intuition for the first time, Husserl thought the great tradition of Western philosophy through to its end." Mentioning Husserl's principle of all principles, Heidegger then proceeds through the history of philosophy—discussing (in order) Kant, Leibniz, Descartes, Aquinas, Hegel—indicating in each instance the determining role assigned to intuition (and, hence, to presence) (Heidegger, *Logik: Die Frage nach der Wahrheit,* vol. 21 of *Gesamtausgabe* [Frankfurt a.M.: Vittorio Klostermann, 1976], 114–23). It is against this background that in *Being and Time* Heidegger writes that "pure intuition has been deprived of its priority, which corresponds noetically to the traditional ontological priority of the present-at-hand [*des Vorhandenen*]" (Heidegger, *Sein und Zeit,* 9th ed. [Tübingen: Max Niemeyer, 1960], 147).

28. Derrida, *La Voix et le Phénomène,* 3.

must be toward showing, toward the showing in which things themselves come to show themselves from themselves and to which belong moments that are constitutive and yet are utterly irreducible either to presence or to some mode of presence. It is not easily—if at all—foreseeable how such a mutated pragmatology will compose its discourse. At most one might extrapolate along very general lines and suppose that in bringing to a kind of presence something irreducibly nonpresent, such a venture would have recourse to imagination.

In a sense the self-showing of things themselves would now also be haunted by a certain insecurity, though not quite the same insecurity that haunts the discourse of philosophy at the limit. In the wake of this mutation, endowing the discourse with binding power and developing its idiom so as to engender sense can no longer be a matter of binding it to the bedrock of presence; now the venture must be to find out how to take up into discourse the self-showing of things themselves. And that requires perhaps that one first of all find out how to discern in the very slightest, momentary gesture what a thing thereby shows itself to be. As the slightest, momentary gesture of the hand can disclose who someone is. As, according to Plato's *Seventh Letter,* from being often with the thing itself, what one pursues can suddenly, in a flash, be brought to birth in one's soul, as light is kindled by a leaping spark.

In this mutation by which it is rigorously reoriented to the self-showing of things themselves, phenomenology as pragmatology could be called monstrology. To be sure, the word is itself something of a monstrosity, a kind of unnatural melding of stems from different languages. But it could serve to emphasize the orientation of the discourse (λόγος) to showing (*monstrare*), while also alluding to the monstrosities to which such discourse will inevitably be exposed: that in which nonsense becomes interior to, rather than the opposite of, sense, an unnatural deviation that appears to confound what nature would set apart; and the divergence from nature within nature that will be called the elemental, the hypernature in nature.

There remains a third way in which the discourse of philosophy at the limit can endure the loss of secure anterior significations and be brought to engender sense anew. It is a way that has been in play from the beginning, since before the beginning. The way consists in grafting the discourse onto a poetic text in such a way as to draw from that text something of its power to engender sense in unheard-of phrases and turns of phrase. In this way one would venture to lend a certain poetic force to the discourse of philosophy at the limit—to lend it a special force of imagination—interweaving it with certain of those flowery bands that poets wreathe so as, in Keats' words, to bind us to the earth.

2

REMEMBRANCE

A. IMAGINATION AT THE LIMIT

It is a very old word, already intact in Middle English and found in Chaucer in the form *ymagynacioun,* common since antiquity in the Latin to which it is cognate, *imaginatio.* In these forms and the others that now would be gathered under—translated into—*imagination,* what was signified was a power that philosophy never quite succeeded in fully appropriating or domesticating. Drawing upon this power, putting it in service to the highest interests, philosophy was always compelled also to exclude imagination, to set it at a distance, and even to reserve a refuge in which finally there would be protection from the threat of imagination. The dynamics of the relation of philosophy to imagination remained one of ambivalence and, though a semblance of reconciliation, even appropriation, was repeatedly made to veil the tension, it invariably broke out again in ever new guises.[1] Imagination has never entirely ceased exerting a kind of oblique force on philosophy, countering it precisely in driving it on, forcing it to diverge from its

---

1. See my discussion in *Delimitations,* chap. 1.

proper destination, interrupting and suspending its smooth operation. In this dynamic sense, imagination remains at the limit of philosophy. Thus it is that a remembrance of what is now gathered in this old word can bring back something that perdures in its force even through the turn that philosophy carries out at the limit.

What does one hear in this old word? What it presumes to name is something inward, something of the soul, of the subject, a certain power with which the soul or the subject is endowed. In the word one would hear named a distinctive power of the soul (δύναμις τῆς ψυχῆς), a particular faculty of the subject. In whatever way it might be specifically determined, *imagination* would name a power possessed by the soul, a faculty belonging to the subject. This general determination would be invariant even with respect to any redetermination of the being previously determined as soul or as subject, its redetermination, for instance, as spirit, as will, or as consciousness.

And yet, if now one returns to the very texts that would seem to have established this general determination, it proves much less stable and certain than one might have supposed. In this regard reference to two recent discussions is pertinent.

One occurs in Eva Brann's monumental study of imagination. It concerns the interpretation of a passage in *On the Soul* in which Aristotle writes about what he calls φαντασία, one of the ancient words that resound in *imagination,* even though its cognate forms remain effective in modern European languages. In the passage in question Aristotle writes of φαντασία in relation to the powers of the soul. Brann underlines the way in which Aristotle's text—this "short text that is long in perplexities"[2]—may be taken to put in question, even to deny, the identification of φαντασία—and so, of imagination—as a power or condition (δύναμις ἢ ἕξις) of the soul. Following Hamlyn, she renders Aristotle's opening sentence as a question: "If *phantasia* is that according to which we say that a *phantasma* comes to be in us (and if we don't speak in a metaphor), is it a power or a condition by which we judge and are correct or incorrect?"[3] While granting that it is grammatically possible to construe the sentence as a statement (the more common rendering), Brann argues that such a rendering would be incoherent with the conclusion that much of the remainder of the passage on φαντασία is devoted to establishing. For, immediately following the opening sentence, Aristotle goes on to give what may be regarded as an exclusive enumeration of the relevant powers: "Such are sensation, opinion, knowledge, intellect [αἴσθησις, δόξα, ἐπιστήμη, νοῦς]." What then follows is a demonstration that φαντασία is not any of these four powers. One may

---

2. Eva T. H. Brann, *The World of the Imagination: Sum and Substance* (Savage, Md.: Rowman and Littlefield, 1991), 40.

3. Aristotle, *On the Soul* 428a. Cf. Brann, *The World of the Imagination,* 41.

conclude, as does Brann, that φαντασία is not a power of the soul, at least not *properly* a power of the soul, though it might be called such metaphorically: "I therefore understand Aristotle to say that those who call it a power speak of it metaphorically."[4] On the other hand, one could regard Aristotle's enumeration to include only the powers by which we judge or discriminate (καθ' ἥν κρίνομεν) and so are correct or incorrect, that is, either present truth or purvey falsity (καὶ ἀληθεύομεν ἢ ψευδόμεθα). Yet even in this case, which would leave open the possibility that φαντασία might be some other kind of power of the soul, the passage would still have left in question, in a certain suspension, any straightforward inclusion of φαντασία with those powers of the soul to which, superficially at least, it appears most akin.

The other discussion occurs in a recent paper by Rodolphe Gasché and concerns the peculiar displacement—Gasché calls it "abysmality"—that imagination (translating *Einbildungskraft*),[5] precisely because of the constitutive role it plays for Kant, undergoes in Kant's text. It is virtually as if imagination were absent, as indeed, literally, it is missing from that table at the end of the Introduction to the *Critique of Judgment* that Kant himself designates as a list of all the faculties of the mind (*Gesamte Vermögen des Gemüts*). Gasché sets about to show that this literal absence is duplicated in Kant's analysis of imagination (especially in the *Anthropology*), concluding that imagination, precisely in empowering all the powers, is never itself except by the grace of those (other) powers, that it "lacks an *itself* while at the same time performing operations without which the other faculties would remain empty or would be deprived of any bearing on cognition or moral action."[6] This lack of an *itself* imparts to imagination a certain resistance to the question of *what* it *is* and thus suspends, in particular, its straightforward determination as a faculty of the subject.

Such return to the texts in which are determined the old words that resound in *imagination* needs to be carried out more extensively. By translating these texts, as it were, back to themselves, one can free the names of imagination to their more exorbitant senses, thus preparing their remembrance at the limit. For in the turn that outlines the limit to which philosophy now cannot but be exposed, *imagination* too suffers the loss of anterior signification. One can no longer take it for granted that what imagination is as such is established anterior to all discourse on imagination, that *imagination* has a predetermined sense to which that which is called imagina-

---

4. Brann, *The World of the Imagination*, 41.

5. Gasché alludes to the failure of this translation to preserve the full semantics of *Einbildungskraft*, referring to "Kant's own definitions of imagination as the power of synthesis in general, of presentation (*Darstellung*), of intuition without the presence of the object, or of forming one image from several others—thus drawing on the semantics of *Einbildungskraft*—" (Rodolphe Gasché, "Leaps of Imagination," in *The Path of Archaic Thinking*, ed. Kenneth Maly [Albany: State University of New York Press, 1995], 35).

6. Ibid., 44.

tion—that to which *imagination* refers—would conform in its concrete determinateness. Without the security of anterior signification, one can no longer propose a mere phenomenological explication of the sense of *imagination*. Rather, what is required is a discourse that, even if also phenomenological or, more precisely, monstrological, is capable of engendering anew a sense of imagination. One of the primary ways of preparing and fostering such discourse is by remembrance of the old words that resound in *imagination*, by a remembrance that begins the labor of freeing the traces of exorbitant sense retained by these words and of translating them into *imagination* so as to lend it now an exorbitant and unheard-of sense.

B. THE NAMES OF IMAGINATION

Drawing upon the force of imagination, philosophy has also been obliged, because of the ambivalence of that force, to set imagination at a distance and to provide itself with protection against the disruptiveness of the force of imagination. Ever again philosophy attests that imagination has a double effect, a double directionality, bringing about illumination and elevation, on the one hand, and deception and corruption, on the other, bringing them about perhaps even in such utter proximity that neither can, with complete assurance, be decisively separated from the other.

Such attestation is conspicuous in the Platonic dialogues. In the *Sophist*, for example, the search for the sophist carried out by the Eleatic Stranger and Theaetetus focuses on a certain practice that could be called—turning the subsequent translations back upon the Platonic text—an exercise of imagination. This exercise consists in a certain making and purveying of images, of what the Stranger terms—not unproblematically—spoken images. He says that the sophist is able to "bewitch the young through their ears with speeches [λόγοι] while they are still standing at a distance from the things of truth [τῶν πραγμάτων τῆς ἀληθείας], by exhibiting to them spoken images of all things [εἴδωλα λεγόμενα περὶ πάντων], so as to make it seem that they are true and that the speaker is the wisest of all men in all things."[7] Since the sophist is thus a purveyor of imitations, the Stranger focuses on imitative practice, on imitation (μίμησις) as such. Through division of it into its two kinds, the Stranger sets out tracking the sophist, trying to corner him so as to expose and illuminate the place in which otherwise the sophist can conceal himself so effectively that he appears to be the wisest of all men in all things, disguising himself even as the philosopher, rendering the difference imperceptible. According to the Stranger, the first of the two kinds of imitation (or of image-making—εἰδωλοποιικὴ τέχνη) has to do with the production of likenesses (εἰκών): likeness-making (εἰκαστικὴ τέχνη) produces an image or imitation by following the propor-

---

7. Plato, *Sophist* 234c.

tions of the original, of the paradigm, and by giving the right color to each part. What such τέχνη produces is other than the paradigm but like it. On the other hand, the second kind of imitation or image-making produces, not a likeness, but only something that *seems* (φαίνεται) to be like its paradigm. Such a product can appropriately be called a semblance (φάντασμα), and the τέχνη that produces such images the Stranger calls semblance-making or phantastic (φανταστική) τέχνη.

In naming the two kinds of imitation, the Stranger introduces the two families of words by which the Greeks designated what later thought—through a complex history of translation, inversion, and exchange—will call imagination, the imaginary, etc. On the one side, the root is the verb εἴκω (*be like*), from which derive εἰκών (*likeness* or *image*) and εἰκασία, one of the words for what will later be called imagination. On the other side, there is the root φαίνω (*seem, appear*), mentioned in its middle-voice form (φαίνεται) by the Stranger; from it derive φάντασμα (*semblance* or *appearance*) and φαντασία, the other word for what will later be called imagination. Yet it will not be a matter of two distinct and parallel histories, as though two distinct things themselves had at the outset been delimited once and for all and would then only be differently designated in the future. Rather, the history of translation that stems from these two families of words is a history of mutations, repressions, inversions, and exchanges, in which the delimitation of what is called by the various names that might be gathered under *imagination* proves to be by no means independent of the way in which the various names are deployed. In a sense this history is foreshadowed by the way in which, having drawn the seemingly rigorous, linguistically precise distinction between two kinds of image-making (εἰκαστική and φανταστική), the Stranger then proceeds. For, rather than being, as he had expected, then assured of having trapped the sophist in one of the two kinds distinguished, he confesses that now, as before, he cannot see clearly just where the sophist is hidden. For the sophist is very difficult to keep in sight and, says the Stranger, has now withdrawn into a kind of place that is impassible (εἰς ἄπορον εἶδος), where it is hard to see one's way, where it is hard to track the prey. The division carried out has not sufficed to contain the sophist in a delimited kind (of τέχνη), and one realizes that the force of sophistry lies not only in producing semblances of other things but also in covering that very operation with a semblance that makes it look otherwise and that prevents its being simply confined to the kind of imitative τέχνη that makes semblances. The force of imagination is attested not only by its twofold productivity but also by the facility with which it can make its semblances seem like likenesses so as to dissemble its own operation, keeping itself withdrawn, in hiding.

This self-dissembling double force of what subsequently will be translated into *imagination* forms one of the primary axes on which the *Republic* turns, installing in this dialogue a tension so originary that it reappears throughout virtually the entire history of Platonism and even beyond. It is a tension pertaining to the originary, the original, the paradigm, specifically to the relation of an image to its original. In the most general but not therefore most forceful formulation, the tension lies in the twofold capacity of the image: on the one side, by imaging the original, the image serves to present it, to draw one's vision to it; on the other side, as other than the original, as removed from it, the image has also the capacity to present the original otherwise than it truly is, to conceal and distort it, while dissembling that very operation, making its semblances look like likenesses.

Although the word εἰκών (*likeness* or *image*) is common in the Platonic texts, the word εἰκασία, which names the apprehension of images in their revelatory capacity, is extremely rare. There are only two occurrences, both of them near the center of the *Republic*.[8] Their locations in the text are not insignificant. The first comes at the very end of Book 6, thus immediately preceding the presentation of the image of the cave with which Book 7 begins. The second occurrence follows that presentation as well as the outline of the course of studies, which in effect amplifies in the form of a curriculum a portion of the ascent just told of in the presentation of the image. Both occurrences come at a point where Socrates summarizes what has been said of the ascent, marking its segments and assigning a name to each, or, more precisely, to the affections in the soul (παθήματα ἐν τῇ ψυχῇ) that arise in relation to each of the four segments: to the uppermost segment there corresponds νόησις or ἐπιστήμη; to the second, διάνοια; to the third, πίστις; to the fourth, εἰκασία.[9]

The sense of these names is determined by the discourses in which Socrates presents the images of the cave and the figure of the divided line to which it corresponds. What is at stake in these discourses is a movement of the soul, and what both the image and the figure represent is the course of this movement. The movement is one of liberation in which the soul, initially in bondage to images, ascends toward the free vision of the original. Bondage to images consists precisely in the failure to see them *as images:* the prisoners chained in the cave are confined to seeing only the shadows on the inner wall, and their condition is determined by their belief that there is nothing further to see, nothing beyond the shadows, which

---

8. The only other occurrence listed by Ast is in the spurious dialogue *Sisyphus*. There is a significant occurrence of the word in Xenophon's *Memorabilia* (III.x.1), in the account of Socrates' conversation with a painter: "Thus, on entering the house of Parrhasius the painter one day, he [Socrates] asked in the course of a conversation with him: 'Is painting a representation [εἰκασία] of things seen, Parrhasius?'"

9. Among the traditional translations are intellection (νόησις), knowledge (ἐπιστήμη), thought (διάνοια), trust (πίστις), and imagination (εἰκασία). Yet in these and other traditional translations there are sedimented so many subsequent determinations—determinations that only became possible starting from what the Platonic texts accomplished—that they serve more to obstruct than to further access to those texts. Today especially there is need to translate Plato back into Greek.

are thus not even recognized as shadows, as images, but rather are taken to be simply the things that are. In order that the prisoner's condition be disrupted, in order that the prisoner escape this bondage to images, a kind of double seeing must come into play: the prisoner must no longer simply see the images on the wall but must come also to see them precisely *as images* of other things, of those objects (all sorts of artifacts and statues of various creatures) being conveyed along behind the prisoner's back, those objects to which, as the ascent begins, the prisoner will turn. What is decisive in this turn is not just that the prisoner, at the moment of release, comes to see things other than those formerly seen on the wall of the cave. What is decisive is not just that the prisoner's vision is displaced from one domain of objects to another but that this very displacement be enacted in the prisoner's vision, which thereby ceases to be a mere apprehending of something present and becomes instead a double seeing. The prisoner comes to see through the image to the original that it images; the new vision that the prisoner achieves, the liberating vision, is constituted in the turning from image to original, the turning in which the image is recognized as image by being apprehended in its imaging of the original. Such double seeing is what Socrates names εἰκασία.

The inception of such double seeing is what launches the ascent. Yet, in turn, the movement up out of the cave, the extending of vision up toward the original of originals, will proceed precisely by repetition, at higher levels, of the double seeing that first launches the ascent. Those objects that cast shadows on the inner wall of the cave come to be seen as images of the things to be seen outside the cave—the statues, for instance, as images of the creatures they represent. And the things above ground, at first seen only as reflected, for instance, in pools of water, come to be apprehended through and beyond those images, that is, in a vision that turns from the image to the original imaged in and through it. Thus, at every level of the ascent double seeing will be in play, and, though εἰκασία explicitly names only the vision operative at the initial stage, in the lowest segment, it *can* name the vision operative at all stages of the ascent.[10] The entire ascent involves operations of double seeing,[11] reiterated turning from image to

---

10. Just as he is about to begin presenting the figure of the divided line, Socrates says, among other things: "I suppose I will leave out quite a bit" (*Rep.* 509c).

This interpretation of εἰκασία, its extension to the entire divided line, was proposed by Jacob Klein (*A Commentary on Plato's Meno* [Chapel Hill: University of North Carolina Press, 1965], 112–15). I have attempted to develop it in the reading of the *Republic* given in *Being and Logos*, chap. 5 (see especially 423–43).

11. Double seeing is not, however, the only force required for the ascent. For, precisely at the point where the transition would be made from sensible to intelligible (thus the transition across the major division of the line), there is within vision a certain coming to rest in the visible, that is, a collapse of double seeing into a simple vision of what is present. The transition to διάνοια requires, therefore, that another moment come into play so as to impel a dianoetic leap. This other moment is λόγος, and thus at this point the *Republic* reaffirms the decisive

original—that is, what can appropriately be called εἰκασία. If—reflecting subsequent translations back upon the Platonic text—one were to render εἰκασία as *imagination,* then one could say that the force of imagination is what preeminently makes it possible to carry out the liberating ascent, the turn to the originary, that is, the engagement in what is to be called philosophy.

Yet one must also say—continuing to translate backward—that imagination is preeminently capable of turning the soul away from the originary, indeed with such force as to conceal the originary and keep the soul utterly apart from it. Such is the accusation that, in Book 10 of the *Republic,* Socrates brings against what will (subsequently) be called imagination. It is precisely the tension between this accusation and the approbation voiced in the central Books that sets the dialogue itself turning between the demands of dialectic and the exigences of poetry.

The unity of the word is lacking in the *Republic,* a unity under which a single word like *imagination* would gather the terms of the tension. In Book 10 the word εἰκασία does not occur, nor is the discourse centered around a designation of images that would accord primary significance to their character as likenesses, as with the designation εἰκών. Though indeed reference to imitation, borne by the frequently occurring word μίμησις, governs the relevant discourse in Book 10, it does not yet have the generic function it assumes in the *Sophist.* At least as an explicit designation, it is reserved for the work—at least some of the work—of poets and painters; it is not extended to philosophy as portrayed in the central Books.

Indeed Book 10 begins by focusing on the part of poetry that is imitative (μιμητική) and by reaffirming the exclusion of such poetry from the city that has been built in λόγος. In order to justify this exclusion and, specifically, the thesis now proposed—that imitative poetry seems to mutilate the thought (διάνοια) of those who listen to it—Socrates addresses, with Glaucon, the question of what μίμησις as a whole is. Sketching the portrait of a wonderful (θαυμαστός)[12] master craftsman (δημιουργός) who is capable of fabricating everything whatsoever—all natural things, the earth, the heavens, the gods, and everything in the heavens and everything in Hades under the earth—Socrates reveals immediately to Glaucon how he too could be such a craftsman: "You could fabricate them quickly in many ways and most quickly, of course, if you are willing to take a mirror and carry it

---

connection posited autobiographically in the *Phaedo* (99d–e) between a turn to λόγος and the beginning of philosophy. See *Being and Logos,* 421, 437.

12. In connection with this designation it would not be out of the question to bring into play a reference to the discourse in the *Theaetetus* (155d) on wonder (θαυμάζειν) as the beginning (ἀρχή) of philosophy. Note that in the present context Glaucon uses the word θαυμαστός twice. Initially he calls the master craftsman strange (δεινός) and wonderful. Then, after Socrates goes on to enumerate all the things this craftsman can fabricate, Glaucon remarks that this man is a wonderful sophist.

around everywhere."[13] Glaucon's response introduces the first link in the chain of words by which he and Socrates will seek to capture the practitioners of imitative art: the things made in this fashion, says Glaucon, would be appearances (φαινόμενα) rather than things that in truth are. The painter is one of these craftsmen, and like all of them he makes things that only seem or appear. This seeming or appearing (the middle-voice form φαίνεται occurs at several junctures in this discourse) proves to be more complex than it initially appears to be, and this complexity contributes to the forcefulness with which—as Socrates' thesis puts it—it mutilates the thought of those exposed to it. For these appearances—fabricated by painters or, most quickly, by anyone who carries a mirror around everywhere—simulate being; that is, they seem to be and they seem to be in truth that as which they appear. Not only does the painter merely imitate the work of other, genuine craftsmen rather than the original things themselves, remaining thus thrice removed from truth, but also he imitates such products not as they are but only as they appear (φαίνεται). Whereas a couch seen from various perspectives only looks different (φαίνεται . . . ἀλλοία) but is not in truth different from itself, the painter is oriented to its looking as it looks, to its looks rather than its truth. Or rather, one could say, the painter imitates its looks in such a way as to make its looks look like its truth.

The word by which Socrates here designates the looks of the thing in distinction from its truth is φάντασμα. The word recurs as Socrates turns from painting to tragic poetry: what the tragedians produce are φαντάσματα, not beings (οὐκ ὄντα). As noted already, this is the word that in the *Sophist* is made to designate the products of the second kind of image-making: *semblances* (as it may be translated) in contrast to likenesses. One could also say, hardly exceeding transliteration: *phantoms*. And one could add what is virtually implied, completing the chain that includes φαίνω (and especially the middle-voice form φαίνεται), the participial form φαινόμενον, the derivative φάντασμα (with the associated verb φαντάζω: *make appear, make visible*): one could add, finally, the word that will most consistently be translated into *imagination*, the word φαντασία.

Socrates focuses finally on the consequences of such imitation: by making images (εἴδωλα) that are far removed from the truth, both the painter and the imitative poet produce a bad regime (πολιτεία) in the souls of individuals. For the phantoms conjured up by imitative artists deceive those exposed to them. The deception effected is complex and self-reinforcing: not only does the mimetic phantom represent the *mere look* of a thing as being, as though it *were*, as though it actually belonged to the thing as such, but also such representation sets the mere look in the place of the thing, displacing the thing into oblivion and thus effectively keeping the souls of

---

13. Plato, *Republic* 596d–e.

those exposed to such phantoms far removed from the truth and oblivious to that very removal. Thus, by the complex deception that imitation puts in effect, it is corruptive and produces a bad regime in the souls determined by it. Socrates is assured—pending a suitable apology—of the need to keep the poets exiled from the good city that has been projected in λόγος. He is assured also of the need for self-protection in the face of imitation, for a kind of countercharm to ward off the phantoms of poetry: "But as long as it is not able to make its apology, when we listen to it, we will chant to ourselves as a countercharm these words we are saying, taking care against falling back again into this love, which is childish and belongs to the many. We are, at all events, aware that such poetry must not be taken seriously as a serious thing laying hold of truth, but that the one who hears it must be careful, fearing for the regime in himself, and must hold what we have said about poetry."[14]

On both sides, imagination—what will be translated into *imagination*—has to do with looks: either with images that look like the original and that, by looking like it, present it and draw one's vision to it; or with images that present only the looks of the original, setting the looks in place of the original, fixing one's vision on the mere image, withdrawing the original from vision in such a way as to confine one's vision to mere shades, as in Hades.

This seminal differentiation persists throughout the history of ancient Platonism, though not without decisive mutations and recurrent shifts of focus. With Proclus, for instance, the focus of the Platonic critique of imitation shifts from a concern with the deceptive character of the appearances produced by it to a denunciation of it as oriented merely to pleasure. This shift is not without some basis in Book 10 of the *Republic*. Once Socrates has established that the imitative artist produces mere phantoms, he continues by considering how such products of imitation affect the souls of those exposed to them. He asks, in particular: On which part of the human being does imitation have the power (δύναμις) that it has? Where in the soul do the dissembling phantoms exercise their force? Drawing a contrast with the soul's calculating part, he answers: the phantoms have power over the soul's foolish part, which is incapable even of distinguishing great from small. In appealing to this part, imitative art is oriented to pleasure. To this extent Socrates can speak of "poetry directed to pleasure and imitation,"[15] as he does in acknowledging the charm of Homer while also holding open the possibility that by a suitable apology the poets might regain entry into the city of good laws.

In his *Commentary on Plato's Republic* Proclus contrasts directly the terms kept apart in the *Republic*: φαντασία and εἰκασία. Referring, for instance, to a passage in the *Laws*, he writes that music "has as its aim, not pleasure,

---

14. Ibid., 608a–b.
15. Ibid., 607c.

but the correctness of the eikastic copies [οὐ τὴν ἡδονὴν τέλος ἔχει, ἀλλὰ τὴν ὀρθότητα τῶν εἰκασθέντων]."[16] Referring to Socrates' discussion of imitative art in Book 10 of the *Republic*, Proclus distinguishes sharply between the operation of φαντασία, which is directed to pleasure, and that of εἰκασία, which is oriented to the correctness of the imitation and thus to its capacity to image the original, to make visible the paradigm: "For the phantastic mode [τὸ φανταστικόν] of imitation falls short of the eikastic [τὸ εἰκαστικόν] in this respect: that, whereas the eikastic looks to the correctness of the imitation, the phantastic looks only to the pleasure that comes to the multitude from phantasy [ἐκ τῆς φαντασίας]."[17] Thus Proclus brings into the discussion of imitation the determination of εἰκασία that in the *Republic* was kept apart in the central Books. On the one hand, then, he lets the distinction between φαντασία and εἰκασία be reflected back on the discourse on the divided line: eikastic imitation he identifies with correct opinion, which he takes to be represented by the third segment on the line (that of πίστις), whereas phantastic imitation he equates with false opinion, which he takes to be represented by the lowest segment (which Plato's text terms εἰκασία). On the other hand, both the eikastic and the phantastic mode are brought into the discourse on poetry in which Proclus comments on Book 10 of the *Republic*. Hence emerges a differentiation, barely if at all discernible in the *Republic*, between two kinds of poetry: "For instance, when the sun is represented as rising from a lake, not as it is, but as it appears to us on account of its distance, we have the phantastic power of the poet. But when he imitates heroes waging war, deliberating and speaking according to life, some discreet, some courageous, some fond of honor, such a work is eikastic."[18] Even a certain appropriation of myth to philosophy is prepared by the connection that Proclus forges between the Socratic discussion of poetry and the delimitation of philosophy in the central Books of the *Republic*. Whereas, in the Platonic text, it is only in the deed of λόγος—and never explicitly in the λόγος itself—that myth is appropriated, the reconfiguration achieved by Proclus makes it possible to regard certain imaginative moments in myth as providing images through which the higher originals become visible. Though one would expect Proclus to designate any such moment as eikastic, his actual reference is to myth as a kind of phantastical operation, a φανταστικὸς νοῦς.[19] It is as if, having differentiated the eikastic from the phantastic, he would go even further and open this very distinction again within the phantastic.

The shift that this differentiation undergoes between Plato and Proclus

---

16. Proclus Diadochus, *In Platonis Rem Publicam Commentarii*, ed. G. Kroll (Amsterdam: Verlag Adolf M. Hakkert, 1965), 1:190.

17. Ibid., 191.

18. Ibid., 192f.

19. Ibid., 2:107.

is indicative of the transformations found in the history of the names of imagination. The transformations occur largely in translation, first of all, within a single language, primarily Greek, and, less directly, in the translations from Greek to Latin and then into the modern European languages. Rarely, if ever, is such translation simply a matter of reproduction; on the contrary, there are typically shifts of focus, mutations in which certain senses get augmented or specified and differentiated, reductions in which certain distinctions get repressed or effaced, and inversions and exchanges between various senses. One would like to be able to say with full assurance: there is the sense of imagination, the signification, which then gets signified or expressed in various ways and in various languages. Yet, in saying this, one remains of course in the order of expression and posits the would-be pure signified only in correlation with its signifier. Even disregarding the loss of anterior signification to which philosophy is exposed at the limit, the possibility still must be left open that an absolute separation of the signified from the signifier may in this case be unsustainable. If so, then discussion of the history of translation would not be a matter of tracing the errant ways in which a determinate sense would have been translated and thus expressed; it would be, rather, a means of entering the circuit of translation, of exchange, between what is said and the various ways in which—in various languages and from various theoretical perspectives—it is said.

Medieval thought does not simply take over the distinction found in the Platonic texts, nor do the Latin translations in which the Greek determinations are appropriated correspond exactly to the terms εἰκασία and φαντασία by which Proclus marks the two modes distinguished by Plato. The relevant history is more complex and involves, most conspicuously, the re-determination that φαντασία undergoes with the Stoics, who transmit to the Middle Ages a configuration of senses and of concerns that diverges considerably from that of ancient Platonism.

Sextus Empiricus gives an extensive report on what the Stoics say of φαντασία.[20] He reports, first of all, that they take φαντασία to be an impression on the soul (τύπωσις ἐν ψυχῇ). Thus one can say, drawing out the contrast: the word now names neither a power (δύναμις) of the soul nor even quite something befallen, suffered, by the soul (the Platonic phrase is: ταῦτα παθήματα ἐν τῇ ψυχῇ γιγνόμενα)[21] but rather an inscriptive occurrence in the soul, one in which there is stamped on the soul an imprint that precisely as such has the capacity to present something. It would seem that φαντασία names both the inscriptive, presentative occurrence and the im-

---

20. Sextus Empiricus, *Against the Logicians I* (= *Adversus Mathematicos VII*), 227–62. For other, corroborating references see Murray Wright Bundy, *The Theory of Imagination in Classical and Mediaeval Thought* (Urbana: University of Illinois Press, 1927), 87–96; also those given below in connection specifically with Epictetus.

21. Plato, *Republic* 511d.

print, the impression, stamped on the soul through such an occurrence. Such imprints, curiously introduced under the title φαντασία, prove to haunt virtually the entire subsequent history of philosophy and, ironically, play a decisive role in repeatedly driving to the margin of philosophy that which would be signified by the names of imagination.

For the Stoics everything depends on what the impressions present. According to Sextus Empiricus, the Stoics take the very criterion of truth to lie in what they call cataleptic φαντασία; it is through the occurrence of such φαντασίαι that one is enabled to determine things in their truth. Sextus Empiricus explains that for a φαντασία to be cataleptic (καταληπτική) means that it arises from something and is distinctly impressed in accordance with that thing itself. Thus the mad Orestes cannot be said to have had a cataleptic φαντασία, for, though his φαντασία arose from Electra, it was not stamped in accordance with her, since he supposed her to be, instead, one of the Furies. For the Stoics a cataleptic φαντασία not only allows correct recognition of that from which it arises (thus such would have allowed Orestes to recognize Electra as herself), but also it enables one to discern the various characteristics of that from which the impression arises. Sextus Empiricus mentions even that such a φαντασία is taken to have, as compared with others, its own peculiarity (ἰδίωμα), an idiomatic trait marking it as cataleptic. It is said to be like the horned serpent, always distinguishable from others, from noncataleptic φαντασίαι, which either do not arise from anything (as with those had by persons in a morbid condition) or, if they do arise from something, are not imprinted in accordance with that thing (as with the mad Orestes). A cataleptic φαντασία would thus bear its own certification as such, and the force with which a noncataleptic φαντασία could deceive would be limited by the possibility of exposing its lack of such self-certification. And yet, Sextus Empiricus notes that there is some dispute regarding the manifestness of the difference: the Academics, he says, assert that a false φαντασία can be found exactly similar to the cataleptic one.

For the Stoics the fundamental distinction becomes that between cataleptic and noncataleptic φαντασίαι. In this distinction one could mark only the most remote affinity to that drawn by Plato or Proclus: not only is the double seeing that was designated as εἰκασία lacking entirely, but also, most decisively, the outwardly directed vision of images (the vision of shadows on the wall of the cave, that of the couch in the painterly work) has been replaced by a τέχνη of imprinting, which has the effect of driving vision back from things, of confining it in such a way that critical attention comes to be focused on the reliability of the impressions, which needs somehow to be discernible in the idiom of the impressions themselves. For this fundamental distinction between cataleptic and noncataleptic φαντασίαι, the Stoics redeploy the words belonging to the group generated from φαίνω, even though, ironically, it is precisely *seeming* and *appearing* that get reduced and displaced in Stoic thought. The otherwise generic φαντασία comes to be reserved for the cataleptic species. For noncataleptic φαντασία the Stoics adopt the word φάντασμα.[22] Therefore, the fundamental distinction that emerges in Stoic thought is expressed as the difference between φαντασία and φάντασμα.

This distinction reappears in the thought of Albertus Magnus: φαντασία and φάντασμα are translated, respectively, into *imaginatio* and *phantasia*, and the distinction itself is thoroughly transformed. At the same time, Albertus Magnus renews the Aristotelian effort, as in *On the Soul*, to distinguish analytically and rigorously between the various powers or faculties. One moment in the translation and transformation reorients *imaginatio* and *phantasia* in such a way that they come to name, not just an inscriptive occurrence or the resulting impression, but rather, in each case, the *facultas* through which such an occurrence is possible. Another moment in the transformation consists in an inversion: for Albertus Magnus it is *phantasia* that is the superior faculty—indeed, precisely because, unlike *imaginatio*, it is not bound to cataleptic impressions nor to the apprehension—even if extended—of sensible things achieved by means of such impressions.

In *De Apprehensione* Albertus Magnus distinguishes five apprehensive faculties: common sense, *imaginatio,* the estimative faculty, *phantasia,* and memory. Along with common sense and memory, *imaginatio* is retentive: it is a faculty for retaining and preserving primary impressions provided by common sense. On the other hand, the essential function of *phantasia* is to compare, unite, and divide; Albertus Magnus notes that it is this faculty that enables one to picture a man with two heads or a being with a human body, the head of a lion, and the tail of a horse. Whereas *imaginatio* is bound to the function of retaining and preserving images of things derived from sense, *phantasia* is more than a sensory power; it freely configures the images provided by the sensible faculties, yet without regard for the truth of the configurations it conjures up. *Phantasia* is the noblest of the apprehensive faculties. Yet, on precisely this account, it is also the most dangerous: for the images and fictions of *phantasia* can easily give rise to error and deception. Thus, it must be held in check, kept subservient to the higher, intellective or rational faculties.[23]

The differentiation of modes corresponding to the various names of imagination, a differentiation carried out almost always in proximity to the question of its force, is thus subject to recurrent shifts and mutations borne

---

22. See Bundy, *Theory of Imagination,* 89.

23. Albertus Magnus, *De Apprehensione,* pts. 3–4, in vol. 5 of *Opera Omnia,* ed. A. Borgnet (Paris: Vivès, 1890), 577–89. In this account Albertus Magnus uses the expression *virtus imaginativa*. In the more extended account given in *Summae de Creaturis* (part 2), this faculty is called *potentia imaginativa* or simply *imaginatio* (*Opera Omnia,* 35:323). The example of the phantastically composed creature is given in the discussion of *phantasia* in *Summae de Creaturis* (ibid., 332).

especially through translation. Thus, when the variously elaborated medieval distinction between *imaginatio* and *phantasia* comes to be translated and developed in English Romanticism as the distinction between imagination and fancy, it is imagination that is considered the superior power. Hence, in Coleridge's celebrated distinction between imagination and fancy, the distinction elaborated by Albertus Magnus has undergone an inversion and a shift of levels: *imagination,* translating *imaginatio,* can aptly name a creative power higher than *phantasia,* since it is free of the connotations of error and deception, which *phantasia* continued to have; at the same time, *phantasia,* translated into *fancy,* seems by comparison to be almost mechanical, bound to the law of association. Yet, remarkably, one can still hear in Coleridge's words an echo of the Platonic εἰκασία, at least of the force of ascent that it would provide. As in the following passage from a lecture that Coleridge delivered in 1795: "Our Almighty Parent hath therefore given to us Imagination that stimulates to the attainment of *real* excellence by the contemplation of splendid Possibilities that still revivifies the dying motive within us, and fixing our eye on the glittering Summits that rise one above the other in Alpine endlessness still urges us up the ascent of Being, amusing the ruggedness of the road with the beauty and grandeur of the ever-widening Prospect."[24]

The force of what is called by the names of imagination is attested even more widely. Although the Platonic discussions refer to the way in which the images fashioned by imitation could prove corruptive, producing a bad regime in the soul, the practical concern with the corruptive force of images is both enhanced and broadened in Stoicism. Such concern is most conspicuous in the *Discourses* of Epictetus. It is, above all, a *practical* concern, a concern directed, not primarily at the philosophical analysis of φαντασίαι and of their corruptive force, but rather at principles and maxims by which one can effectively oppose their force and escape having one's actions corrupted by them. The theoretical attitude, which Epictetus tends to reduce to a kind of bookishness, is to be subordinated to life, to living. Epictetus illustrates this subordination with a contrary example that has to do precisely with φαντασίαι: "It is as if, when in the sphere of assent we were presented with φαντασίαι, some of them cataleptic and others noncataleptic, we should not wish to distinguish between them but to read a treatise *On Catalepsis.*"[25] Thus, Epictetus accepts the basic Stoic distinction and himself offers only the most meager, indeed quite formal analysis of φαντασίαι, remarking that they come to us in four ways, then indicating these ways by merely enumerating the possible combinations of the members of

---

24. "Lecture on the Slave-Trade," in *Imagination in Coleridge,* ed. John Spencer Hill (Totowa, N.J.: Rowman and Littlefield, 1978), 27. In a letter written in 1804, Coleridge describes imagination as "a dim Analogue of Creation" (ibid., 50), anticipating the concept of imagination that he was to develop in *Biographia Literaria* (1815, published 1817).

25. Epictetus, *Discourses* IV.iv.13.

the two pairs being/not being and seeming/not seeming.[26] Even when he addresses the question of cataleptic φαντασία, his concern is with assent: as when, in a chapter entitled "How We Must Exercise Ourselves against Φαντασίαι," amidst discussions of how to form the right habits for dealing with situations of death, disinheritance, condemnation, etc., he asserts that "we will never assent to anything but that of which we get a cataleptic φαντασία."[27]

Epictetus regards all action (πρᾶξις) as originating in φαντασίαι—hence their force, hence the need also to exercise oneself against them, lest they determine one's deeds in the wrong direction. More precisely, Epictetus says that "the measure of every human action is the φαινόμενον," that is, the operative appearance (appearance regarded in the way typical of Stoicism, as a presentative impression). In a remarkable passage he goes on to write of the great and terrible deeds that have their origin (ἀρχή) in φαντασία: "The *Iliad* is nothing but φαντασία and the use of φαντασίαι. To Alexander there came the appearance [ἐφάνη—from φαίνω] of carrying off the wife of Menelaus, and to Helen there came the appearance of following him. Now if an appearance had come that led Menelaus to feel that it was a gain to be deprived of such a wife, what would have happened? Not only the *Iliad* but also the *Odyssey* would have been lost."[28]

Since all deeds originate from φαντασίαι, all well-being depends on exercising control over the appearances that come: control, when possible, over their coming, control, in any case, over their use, over their governance of action. It is thus, says Epictetus, that we have received λόγος from nature, namely, in order that through this power a proper use might be made of φαντασίαι. By means of λόγος the philosopher is enabled to carry out his first and greatest deed: to test the φαντασίαι and discriminate between them, letting action originate only from those thus legitimated as sources of action. Epictetus advises all, when struck by φαντασία, to fight against it with λόγος, to beat it down so that it does not grow strong and make come whatever appearance it likes.[29] Every means is advised for preventing one's being carried away by, for instance, the vividness of the appearances that come. Every means should be employed against the situation in which, failing to test them, one lets originate from them deeds that are base or corruptive. One of the means that Epictetus urges is that, having exposed a sordid appearance, one "introduce and set over against it some fair and noble φαντασία and throw out the sordid one,"[30] practicing thus an art of displacement and substitution, letting noble appearances come to drive out base ones, redirecting the lines of force.

---

26. See ibid., I.xxvii.1–2.
27. Ibid., III.viii.4–5.
28. Ibid., I.xxviii.10–14.
29. See ibid., I.xx.5–7 and III.xxiv.108.
30. Ibid., II.xviii.25–26.

Yet even in the practice of this art there is a difficulty with beginning, one that needs to be marked. The practice of displacement and substitution will be difficult simply to take in hand, for one will be able to use a fair and noble φαντασία to drive out a sordid one only if a fair and noble φαντασία *phantasia* comes before one's vision. The force of φαντασίαι lies not only in their originating of action but also in their inherent resistance to being simply produced, in their character as *coming* before one's vision. There comes an appearance, and then, depending on one's intervention through λόγος or through substitution of other appearances, it may or may not determine one to action and originate the particular deed. But, first of all, appearing must occur—that is, all begins with a "there comes."

Neoplatonism shares with Stoicism an insistence on the danger of φαντασίαι, on their capacity, even their positive tendency, to gain the upper hand in determining human action. This tendency is furthered all the more if, as Plotinus stresses, φαντασίαι are usually excited by the passions of the body. Only the rare individual, one elevated by the self-determining operation of intellect (τὴν τοῦ νοῦ ἐνέργειαν), will succeed in escaping enslavement to φαντασίαι and the passions that excite them.[31] For Plotinus the decisive ascensional force is not φαντασία but rather that which draws the soul beyond the sphere of φαντασία. To be sure, Plotinus does grant that under certain harmonious conditions φαντασία may operate as something of a mirror in which images of thought and intellect come to be reflected; yet, for him, there is no question but that these can operate—and in the more excellent souls do operate—without any admixture of φαντασία.[32] The proper name of the ascensional force is contemplation (θεωρία), which thus comes to displace φαντασία: "One who wishes to see the intelligible nature will, without any φαντασία of sense, contemplate what is beyond the sensible."[33] It is likewise with εἰκασία: "One does not bring the intelligibles to appear by εἰκασία or syllogistics ... but by the power [δύναμις] of contemplation [θεωρεῖν], which alone enables us to speak of them while we are here below."[34]

Other Neoplatonists attest to an ascensional force of φαντασία, while introducing a kind of transposition that reverses in some measure the directionality of the figure: instead of driving the soul upward, instead of constituting the motive force by which the soul could elevate itself, φαντασία becomes primarily the means by which what is intrinsically elevated descends into the soul; only as a result of this descent from above does the soul come to be itself drawn upward. It is through φαντασία that one is

---

31. See Plotinus, *Enneads* VI.8.3.
32. Ibid., I.4.10. Thus Plotinus also distinguishes in some passages between two kinds of φαντασία, one belonging to the higher soul, the other to the lower. See ibid., IV.3.31.
33. Ibid., V.5.6.
34. Ibid., IV.4.5.

receptive to illumination sent from above. For instance, Synesius regards φαντασία as the great mediator between matter and spirit; he writes of τὸ φανταστικὸν πνεῦμα (the phantastical spirit) and compares it to a boat by which the cosmic soul crosses over from above, coming into communion with the corporeal and material.[35]

A similar transposition, though much more highly elaborated, is found in Iamblichus' *On the Mysteries*. Here another approach becomes decisive over against Plotinian contemplation, namely, that of theurgy, of theurgic ritual as taught in the *Chaldaean Oracles*.[36] Iamblichus insists that, while bound in the body and exposed to generation, human beings need a form of worship that involves the body as well as the soul; they need an approach to the gods that is exercised within the sphere of generation and materiality, even if absolutely irreducible to that sphere alone. Thus, he argues, philosophical contemplation alone does not suffice to enable one to approach the divine; rather, for embodied beings, there is needed the performance of the appropriate ritual actions, that is, theurgy.[37]

On the Mysteries is written, then, in defense of theurgy. Specifically, it is written in the form of a reply to a letter from Porphyry expressing some scepticism—and, as Iamblichus attempts to show, considerable misunderstanding—regarding various aspects of theurgy. There is one point that Iamblichus repeatedly stresses from the outset: the utter inferiority and dependence of the theurgist with respect to the higher powers invoked in theurgic ritual. Here especially Iamblichus addresses Porphyry's scepticism: the theurgists do not induce the gods to appear and to descend into the human soul but only receive the free gift of light imparted by the gods. It is this gift of light, flowing from the benevolence of the gods and brought to shine forth in abundance, that can draw human souls upward, "accustoming them, while they are still in the body, to being separated from bodies and to being led around to their eternal and intelligible origin [ἀρχή]."[38] Iamblichus emphasizes, therefore, not the ritual practices of the theurgists but rather the gift of light on which they are utterly dependent.

---

35. Bundy, *Theory of Imagination*, 147–53. See also Brann, *World of the Imagination*, 50f.

36. Wallis gives the following brief account of the *Chaldaean Oracles* and of its relation to Neoplatonism: It is "a collection of turgid and obscure hexameter oracles composed or collected during the reign of Marcus Aurelius by a certain Julian and his son of the same name (entitled respectively the Chaldaean and the Theurgist) and probably originating in the revelations of an ecstatic prophet or prophetess. The first philosopher known to have quoted the *Oracles* was Porphyry; for Plotinus either did not know them or deliberately ignored them. Porphyry further equipped them with a commentary harmonising their teaching with Neoplatonism, and for Iamblichus and the Athenian School they became the supreme authority, exceeding even Plato" (R. T. Wallis, *Neoplatonism*, 2nd ed. [Indianapolis: Hackett Publishing Co., 1995], 105).

37. Iamblichus, *On the Mysteries* II.11. See Wallis, *Neoplatonism*, 118–21; and Beate Nasemann, *Theurgie und Philosophie in Jamblichs De Mysteriis* (Stuttgart: B. G. Teubner, 1991), 198.

38. Iamblichus, *On the Mysteries* I.12.

This light constitutes an appearance of the gods, their epiphany (ἐπιφα-νεία). Distinguishing such appearances from those of other superior be-ings (daimons, angels, heroes), Iamblichus declares that the appearances of the gods are uniform and immutable and that they shine with such im-mense splendor that spectators are transfixed in wonder. The divine epiph-anies are of such magnitude "as sometimes to conceal the entire heaven, the sun and the moon; and the earth itself, as the gods descend, is no longer capable of standing still."[39] The gift of light, the epiphany of the gods, is so great, so overpowering with respect to everything on earth and in the visible heaven, that all is reversed: that which otherwise illuminates is concealed, and that which otherwise always stands still (to such an extent that it is ordinarily the very measure of the stationary) is set trembling. It is because the appearance is overpowering that it can and does empower the theurgist, who, rather than commanding it (as Porphyry assumes), sub-mits to it. Iamblichus stresses the truthfulness of the divine epiphanies, while, at the same time, insisting on their difference from images in the ordinary sense. A divine epiphany is not an imitation (μίμημα) in the sense of those indicated in the *Republic* for being deceptive. Rather, the gods "dis-close true images of themselves [τάς ἀληθινάς ἑαυτῶν εἰκόνας ἀποκαλύπ-τουσιν], but by no means do they extend semblances [φαντάσματα] of themselves such as those produced in water or in mirrors." Such sem-blances, he adds, would cause deception in those to whom they were ex-tended and would only withhold the spectators from true knowledge of the gods. Abjuring all imitations and semblances, a god "shines [ἐλλάμπει] truthfully in the true manner of souls."[40]

In response to Porphyry's inquiry about dreams in which one receives a knowledge of future events, Iamblichus insists on distinguishing between merely human dreams, which portend things that sometimes prove true but sometimes are false, and dreams that are sent by the gods (θεόπεμπτοι), which are thus submitted to divine epiphanies. Such god-sent dreams are capable of illuminating the embodied soul in such a way that, correspond-ing to soul as such, it contains in itself the λόγοι of all generated natures; it is through these λόγοι, which comprehend also future events, that a fore-knowledge can be granted in such dreams.[41] What is decisive in this re-sponse to Porphyry is Iamblichus' insistence on the utter antecedence of the divine appearance. Indeed, he continues to stress this antecedence as he turns to discussions of enthusiasm (which is produced neither by human powers nor by nature but rather from the gods) and of divine madness (which is caused by the illumination proceeding from the gods). It is like-wise with oracles, as at Delphi: "But the prophetess in Delphi . . . entirely

---

39. Ibid., II.4.
40. Ibid., II.10.
41. See ibid., III.2–3.

gives herself up to a divine spirit [τῷ θείῳ πνεύματι] and is illuminated by a ray of divine fire. And when fire, ascending from the mouth of the cave, embraces her from all sides, she becomes filled from it with divine light. But when she places herself in the abode [ἕδρα—also: temple, altar, seat] of the god, she is united with his calm prophetic power. From both these preparatory operations she becomes wholly possessed by the god. And then the god, in a separate manner [χωριστῶς], is present with her and shines forth in her, and is different from the fire, the spirit, the proper abode, and all the visible apparatus of the place, whether natural or sacred."[42]

Iamblichus insists no less on the antecedence when, again responding to Porphyry's letter, the discussion turns to the reception of divine images by that human power that is most properly oriented to images, φαντασία or what Porphyry terms τὸ φανταστικόν. Iamblichus explains that divine inspiration according to τὸ φανταστικόν—*phantastic inspiration,* one might call it—can take place in two ways: either by the gods coming to be present with the soul or by their illuminating the soul, literally, shining forth light from themselves into souls. Yet in both cases what is decisive, utterly decisive, is the illumination, whether produced by the presence of the gods or made to shine into the human soul by them—or both, as with the prophetess in Delphi. Beginning with the divine delivering of light, Iamblichus describes phantastic inspiration: "This illuminates with divine light the ethereal and shining support [ὄχημα—also: chariot] surrounding the soul, from which divine φαντασίαι take possession of the phantastic power in us [τὴν ἐν ἡμῖν φανταστικὴν δύναμιν], these being excited by the will of the gods. . . . But the phantastic power [τὸ φανταστικόν] is divinely inspired, for it is excited to the ways of φαντασία not by itself but by the gods, [this power] being wholly strange to human customs."[43] Unlike the kind familiar to human customs, this φαντασία is suspended from the gift of light. At the same time, its effect is to elevate the soul, to draw it toward the source from which the gift comes, a source that, even when present with the soul, remains perfectly in itself, not itself drawn down to the sphere of generation and materiality. The gods remain separate; they perdure, as Iamblichus says of Delphic Apollo, in a separate manner. The gods and their epiphany remain utterly antecedent to all that would be effected through their gift of light, the true images they send of themselves coming always in advance of the humanly strange φαντασία capable of drawing the human soul toward them.

Thus, outside the φαντασία familiar to human customs, Iamblichus locates another, strange φαντασία, a φαντασία that can take place only when the human soul is overcome by the divine gift of light, only when there comes an epiphany of the gods. All begins with this coming—which is to

42. Ibid., III.11.
43. Ibid., III.14.

say that in this regard one will never simply have begun. Iamblichus stresses that, though in their epiphany the gods send true images of themselves, they are not thereby assimilated to the sphere of generation and materiality but rather remain separate, apart; even when present in the human soul, they remain withdrawn in such a way as to draw the phantastically inspired human soul toward them.

For Iamblichus, then, the division of φαντασία into proper kinds depends entirely on whether or not it is suspended from the divine gift of light. If not, then it is the φαντασία familiar to human custom; it is a merely human φαντασία, and, as in dreams that are of this kind, what is foreseen will be sometimes true, sometimes false. The other kind, submitted to divine truthfulness, involves the structural differentiation between, on the one side, the free gift of light, the coming of the divine epiphany, which nonetheless leaves the gods separate, and, on the other side, the phantastic inspiration, the strange φαντασία, produced in the human soul through reception of the gift.

Nowhere is the double effect of that which is called by the names of imagination, the double directionality of its force, more openly attested than in Pico della Mirandola's treatise *On the Imagination;* written in 1500, it gathers up into a sustained statement much of the complicated, entangled history of thought and translation that ancient and medieval philosophy had produced on the terrain of what would come to be called *imagination.* Pico mentions that the faculty that is the topic of his treatise was called φαντασία by the Greeks. He notes that in Latin it has been called both *imaginatio* and *phantasia,* and, though referring to certain distinctions drawn between these (Avicenna is mentioned), he puts these aside and uses almost exclusively *imaginatio* as the name for this power (*vis*), force (*potestas*), or faculty (*facultas*). At the very beginning of his treatise Pico launches a reflection that can indeed be heard as a remote echo of what was sounded by Platonism in the word εἰκασία, but this too he puts aside abruptly and emphatically.[44] Though he grants the need for further investigation, for example, concerning its relation to common sense and to memory, he treats *imaginatio* as a single faculty.

He offers a kind of definition of *imaginatio:* "It is that motion of the soul that actual sensation generates; it is a power of the soul [*animae vis*] that from itself produces forms; it is a force [*potestas*] related to all the powers; it fashions all the likenesses of things and transmutes the impressions of some powers to other powers; it is a power [*potentia*] of assimilating all other things to itself."[45] The Aristotelian background, explicitly mentioned

---

44. See my discussion of Pico and especially of this opening reflection in *Delimitations,* chap. 1.

45. Gianfrancesco Pico della Mirandola, *Liber de Imaginatione/On the Imagination,* Latin text with English translation by Harry Caplan (New Haven: Yale University Press, 1930), 32f.

by Pico, is evident. Like the φαντασία of Aristotle's analysis, *imaginatio* has, for Pico, an essential connection to sensation; as in *On the Soul,* it is a *motion* of the soul, a motion generated by sensation.[46] Yet it is not merely determined by sensation nor bound simply to reproduce sense. Again as in Aristotle's analysis, it has its own productivity:[47] from itself it produces forms. Set in motion by sensations, indeed generated as a motion by sense, it has then the power—it *is* the power—to produce forms from itself, to fashion likenesses, images, of the things given to sense but *not as* they are given in sense. In fashioning these images, *imaginatio* relates to the other powers of the soul. Taking up the impressions of sense, *imaginatio* transmutes them in such a way as to purify them and pass them on to the higher powers of the soul. Its force is such as to draw forth the images indispensable to knowledge and opinion, and thus it mediates between the lower powers of sense and the higher powers of *ratio* and *intellectus,* which relate to the universal. Such mediation is a necessity for human beings, as Pico observes, curiously substituting *phantasia* for *imaginatio,* as though, denoting the single faculty, they were interchangeable: "Nor could the soul, fettered as it is to the body, opine, know, or comprehend [*intellegere*] at all, if *phantasia* were not constantly to supply it with the images themselves."[48]

Yet in its power to assimilate all things to itself, its power to transmute them in such a way that they can be conveyed across the divide separating sense from intelligence, *imaginatio* also has the power to distort and conceal all things in such a way as to corrupt the very soul that it empowers. This other moment of the double effect is decisive for Pico: he writes his treatise on *imaginatio,* not to celebrate its force, but, as he says, to "pass sentence upon the treacherous *imaginatio*": "But *imaginatio* is for the most part vain and wandering; for the sake of proving this to be so I have assumed the present task of demonstration."[49] When he comes to stand witness against the treacherous *imaginatio,* there are hardly any evils omitted from the enumeration he gives of those that come from *imaginatio:* not only ambition, cruelty, wrath, lust, etc., but also "all monstrous opinions and the defects of all judgment," including the perversion of opinion even in philosophy itself.[50] And yet, though its force gives rise to such evil, perversion, and corruption, *imaginatio* is also a prime, indispensable force for the knowledge and right opinion that are required both for achieving a better state and for opposing the manifold evils. Even in opposing *imaginatio* itself, in passing sentence upon the treacherous *imaginatio,* one will have drawn

---

46. "Φαντασία appears to be some kind of motion and not to occur without sensation" (Aristotle, *On the Soul* 428b).

47. "Φαντασία is that by which an image [φάντασμα] occurs for us" (ibid., 428a).

48. Pico, *De Imaginatione,* 32f.

49. Ibid., 46f., 28f.

50. Ibid., 48f. The enumeration is given in chap. 7, entitled "On the Numerous Evils That Come from *Imaginatio.*"

upon its force, dividing the force so as to turn it against itself, transforming the line of force into a more complex configuration.

Modern thought too focuses on the implication: precisely as the paradigmatic mediator, what is called by the names of imagination engages a double directionality and produces a double effect. Nowhere is this implication more directly expressed than in the words Rousseau writes in *Emile* about what he calls *imagination*. Now it is not out of the question to translate the word directly, rendering as follows what Rousseau says of that faculty that is awakened as soon as one's potential faculties are put in action, the faculty that is most active of all and that outstrips the others: "It is imagination that extends for us the measure of the possible, whether for good or bad. . . ."[51] In extending the measure of the possible, in enlarging the bounds of what appears as possible, imagination opens possibilities, opens them beyond one's immediate sensible condition; it brings forth possibilities and induces a movement toward them.

For good or bad.

How for bad? The entire sentence reads: "It is imagination that extends for us the measure of the possible, whether for good or bad, and that consequently excites and nourishes the desires by the hope of satisfying them." Rousseau promptly warns that such hope is ill-founded. Kindling the passions, imagination has the effect of exposing us (Rousseau uses the personal pronoun frequently in this context) to the difference between the limited real and the virtually unlimited imaginary: "It is from their difference alone that are born all the pains that make us truly unhappy."[52]

How for good? By the way in which imagination adds charm to nature so as, in turn, to warm our hearts. The force of imagination, its force for good, lies in its exceeding of what is: "The existence of finite beings is so poor and so limited that, when we see only what is, we are never moved. Chimeras adorn real objects; and if imagination does not add a charm to what strikes us, the sterile pleasure one takes in it is limited to the perceiving organ and always leaves the heart cold." Whereas: "In spring the countryside, almost naked, is not yet covered with anything, the trees provide no shade, the green is only beginning to sprout, and the heart is touched by its aspect. In seeing nature thus reborn, one feels revived oneself; the image of pleasure surrounds us. Those companions of voluptuousness, those sweet tears always ready to join with every delicious sentiment, are already on the edge of our eye-lids. . . . Why this difference? It is that imagination joins to the spectacle of spring that of the seasons that are to follow it. To these tender buds that the eye perceives imagination adds the flowers, the fruits, the shadows, and sometimes the mysteries they can cover. It concen-

---

51. Jean-Jacques Rousseau, *Oeuvres Complètes* (Paris: Gallimard, Pléiade, 1959), 4:304.

52. Ibid., 305. Rousseau is explicit regarding the link between imagination and the passions: "It is only at the flame of imagination that the passions are kindled" (ibid., 384).

trates in a single moment the times that are to succeed one another, and it sees objects less as they will be than as it desires them to be. . . ."[53] On both sides imagination exceeds what is present, extending our gaze beyond the immediately visible (the sparse traces of spring), beyond to the stages to come (flowers, fruits, shade), opening to the future precisely in and through the profusion of sense to come. In this very movement imagination draws us beyond ourselves, displaces us from the simple feeling of self given in and through sensations, makes us exceed the bounds of the self-apprehension produced merely through sense and feeling.[54]

For Kant too imagination exceeds sense on the side both of nature and of the self, both of outer and of inner appearance. Or rather, what exceeds sense is what Kant calls *Einbildungskraft:* precision would require that one call it *force of imagination* or at least note that in rendering it simply as *imagination* one is translating elliptically, as also in passing over the fact that alongside *Einbildungskraft* and *Einbildung* (and *Phantasie*) the German language also provides the Latinate form *Imagination,* thus deploying (in relation also to other words such as *Vorstellungsvermögen* and *Darstellungskraft*) a configuration of names of imagination that cannot simply be mapped onto those of Latinate languages or of English. Only on condition of having marked this ellipsis and of continuing to allude to it, can the translation of *Einbildungskraft* as *imagination* be sustained in reference to the texts of Kant and of his successors. Writing under this condition, one can, then, observe that through Kant's so-called Copernican revolution imagination is brought to the fore not just as mediating between sense and intelligence but as the power of synthesis that yokes sense and intelligence together in the knowledge or experience of objects. The critical turn requires that this yoke also be carried over to the object of knowledge or experience, that imagination therefore effect also a synthesis of the intelligible and the sensible elements in the object.

An indication is given in Kant's statement that "Synthesis in general . . . is the mere result of imagination [*Einbildungskraft*], a blind but indispensable function of the soul, without which we would have no knowledge whatsoever, but of which we are scarcely ever conscious."[55] Although synthesis occurs also at the empirical level, the synthesis on which the *Critique of Pure Reason* focuses—and *must* focus, granted its aim—is pure synthesis, a synthesis in which the elements being united through synthesis involve nothing empirical, nothing derived from sense. Hence, in this capacity, as effecting pure synthesis, imagination operates entirely beyond sense, ex-

---

53. Ibid., 418.

54. Rousseau refers to this sentient self-apprehension in such statements as the following: "I exist and I have senses through which I am affected. . . . My sensations take place in myself, for they make me feel [*sentir*] my existence" (ibid., 570f.).

55. I. Kant, *Kritik der reinen Vernunft,* A 78/B 103. My remarks here are limited to the merest of indications. I have discussed at length Kant's theory of imagination in relation to the critical philosophy as such in *The Gathering of Reason* (Athens: Ohio University Press, 1980).

ceeding it, or rather, absolutely preceding it, indeed with a precedence that is archaic rather than temporal or logical. As pure imagination it unites the categories (pure concepts) of the understanding (*Verstand,* Kant's translation of *intellectus*) with the pure forms of intuition; that is, it brings the manifold of pure intuition, ultimately of time itself (or of time not yet quite itself), under the forms of unity that are thought in the categories. What imagination produces in and as the pure synthesis are transcendental determinations of time. Kant calls them transcendental schemata. The *Critique of Pure Reason* undertakes to demonstrate that it is only through this pure synthesis effected by imagination that experience of objects becomes possible. It undertakes to show also that the conditions of the possibility of experience are likewise conditions of the possibility of objects of experience. Thus, imagination proves essential to the very conditions of possibility of objects: it is through the pure synthesis effected by imagination that objects first come to be constituted as objects. To this degree, imagination can be regarded as that which brings them forth as objects, even if it is not imagination alone that conditions their possibility, even if, most emphatically, a certain empirical, sensible content must also in every case be given.

Although it is not his primary focus, Kant insists that even at the empirical level imagination is essential in the constitution of experience. Thus, in discussing, at the empirical level, the moment of synthesis that he terms the synthesis of reproduction, he explains that this moment of synthesis gives form to the sense-manifold, that it brings the manifold into a certain form. The form into which imagination forms it is that of an image: "Imagination [*Einbildungskraft*] has to bring the manifold into the form of an image [*Bild*]." For this reason Kant maintains that "imagination is a necessary ingredient of perception [*Wahrnehmung*] itself."[56]

Such is its force that without imagination there would be neither objects nor experience. It is, says Kant, "a fundamental faculty [*Grundvermögen*] of the human soul."[57]

Fichte draws the radical consequences of the critical turn. It is precisely in order to do so that he adheres with such rigor to the Kantian system. He insists on this adherence: "my system is nothing other than the Kantian; this means that it contains the same view of things but is in its method completely independent of the Kantian presentation." This independence in method and presentation is what allows Fichte to carry through the Kantian revolution in such a way as to produce a "complete reversal [*Umkehrung*]" in which "the object will be posited and determined by the cognitive faculty, and not the cognitive faculty by the object."[58]

This complete reversal focuses above all on the thing-in-itself, which to

---

56. Kant, *Kritik der reinen Vernunft,* A 120.

57. Ibid., A 124.

58. J. G. Fichte, *Erste Einleitung in die Wissenschaftslehre,* in vol. 1 of *Werke,* ed. I. H. Fichte (Berlin: Walter de Gruyter, 1971), 420f.

such critics as Jacobi could only appear to be a remnant of dogmatism in the Kantian presentation. In Fichte's *Wissenschaftslehre* the signification of that which Kant had called *thing-in-itself* is progressively reduced, assimilated step by step to what Fichte calls—distinguishing it from the subject, for reasons that will become apparent—the I (*das Ich*). Instead of designating a real, externally existing cause of representation, it can only signify the ground of a passivity in the I, of something given to its representational activity. But, in turn, rigorous critique restricts it to indicating only the passivity itself, only the limitation in the I, eliminating the further, critically unjustifiable step by which a ground for the limitation would be posited, whether as an existing object or otherwise. But then, finally, all that remains for it to name—and which therefore it does not name appropriately— is that which merely sets, for the I, the task of self-limitation, of self-determination, without itself introducing any limits or determinations into the I. The name that comes finally to replace *thing-in-itself* is *Anstoss:* it refers to an impulse or impetus, not grounded in the I, which drives the I to set self-determining bounds for itself by positing the not-I over against itself.[59] Thus, the reduction of the signification of the thing-in-itself leaves neither an independently existing thing outside the I (such as would cause representations by producing sense-content in the I); nor a ground (even if not an existing thing) for such content; nor even such content itself, interior to the I without having been produced by the I. It is not even a matter of merely declaring there to be some passivity in the I, some content present unaccountably in what will be called experience. On the contrary, there is *nothing* in experience, not a single moment, that is not brought forth from the side of the I. There is—in a sense (the sense of being) that is displaced—only the impetus to limit itself by bringing forth something other—but also, then, not finally other—than itself. The very distinction between a priori and a posteriori, which seems to stabilize the entire Kantian presentation, comes to be reduced to no more than the difference between two ways of considering the same thing, between two approaches[60]— hence a difference that is, in the end, no difference. Hence the complete reversal: the object is posited and determined by the cognitive faculty, not the cognitive faculty by the object.

The consequence is quite direct as regards the force of imagination, its originary, archaic force. For, as producing the synthesis in which objects are first brought forth as such, it proves, in this completed reversal, not to be limited by anything over against the I, by any alien causality or content. Thus Fichte writes of the force of imagination: "It is therefore here taught

---

59. See Fichte, *Grundlage der gesammten Wissenschaftslehre*, in vol. 1 of *Werke*, 145–211. See also my discussion in *Spacings—Of Reason and Imagination* (Chicago: University of Chicago Press, 1987), chap. 2, esp. 61–63.

60. See Fichte, *Erste Einleitung in die Wissenschaftslehre*, 447.

that all reality [*Realität*]—*for us* being understood, as it cannot be otherwise understood in a system of transcendental philosophy—is brought forth solely by the imagination [*bloss durch die Einbildungskraft hervorgebracht werde*]."[61]

This teaching echoes throughout English Romanticism, though in diverse registers. Its reception is perhaps most direct in Coleridge: "The primary IMAGINATION I hold to be the living Power and prime Agent of all human Perception, and as a repetition in the finite mind of the eternal act of creation in the infinite I AM."[62]

Yet there is an even more radical consequence. For, having declared that all reality is brought forth solely by the imagination, Fichte reflects this consequence back upon the subject: "On this act of imagination is grounded the possibility of our consciousness, of our life, of our being for ourselves, that is, of our being as an I."[63] There is consciousness only in relation to an object, life only in opposition, being for ourselves only in relation to another; one can *be* an I only insofar as one is limited—rendered finite—by something not-I, becoming thus a subject over against an object. Thus, the very constitution of consciousness, of a finite I, of a subject, requires the bringing-forth of objects, of reality, that is the accomplishment solely of imagination. Consequently, imagination is the ground of the possibility of the subject. Hence another complete reversal: subjectivity will belong to imagination rather than imagination being a faculty of the subject. Undermining the determination of imagination as a faculty of the subject, reversing the connection in a way that cannot but expose it to still more radical questioning, Fichte also abolishes the ultimacy that otherwise tends, especially in modern thought, to be given to the opposition between subject and object. The originary force thus granted to imagination is nowhere more directly expressed than in Hegel's early text *Faith and Knowledge:* "we must not take imagination [*Einbildungskraft*] as the middle term that gets inserted between an existing absolute subject and an absolute existing world; it must rather be recognized as what is primary and original and as that out of which the subjective I and the objective world first sunder themselves."[64]

C. EXORBITANT TRAITS

It is a matter now of drawing, of drawing out toward the limit what is said in the names of imagination. It is a matter of a drawing that would trace,

---

61. Fichte, *Grundlage der gesammten Wissenschaftslehre*, 227.

62. Samuel Taylor Coleridge, *Biographia Literaria*, vol. 7 of *The Collected Works*, ed. James Engell and W. Jackson Bate (Princeton: Princeton University Press, 1983), 1:304.

63. Fichte, *Grundlage der gesammten Wissenschaftslehre*, 227.

64. Hegel, *Glauben und Wissen*, in vol. 4 of *Gesammelte Werke*, 329.

along the edges of these old words, the exorbitant senses that begin to take shape there, that will always have haunted the names of imagination, returning ever again across the space of translation and redetermination. A drawing out (protraction) as well as that which is drawn or drawn out—for instance, a line, a trace, a stroke made with pen or pencil, hence something penned, a piece of writing—is called a trait.

It is not—nor can it now be—a matter of the sense of imagination being enclosed in some allegedly essential signification. That it has been attested to be nonenclosable by λόγος or by politics, nonenclosable within the human sphere or within presence, only presages how forcefully it resists significational closure. Even in remembrance it is a matter not of enclosure but of beginning to free the exorbitant traits by which what is called by the names of imagination eludes and resists the closure of philosophy.

The most conspicuously exorbitant trait consists in the detaching of imagination from the soul or the subject, that is, in those texts that, in renewed remembrance, prove to trace the lines of such a detachment. As in Brann's reading of Aristotle, which construes the pertinent text as setting φαντασία aside from the powers of the soul, detaching it at least from those powers by which one judges and discriminates, displacing it toward the limit of the soul. Also, as in Gasché's reading of Kant, which points to the absence of *Einbildungskraft,* to its lack of an *itself* that would allow it to be included straightforwardly among the faculties of the subject. And, above all, as in the radical consequence that Fichte draws concerning the relation between *Einbildungskraft* and subjectivity. Because all things, including the subject in its correlation with objects, are brought forth by *Einbildungskraft,* the latter cannot be determined as a faculty of the subject. By twisting it free of the subject, Fichte opens the possibility of engendering a sense of imagination outside the orbit of subjectivity. In opening this possibility, in thus extending the measure of the possible, Fichte's thought is moved by the force of imagination to a greater degree perhaps than even he realized.[65]

The most far-reaching trait is the line drawn in the Platonic text, the line along the entire length of which εἰκασία is in effect extended. Along almost its entire extent, this line involves an irreducibly dyadic structure, that of present image and absent original. Thus, as a double seeing, εἰκασία is distinguished from the mere intuition of something present. It consists in seeing the absent original in and through seeing the image; that is, in and through the image present to one's immediate seeing, one sees the original that is remote from the image, that is absent from one's field of immediate vision. In εἰκασία one makes present (in and through the image) the ab-

---

65. Fichte says of the "creative imagination": "It is this faculty [*Vermögen*] that determines whether one philosophizes with, or without, spirit [*Geist*]" (*Grundlage der gesammten Wissenschaftslehre,* 284).

sent original, and indeed not just by gazing upon the image but by grasping it *as* an image so as to enact in one's seeing the very turn from image to original. What allows such vision to become deceptive, especially when stabilized in mimetic productions, is that what it makes present (in the image) remains nonetheless absent (distinct, remote from the image); μίμησις can deceive so forcefully because a possible confounding of image and original belongs to its very constitution as making the absent original present in the image. As making present something absent, εἰκασία involves a peculiar mixing of presence and absence that does not occur in the mere beholding of something simply present. It is precisely this mixing that the Platonic text, inscribing the line, draws out as a trait of εἰκασία.

With the Stoics this mixing, this making present of something absent, is installed on a very different terrain, that of interiority with its impressions, its φαντασίαι. These are inscribed in the soul in precisely such a way that they can present things that do not lie in the soul. It is through the force of these φαντασίαι that things removed from the soul itself come to be present to its vision. But only as long as this presentative operation remains self-certifying is there assurance that things are presented and are presented as they in truth are. Ancient scepticism recognized the consequences of letting this self-legitimating function begin to erode. For then the possibility of deception will be no more controllable than Plato found it to be in mimetic products. As soon as the self-certification of the φαντασίαι slips away, false φαντασίαι will be able to dissimulate their operation and escape confinement within the rubric noncataleptic. This side of scepticism, Epictetus recognizes a force of φαντασία over which there is the utmost practical need for control, even if limited, even if exercised only by way of displacement and substitution. The force is that of originating action, an operation that will always be linked to one's holding present to one's inner vision something pertinent to the effect that the action to be originated will produce, thus making present something that is not yet, something not yet present, something that, though present to one's inner vision, will remain absent until that decisive moment when action comes to be originated and its effects are actualized.

The same operation of making present something absent can be glimpsed in the operations that Albertus Magnus ascribes to *imaginatio:* retaining images, bringing back to presence images that, as sense-images, will always have disappeared with the very moment of their presence; and preserving images, keeping them present even as time carries them away. In *phantasia,* too, as Albertus Magnus determines it, the trait is discernible: in the operation by which *phantasia* brings forth freely combined images that would otherwise never be present as such. Pico, too, assigns to *imaginatio* the operation by which images are retained and preserved, that is, delivered from their perpetual passingness (from presence to absence). But Pico stresses that it is the productivity of *imaginatio* that enables it to carry out these operations, the productivity by which it can produce from itself images of what is given in sense but *not as* given in sense, rather, purified images such as can be taken up by the higher faculties of the soul. Through its own force of production, *imaginatio* would be the soul's mediating faculty.

One can catch sight of this trait being drawn out also on the strange terrain of Iamblichean Neoplatonism, in that phantastical inspiration strange to human custom. In the absolutely antecedent gift of light, in divine epiphany, the gods come to be present to the human soul, to its phantastical vision. They are either directly present with the human soul or else they shine forth light from themselves into the soul, in both cases filling its phantastical vision with the divine appearance. Such appearance does not assume the form of images in the ordinary sense, which can distort and deceive. Rather, the appearance is truthful: it presents, brings to presence, the gods as they, in truth, are. And yet, in truth, the gods remain always separate; even when present with the human soul so as to let themselves be presented, they remain apart, never being assimilated to the human sphere they enter, always, in human phantastical inspiration, bringing themselves to presence as beings that remain nonetheless absent.

With Kant and Fichte the trait is drawn in a way that, at once, simplifies and radicalizes it. In the reversal carried out in the *Wissenschaftslehre*, *Einbildungskraft* proves to operate most fundamentally, not in making present any particular object, but in effecting all coming to presence, that is, in bringing forth all reality. Yet, even as such it does not bring things to presence without there remaining a trace of withdrawal, of an absent reserve that touches imagination without ever being assimilated to it. Thought by Kant as the thing-in-itself, this reserve is rethought, within the complete reversal ventured by Fichte, as the *Anstoss*, the impulse that releases the entire round of presentation and that is the only limit that still can bear on *Einbildungskraft*.

One could multiply the examples in which this trait is discernible. Quintilian, teacher of rhetoric, writes: "In what the Greeks call φαντασίαι and we call visions [*visiones*], things absent are presented to the soul through images [*imagines*] in such a way that they seem actually to be before our very eyes. Whoever understands these well will have the greatest power over moods."[66] Boethius, too, writes of the operation of *imaginatio* in the absence of sense and of sense-objects: "Although *imaginatio* begins by seeing and forming figures with the senses, nevertheless it can, without the aid of the senses, behold sensible objects by an imaginative [*imaginaria*] rather than a sensible mode of knowing."[67] As does Richard of St. Victor, who describes it as "that power of the soul by which it is able to picture to itself anything

---

66. Quintilian, *Institutio Oratoria* VI.ii.29–30.
67. Boethius, *Philosophiae Consolationis* V.iv.

whatsoever, whenever it wishes."[68] As does Kant, in the *Anthropology:* "Sense is the faculty [*Vermögen*] of intuiting in the presence of the object, imagination [*Einbildungskraft*] without its presence."[69] And in the *Critique of Pure Reason:* "*Imagination* [Einbildungskraft] is the faculty of representing in intuition an object *that is not itself present*"[70]—that is, of making present to intuition an object that in another respect is not present and that in that respect remains absent even when it is brought to presence by force of imagination.

In linking what is called *imagination* to an extending of the measure of the possible, Rousseau reinscribes this trait in the most openly exorbitant direction. For when he writes of imagination's bringing to presence possibilities that otherwise would have remained impossibilities excluded from the bounds of the possible, the turning that he describes, the turning from the sensibly present, is not a turning toward the intelligible, is not a turning that, even if from afar, would be oriented to the intelligible. Rather, it is a turning as in early spring when one's vision is transported by force of imagination, when it is carried away toward that which is not yet present but is to come. It is a turning beyond the sensibly present to a coming profusion of sense, a profusion to come that indeed already comes, before its time, to fill out with all that imagination envisions the sparse traces actually seen. Proceeding from the sensible, it is a turning, not to the intelligible, but to a profusion of sense to come, which indeed already comes by force of imagination. It is a turning within the sensible, a doubling of and within the sensible. It is the turning of imagination in an exorbitant sense allied in advance to the turning of philosophy at the limit.

The figure that this trait assumes with Rousseau is indicative of the way in which it can be freed to its exorbitancy across the interval back to the Platonic text. Especially in the Platonic text the trait is drawn as a making present of something absent, as a mixing of presence and absence. But also—and this is decisive—it is drawn as an ordered mixing, as a mixing oriented to and by an end. It is drawn as a making present that progresses toward the absent original that comes to be made present; and yet, it is prohibited from regressing to the image, especially in view of the possibility of confusing image with original, that is, in view of the danger posed by imitation. To free the trait to its exorbitancy would require, then, releasing it from the orientation to the end, that is to say, finally, to the intelligible and, most decisively, to the end—or beginning—of the intelligible, that point at which the reiterative dynamics would cease and the original would not again become the image of a more remote original. To twist the trait

---

68. Richard of St. Victor, *Benjamin Minor* XVII.

69. Kant, *Anthropologie in Pragmatischer Hinsicht,* in *Werke: Akademie Textausgabe* (Berlin: Walter de Gruyter, 1968), 7:153.

70. Kant, *Kritik der reinen Vernunft,* B 151.

free of its intelligible end is to open the possibility of other ways of mixing, the possibility of circulation along new ways between things present and things absent, or, at the more radical level broached by Fichte, between coming to presence and retreating into absence, between bringing to presence and withdrawing into absence. To twist the trait free of its intelligible end, installing the circulation within the sensible and yet at the level of its very coming to pass, is to begin tracing an exorbitant sense of imagination allied to the turning of philosophy at the limit.

Iamblichus withdraws the circulation from the human orbit, or rather, he construes circulation in the human orbit as utterly dependent on another circulation quite withdrawn from that orbit. The gift of light, its absolute antecedence, precludes there being any force within the human soul capable, through itself alone, of drawing the soul into the ascent. To the divine epiphany there belongs a double directionality: the gods descend to the human soul, coming to be present with it or shining light forth into it; while thus conveying true images of themselves down to the human soul, the gods also remain utterly ascendant, completely above and apart from the human sphere. Only secondarily, then, do human souls become, in their proper way, ascensional; in phantastic inspiration they are drawn upward by the gift sent down from above by the withdrawn gods. What sets in motion the phantastic power in the human orbit is the divine φαντασία, which remains utterly apart. In order to free the exorbitant sense that takes shape in the Iamblichean inscription of this trait, what must be interrupted is the philosophical appropriation of this exorbitancy that would be enforced by the assimilation of the orbit of the gods to the intelligible. What would be required in the turning of philosophy at the limit is that this exorbitant orbit be thought as pure gift, or rather, not simply thought but freely and responsively received—enacted, as it were, in a kind of proto-theurgy.

Along these lines the trait first drawn in the Platonic text and freed as circulation within the sensible comes in the Iamblichean text to mutate into another, which one could call the trait of coming. If one stresses that even in divine epiphany, even in the appearance of the gods, the gods themselves remain withheld, then what will figure primarily is the *coming* of the gift of light, its being sent or somehow conveyed by beings that keep themselves aloof and concealed as such. What will count primarily is the coming of the gift, the coming that belongs to the very constitution of a gift (since a gift always comes, arrives, to such an extent that it would be no gift at all if one merely took it or procured it for oneself). Only through this coming is φαντασία enlivened by inspiration and, filled with the gift of light, then drawn up in the direction from which the gift will have come.

In Epictetus, too, though, in a very different register, this trait of a coming to φαντασία can be marked. The very need to control φαντασίαι in behalf of right action leads Epictetus toward the limit of control, toward the point where the force of φαντασία exceeds the possibility of control, where even displacement and substitution do not suffice. The coming of φαντασίαι constitutes this limit.

Thus it is that the trait of coming is not simply another trait but rather the limit of the trait of imagination as bringing to presence. If all begins with a "there comes," then even bringing to presence in the most radical sense will have been submitted in advance to this coming. In these exorbitant senses, imagination will have come as if from nowhere to broach the circulation belonging to things that come to pass.

In releasing things into this circulation, imagination draws them into time and is itself drawn into relation to time. This trait, the trace from imagination to time, is drawn repeatedly, and not infrequently it has a special bearing on the future. For example, with Albertus Magnus, *imaginatio* has precisely the function of retaining and preserving the sense-images that otherwise (and, indeed, as such) come only to be carried away—at their very moment of arrival—in the incessant passingness of time. By retaining and preserving these images, *imaginatio* lifts them out of this passingness, that is, it extends their presence into the future, confers on them a future present.

With Kant the relation of imagination to time comes to determine time itself. The objectivity of time, its categorial articulation, if not indeed its very constitution,[71] depends on the function that Kant calls transcendental schematism. Only through the production of pure schemata by the pure imagination does the pure manifold of time (which one could regard as pure receptivity as such) come to be determined as that in which objects can appear, can come to presence. Fichte only echoes Kant—even if in a more radical voice—when he says: "Only for the imagination is there time [*Nur für die Einbildungskraft giebt es eine Zeit*]."[72]

And yet, as things come to pass within the orbit of sense to which philosophy at the limit turns, their time does not show itself as a pure manifold or as pure receptivity. When Rousseau tells how imagination extends the measure of the possible, it is to a season, to a time of year, that imagination is drawn. It is in its relation to this time of year that imagination brings its extension of vision beyond the merely sensibly present. In fact, Rousseau

---

71. There are passages in the Transcendental Analytic that support an interpretation by which pure intuition would be regarded as not simply prior to the synthesis effected by imagination, as not merely a material to which a synthesis would be applied. For example, in regard to the moment of synthesis that he terms the pure synthesis of apprehension, Kant writes: "For without it we would never have a priori the representations either of space or of time" (*Kritik der reinen Vernunft*, A99). See also the important note at B160f., which suggests that the treatment of space and time in the Transcendental Aesthetic is only provisional and that, as the Transcendental Analytic then presumably shows, each pure form "presupposes a synthesis."

72. Fichte, *Grundlage der gesammten Wissenschaftslehre*, 217.

contrasts the expansion of imagination in the spring with its retreat in the autumn when "one can see only what is [*on n'a plus à voir que ce qui est*]" and when, though "the earth adorned with autumn's treasures displays a richness that the eye admires," the heart remains cold.[73] The time of imagination is a time of sense. It is a time of earth and sky in an exorbitant sense.

---

73. Rousseau, *Oeuvres complètes,* 4:418.

3

DUPLICITY OF THE IMAGE

A. SENSE IMAGE

Beginning with sense requires both turning to it and letting it go. It requires turning to the expanse open to sense while releasing the sensible from the imperative of being only the appearance of another, remote truth. It requires also that in turning to the sensible one let go of sense in another sense, in the sense heretofore determined as that other, remote truth: its retreat is now to be granted, endured, as one ventures to engender sense. As in remembrance.

In beginning with sense, one needs also to mark another doubling in *sense: sense* and certain variations on it can name both prehending and prehended, allowing one to say that someone has a sense of how things look, of their significance, a sense of direction, and also that someone senses the presence of something (its presence to the senses) or senses certain of its sensible qualities. In the dyad of prehending sense (sensing) and prehended sense (sensed), what occurs is a presence of sense to sense; or rather, within the limit of the sensible, what primarily occurs (even if doubled in another register) is that something sensible comes to be present to the senses. Such

77

sense comes to be present to sense in and as an image, a sense image. Or rather, it is appropriate in this connection to resume the word *image*, to invoke it to signify that in and as which sense comes to be present to sense—appropriate, considering what remains of the sense that εικών, *imago, Bild*, etc. as well as *image* bore in philosophical discourses from Plato to Husserl. And yet, in resuming the word, it will be a matter of reinscribing it within the zone of its exorbitant trait, which is discernible already in the trait of *imagination*. As that in and through which anything like εἰκασία occurs, the image is that in and as which a making present of something absent takes place. Or, more exorbitantly, it is a mixing of presence and absence that is not oriented in advance to the allegedly pure presence of a final intelligible; it is a freer mixing, as in the sheer upsurge of presence, which one cannot simply have initiated or effected but can only have welcomed in advance. It goes without saying that such connection as might otherwise be assumed to hold between what are called *imagination* and *image* is, in their exorbitancy, suspended: it is not to be supposed that imagination generates, produces, reproduces, reconfigures, or synthesizes images, nor of course that it does *not* carry out any of these operations on images.

In turning to the sensible, one begins, then, with the sense image, beginning to double the sensible in a discourse oriented to *sense* and to *image*. In the image sense comes to be present to sense, and the image is nothing but this coming to presence—and being present—of sense to sense. It is in and as the sense image that sense comes to be—and thus is—present to sense. Or, more precisely, granted that the turn is to sense in the sense of the sensible, it is in and as the sensible image that the sensible comes to be—and thus is—present to sense prehension, to sensible intuition. Leaving suspended for now the question whether there are other kinds of images that would need eventually to be distinguished, let *image* function as shorthand for *sensible image* in precisely the sense here specified.

Image would name, then, the occurrence, means, and locus in which the sensible becomes present to sensible intuition. As the discourse thus begins to be oriented around the presence of sense to sense, one will be prompted to inquire about the sense of *presence*, to ask: What is presence? Or rather, this is the question one would like to ask, were it not set spiraling out of control by the necessity of presupposing presence in any rigorous determination of the *what* (as essence, as εἶδος, etc.), to say nothing of the *is*, which has perhaps never been determined otherwise than as presence or at least in reference to presence. Nonetheless, one will, without question, need to remain vigilant about the word, which, like its Latin root, threatens to condense, and hence to efface, a differentiated chain of senses expressed in various Greek and German words.[1]

---

1. In a note to "Ousia and Grammē," Derrida elaborates: "Here the question would be the following: how to transfer into, or rather what happens when we transfer into the single Latin

But still, without pressing the question, without releasing its spiraling, can one not somehow delimit the sense of *presence*? Can one not say what is meant when one speaks of presence? Here precisely is the most pertinent difference: presence is otherwise than speech—these five words, by virtue of what they say (which is irreducible to a *what*), imposing the demand that they also be crossed out, as would needs be every other such saying of this otherness. Such as: presence is precisely what speech lacks and what it requires for its legitimation. As the other of speech—continuing here to write under this demand also to cross out—presence is unassimilable to a linguistic signification, to a signified of a signifier. What the word would say escapes the saying, escapes what the word does indeed say. One will never have said what *presence* means, for presence is other than what can be meant through speech. The very understanding of the word requires that it be displaced from the order of speech, translated toward the sensible, and through this translation be made to outdistance itself.

In order to prepare a phenomenological, or rather, monstrological, discourse, *image* is to be brought to signify the occurrence, means, and locus of the coming to presence of the sensible to sensible intuition. Even if in what the word signifies it must somehow also allude to the retreat of presence from signification, the sense of *image* needs to be stabilized and delimited in order for the word to function as one anticipates it must in the development of monstrological discourse. Does it suffice to this end to resume what remains of its philosophical sense and to reconfigure the sense along the lines of the exorbitant trait? Or has the sense of *image* not been extended today beyond all limits so that now anything and everything can be called an image? Is this inflation of the word *image* not also powerfully reinforced today by the most compelling and far-reaching transformations in social practices and in the theoretical discourses that have arisen in relation to these practices? Can one set about to engender a sense of *image* and to determine it monstrologically without running the risk that such a discourse will be swamped or hopelessly diverted by the inflation of the word? One could of course simply decide to take the risk, insisting that in any case a new and more precise discourse would be produced, even if it proved powerless to counter the uncontrolled inflation of *image*. And yet, in taking the risk one would also incur the risk that such a discourse might prove unable to keep itself apart from the inflation of *image* and all that is

word *presence* the entire differentiated *system* of Greek and German words, the entire *system of translation* in which Heideggerian language (*ousia, parousia, Gegenwärtigkeit, Anwesen, Anwesenheit, Vorhandenheit*, etc.) is produced? And all this taking into account that the two Greek words and the words associated with them already have translations charged with history (essence, substance, etc.). Above all, how to transfer into the single word *presence*, at once too rich and too poor, the *history* of the Heideggerian text, which associates or disjoins these concepts in subtle and regular fashion throughout an itinerary that covers nearly forty years" (Jacques Derrida, *Marges de la Philosophie* [Paris: Les Éditions de Minuit, 1972], 35f.).

linked to that inflation; the risk is that the inflation might prove not merely something external that would come to swamp or divert the less enforced discourse, the discourse enforced only by the appeal to the things themselves. For the inflation is precisely such as to put in doubt that there are things themselves and hence to put in question the very possibility of a discourse determined by reference to them. In the inflation of *image* the very rigor of discourse—the very possibility of rigor—is at stake. The difficulty of keeping would-be rigorous discourse apart from the discourse of inflation is grounded in the fact and the implications of their common origin.

Today the word *image* has become so inflated that its sense is extended to cover all things; that is, all things can now be designated as images, and yet precisely as a result of this extension they are effaced as things, as things themselves in distinction from images. In this extension of sense to the point where it covers all things, the most unsettling moment arrives when the sense of *image* comes to cover itself, that is, to efface or disfigure itself. Even though, in the field of social practice and its theoretical discourse, this self-disfiguring inflation is inextricably linked to modern technology, mass communications, and the thoroughgoing reorganization of human life and society brought about through them, the inflation of *image* has its motivation, its theoretical prefiguration, in the history of philosophy. The figure is there from the beginning: in the figure of the line and the image of the cave there is figured and imaged an almost continuous, almost unlimited extension of the dyadic structure of imaging. Although εἰκασία literally designates only the lowest segment of the line and the doubled vision of the just released, still caverned prisoner, there are unmistakable indications that the dyadic structure of image and original and thus the turning of vision through the image toward the original are determinative at all points of the ascent except that at which it would come to its end. The dynamics of this reiterative structure is what preeminently drives the ascent, even though it alone does not suffice. Except for the terminal point, everything on the way up the line and out of the cave thus takes on the character of an image, and all vision along this way turns through image toward original, enacting, in repetition, the transition that begins with an original only to discover that it is itself only an image from which, then, the move upward to its original must be carried out. Thus it is that the philosopher's persistent engagement with images remains a constant theme repeatedly staged throughout the *Republic:* as when, urged to give an apology for the effect of philosophy on the city, Socrates prefaces his account (which presents the image of a ship's pilot) with a self-account describing himself as greedily forming images (γλίσχρως εἰκάζω).[2] When pressed later to speak of the

2. *Republic* 488a. On the interpretation of the phrase ὡς γλίσχρως εἰκάζω, see James Adam, *The Republic of Plato,* 2nd ed. (Cambridge: Cambridge University Press, 1965), 2:9.

would-be terminal point of the philosophical ascent, he refuses to disengage his discourse from images. Even the original of originals, the original that could not in turn become an image of a still more original original, is made to appear in the guise of an image: leaving aside what the good itself is, Socrates agrees only "to tell what looks like a child of the good and seems most similar to it."[3] Begotten by the good and most similar to it, the sun is an image of the good. Thus is the would-be terminal point of the ascent, the original of originals, determined in the end from the point of view of its image and as itself possessing the power of image-making, as making images—at least *an* image—of itself, fathering it. Retreating before the original of originals, Socrates' discourse remains engaged with images even in addressing what would be the pure original.

Thus prefigured in its extent, the inflation of *image* has today produced virtually unlimited engagement with images in the field of social practices. Now even the restraint of Socratic irony is gone: if anything and everything has the character of an image, then all comportment will be image-determined; whether it is a matter of psychological and social development, of politics, or of education, everything will depend on the appropriate engagement with images, on forming, cultivating, and maintaining the proper image. Even outside all nostalgia, one wonders what remains today that is not thoroughly determined by the incessant flow of images. The stakes are limitless, for the images to which one is exposed also become invasive, binding one to their flow to such an extent that the veil with which one would keep oneself apart begins to shred under the force of the gale. There results what Baudrillard calls a nuclear contraction of the opposing poles,[4] an effacement of the difference one would have posited between oneself and the flow of images. One is confined ever more securely to the cave.

In the very era in which the sense of *image* has come to be extended without limit, the structure determining that sense has undergone deformation, that is, first, reduction, and then, disfigurement. Technological innovation has provided the means for the reduction, for a massive reduction of the relation between image and original. Simplifying to the extreme while leaving the relation still intact, this reduction occurs through the transformation of images into copies. Within the framework of the classical concept of production, the artisan envisions the original in advance in order then to produce an image of it. In the case of artisanal production every such product, every such image, will be somewhat different, de-

---

3. *Republic* 506e.

4. "Now, one must conceive of TV along the lines of DNA as an effect in which the opposing poles of determination vanish, according to a nuclear contraction, retraction, of the old polar schema that always maintained a minimal distance between cause and effect, between subject and object" (Jean Baudrillard, *Simulacra and Simulation*, trans. Sheila Faria Glaser [Ann Arbor: University of Michigan Press, 1994], 31).

pending on the skill of the artisan and on the particular appropriateness and qualities of the materials employed. Today, on the other hand, in technological production such variation disappears almost entirely: every image tends toward utter identity with every other, and, once images have become mere copies, their relation to the original is regulated with a strictness both unknown to artisanal production and indeed alien to it.

A further development comes to disfigure the dyadic structure of image and original: today there regularly occur instances in which a nuclear contraction effaces the very difference between image and original. Now it is technologically possible to generate images that are virtually, if not entirely, indistinguishable not only from one another but also from their original. Even further, there are images to which no original other than a thoroughly disseminated one corresponds: as when a musical recording, for instance, is constructed not only by splicing together recordings of various parts of different performances but also by means of technical interventions and alterations that disrupt even the partial correspondences that would otherwise obtain. Such an image no longer images a real performance; itself indefinitely reproducible, it becomes—says Baudrillard—the real itself, or rather, a hyperreal. In this case the difference between original and image ceases to be operative: there is no real performance but only simulation of it, and the image is not so much a copy as rather a simulacrum.

The disfiguring of the image-original structure thus results in a reign of simulacra posing as hyperreal. The extent of this reign is, according to Baudrillard, practically unlimited: the mutation of images into simulacra is no mere isolated, technologically contrived occurrence but rather has now taken place across the entire field of social practice and its theoretical discourse, and beyond. Baudrillard is not alone in his appraisal of the extent of this deformation. Deleuze declares: "Everything has become simulacrum, for by simulacrum we should not understand a simple imitation but rather the act by which the very idea of a model or privileged position is contested, overturned."[5] Reference to a model or original is liquidated, and in place of a reality determined as originary there remain only images, which, stripped of their originals, mutate into simulacra, into the hyperreal. Baudrillard is explicit about the consequences for (as he calls it) the imaginary: once the reign of simulacral hyperreality has set in, there is no longer any imaginary enveloping the real. What remains is only "a hyperreal henceforth sheltered from the imaginary, and from any distinction between the real and the imaginary, leaving room only for the orbital recurrence of models and for the simulated generation of differences."[6] On the other hand, Baudrillard marks also a kind of return of the imaginary to the scene of hyperreality, though of an imaginary that, like Disneyland, would

---

5. Gilles Deleuze, *Différence et Répétition* (Paris: Presses Universitaires de France, 1968), 95.
6. Baudrillard, *Simulacra and Simulation*, 2f.

represent only a futile attempt to conceal and deny the reign of simulacral hyperreality.[7]

A discourse such as Baudrillard's would, on the contrary, expose this
reign. It would expose hyperreality as simulacral, confirming everything
that would have prompted one to doubt whether the image revealed something originary or only concealed the void on which it was cast. Confirming
the doubt itself, vindicating it, such a discourse would thus demonstrate
how pervasively the operation of simulacra figures in various areas of social
practice. And yet, this figure—or disfigure—is less compelling if, margin-
alizing the effects of technology and social interaction, one turns to what
remains of what has been called nature. For one can detach oneself from
social interaction and its instruments, and one can solitarily discover places
that, if never virginal, are sufficiently remote to keep at bay the operations
and effects of technology. Within the space of these suspensions, what remains of nature can still appeal in a way capable of countering the figure
of the all-pervasive reign of simulacra. As when, in early spring, detached
to such a place, wandering through the countryside, one comes upon a
tree just beginning to put out its tender buds: not only will one feel the
earth beneath one's feet and sense the support it grants, as one gazes beyond to the distant mountains outlined against the sky, but also one will
add, in imagination, the profusion of sense that is to come with the blossoms of spring and the fruit of summer. Will one then readily agree that
earth and sky, tree and mountain are only simulacra floating on a surface
of nothingness? Will one not insist that in such a place imagination plays
otherwise than on a visit to Disneyland? What would be required in order
to close off such spaces and declare an unlimited reign of simulacral hyperreality? Under what conditions—for instance, under what preconcep-
tions—could one, would one, simply begin ("undo all the opinions I had
previously accepted among my beliefs and begin anew from the beginning
[a primis fundamentis]")[8] by turning away from sense ("Now I shall close my
eyes, I shall stop my ears, I shall turn away all my senses"),[9] submitting to
thoroughgoing doubt all that becomes manifest through sense, the sensible itself ("the earth, the sky, the stars, and all the other things I perceive
through the mediation of my senses")?[10]

---

7. "Disneyland exists in order to hide that it is the 'real' country, all of 'real' America that
is Disneyland (a bit like prisons are there to hide that it is the social in its entirety, in its banal
omnipresence, that is carceral). Disneyland is presented as imaginary in order to make us
believe that the rest is real, whereas all of Los Angeles and the America that surrounds it are
no longer real, but belong to the hyperreal order and to the order of simulation. It is no
longer a question of a false representation of reality (ideology) [Baudrillard is referring here
to Louis Marin's analysis] but of concealing the fact that the real is no longer real, and thus
of saving the reality principle" (ibid., 12f.).

8. Descartes, *Meditationes de Prima Philosophia*, in *Oeuvres*, 7:17.

9. Ibid., 34.

10. Ibid., 35.

Not only the inflation of *image* but also the deformation that would institute a reign of simulacral hyperreality is prefigured in the Platonic text. Especially if the retreat of the Socratic discourse from the finally original original is integrated into the figure, suspending its endpoint, the Platonic line figures a structure of deferral that in effect already programs the deformation: short of the end, every original turns into an image of a still more original original in the reiteration of the advance from image to original. In this turning of each original into an image of a more original original that, in turn, proves to turn into merely an image of still another, still more original original, the line figures the indefinite deferral, the unlimited retreat, of the original and to this extent programs its escape, its loss, as well as the mutation to which the image is then submitted. To be sure, the overturning of Platonism can be construed as simply a matter of denying the original and of promoting the mutation of all images, released from every bond to an original, into simulacra.[11] But such a construal is one-sided: it fails to observe that this very outcome is already programmed precisely by Platonism—that is, it construes the overturning in a form that remains under the control of precisely what it would overturn, failing to carry out a displacement or reinscription that could erode the very schema of the opposition within which it turns. If one would decisively overturn Platonism in this regard—overturn it in such a way as to turn away from it—what is required is that the reiterated turning of original into image be interrupted. One must turn to the sensible in such a way as to deconstruct the opposition between truth and appearance, that is, in a way that no longer takes the sensible as the appearance of another, remote truth, that is, that forgoes turning the sensible into an image of something other, even of something that would itself turn into an image. Outside the nostalgia for an indefinitely deferred, or even lost, original, the sensible will be approached neither as image nor as simulacrum.

---

11. Deleuze writes: "Overturning Platonism means denying the primacy of original over copy, of model over image; glorifying the reign of simulacra and reflections." Construed in this way, the overturning of Platonism links up directly with Nietzsche's idea of the eternal return. Referring to Klossowski's interpretation of the latter, Deleuze continues: "Taken in its strict sense, eternal return signifies that each thing exists only in returning, copy of an infinity of copies that allows neither original nor even origin to subsist. This is why the eternal return is called 'parodic': it qualifies as simulacrum that which it causes [*fait*] to be (and to return). When eternal return is the power of (formless) Being [*la puissance de l'Être (l'informel)*], the simulacrum is the true character or form of that which is—'the being' [*l' étant*]" (Deleuze, *Différence et Répétition*, 92). One should note further how the eternal return, taken thus, constitutes the schema of technological production (in contrast to τέχνη in its classical sense). In this connection it becomes crucial to differentiate between what results from the overcoming of Platonism and what is already programmed by it—crucial even if only to show how these moments coincide and how their coincidence exposes the incompleteness of such an alleged overturning of Platonism.

If in the reign of simulacra one hears still the mourning of the death of God, in the specific deformation involved one can trace the lines of a translation of the modern philosophical theory of the image. In other words, the modern theory of the image—at least that strain of it that reaches its culmination with Berkeley—supplies the theoretical figure that, by the means provided (but also directed, steered) by technology, comes to be translated into the reign of simulacra that would constitute the field of contemporary social practices and would tempt contemporary theoreticians with the prospect of wider, even unlimited extension.

By the time of Descartes the Stoic determination of image as imprint or impression had long since become established. In contrast to the outwardly directed vision of images on the wall of the cave, images are now assumed to be imprinted or impressed (stamped) on the soul (mind, spirit) by a printing or stamping technique that will become ever more problematic before finally being placed in the hands of God. The general effect of this determination is to drive vision (and the other senses) back from things, confining it apart from them; marking the specific effects and the end result is one of the great accomplishments of Prekantian modern philosophy.

The *Meditations* refers thus to the "images of things [*rerum imagines*]" as "formed in our thought."[12] To another passage, which mentions that things "send into me [*mihi immittant*] their images or ideas," the French version adds the gloss: "and imprint there [*y imprimoient*] their resemblances."[13] Yet Descartes mentions this printing of the images of things by things only in order to denounce it as a belief held out of blind impulse. Already, then, with Descartes the connection of image to original—the connection that, sustained by the printing technique, would insure also that the idea is an image resembling the thing—has become precarious. Descartes declares that, in truth, he does not perceive at all that there are "things outside of myself from which these ideas came and to which they were completely similar."[14] Even though Descartes does presume to speak of the difference between an object and its idea, it turns out that—as in the contrast he draws between the sensible idea of the sun as extremely small and the idea of it, drawn from astronomical considerations, as much larger than the earth—his claim to have access to the object itself can be supported only by recourse to intellection or even to innate ideas. But the Sixth Meditation seems conclusive: "Of these things I have no knowledge whatsoever, except that derived from the ideas themselves."[15] The only escape is through a system of indirect assurances regarding clear and distinct ideas and based

---

12. Descartes, *Meditationes de Prima Philosophia,* in *Oeuvres,* 7:20.

13. Ibid., 7:40, 9:31.

14. Ibid., 7:35.

15. Ibid., 7:75.

on appeal to the divine. Only by way of knowledge of God can one arrive at assured knowledge of any things, that is, of what one impulsively believed to be the originals imaged by one's ideas.

With Locke there occurs a subtle, yet decisive shift, one that tends toward effacing the difference that Descartes could finally negotiate only through the divine detour. At the outset of *An Essay concerning Human Understanding,* Locke defines *idea* as serving best "to stand for whatsoever is the *object* of the understanding when a man thinks." Such ideas, he writes, are "in men's minds."[16] Now it is almost as if there were no objects: when the mind is directed to something, its very object is the idea, rather than the idea serving only as the means by which the understanding would come to know an object outside the mind. On the other hand, the determination of the idea as imprint or impression remains somewhat in force, though Locke's text oscillates between regarding the impression as one made on the body and regarding it as an impression on the mind.[17]

In any case, though Locke writes of "the existence of things actually present to our senses,"[18] it is only by the most extreme means that he can impede the retreat of things beyond all reach of the human understanding. Locke's formulation of the problem could not be more direct and succinct: "It is evident the mind knows not things immediately, but only by the intervention of the ideas it has of them. Our knowledge, therefore, is real only so far as there is a *conformity* between our ideas and the reality of things. But what shall be here the criterion? How shall the mind, when it perceives nothing but its own ideas, know that they agree with things themselves?"[19] Faced with what he grants seems a "difficulty," Locke has recourse to the naturalness of the printing technique by which simple ideas arise from

---

16. John Locke, *An Essay concerning Human Understanding,* ed. Alexander Campbell Fraser (New York: Dover Publications, 1959) [unabridged, unaltered republication of the First Edition of 1690], 1:32f.

17. Consider the passage in which Locke writes: "I conceive that ideas in the understanding are coeval with *sensation;* which is such an impression or motion made in some part of the body, as makes it be taken notice of [after the third edition it reads: produces some perception] in the understanding"—in comparison with the passage in which he writes "that the mind is fitted to receive the impressions made on it" (ibid., 1:141f.). In a note to a later passage on perception as "being the *first* step and degree towards knowledge, and the inlet of all the materials of it," Fraser offers the following remark: "Indeed with Locke perception of presented phenomena is throughout an inexplicable fact." Fraser then cites a passage from Locke's posthumous *Examination of Malebranche:* "Ideas it is certain I have, and God is the *original* cause of my having them; *but how I come by them, how it is that I perceive, I confess I understand not.* . . . Ideas are nothing but perceptions of the mind, annexed to certain motions of the body by the will of God, who hath ordered such perceptions to accompany such motions, *though we know not how they are produced.* . . . That which is said about objects exciting perceptions in us *by motion* does not fully explain how this is done. *In this I frankly confess my ignorance*" (ibid., 1:192 n. 1).

18. Ibid., 2:191.

19. Ibid., 2:228.

things (by which ideas are "the product of things operating on the mind, in a natural way . . ."), and, in turn, he guarantees this naturalness by capitalizing on divine sapience and benevolence (". . . and producing therein those perceptions which by the Wisdom and Will of our Maker they are ordained and adapted to").[20]

As, short of such an appeal, everything about the thing tends toward being taken as nothing but an idea, a point is reached where there is need to suppose, beyond the ideas, little more than the mere substance in which everything would inhere—"a supposed I know not what, to support those ideas we call accidents."[21] The stage is set for the complete denial of the thing, of the original otherwise believed to be imaged in the imprinted idea.

This is the step ventured by Berkeley. One of the primary means to which he has recourse in order to make this advance is called *imagination*. The force by which imagination drives the advance is that of making present something singular. Such a determination of imagination is already prepared by Descartes, as in a passage of the *Meditations* where he focuses on the difference between *imaginatio* and *intellectus*: "For example, when I imagine a triangle, not only do I conceive that it is a figure composed of three lines, but along with that I envision these three lines as present [*praesens*] by the force [*acies*] of my mind [expanding this, the French version reads: *par la force et l'application interieure de mon esprit*]; and it is just this that I call imagination."[22] The force of the mind, the force called imagination, lets one envision something *as present*, lets one bring it to presence to the mind. Descartes is distrustful of this force and regards it as continually threatening to disturb the freedom from attachment to the senses that he considers the prerequisite for philosophy itself; for imagining has precisely the effect of turning the mind toward the things of sense ("since to imagine is nothing else than to contemplate the shape or image of a corporeal thing").[23] But whereas, as a result, Descartes repeatedly struggles to restrain the force of imagination and to restrain himself from relying on it, Berkeley mobilizes this force through two further determinations. First, he insists that what imagination brings to presence is always something particular, singular: "I find indeed I have a faculty of imagining, or representing to myself, the ideas of those particular things I have perceived. . . . But then whatever hand or eye I imagine, it must have some particular shape and color." Then, second, he identifies the power of abstracting or conceiving with the force of imagination: "Likewise the idea of man that I frame to myself must be either of a white, or a black, or a tawny, a straight, or a crooked, a tall, or a low, or a middle-sized man. I cannot by any effort of

---

20. Ibid., 2:229.

21. Ibid., 1:406.

22. Descartes, *Meditationes de Prima Philosophia,* in *Oeuvres,* 7:72; French translation in *Oeuvres,* 9:57.

23. Ibid., 7:28; cf. 7:73.

thought conceive the abstract idea [of man]."[24] Imagination is thus placed in service to Berkeley's thoroughgoing critique of abstraction: that one cannot imagine—represent in its presence to the mind—the abstract general idea of man demonstrates that such ideas are inconceivable. It is with this rejection of such abstract ideas that Berkeley deals the death blow to what remains of the thing itself, to that "supposed I know not what" to which Locke still clung.

Berkeley is even more insistent than Locke that ideas are the objects of human knowledge. He is also more consistent as regards the consequences of this identification: "It is indeed an opinion strangely prevailing amongst men that houses, mountains, rivers, and, in a word, all sensible objects have an existence, natural or real, distinct from their being perceived by the understanding." This opinion, Berkeley declares, involves a manifest contradiction: "For what are the fore-mentioned objects but the things we perceive by sense? And what do we perceive besides our own ideas or sensations?"[25] If ideas are the objects of human knowledge, then there is no need to assume other objects beyond these, objects existing outside the mind and its perceptions. Berkeley observes that such an assumption depends indeed on the legitimacy of abstract ideas, on the possibility of the abstract distinction between the existence of sensible objects and their being perceived. But one cannot conceive—that is, imagine—them existing unperceived, for "my conceiving or imagining power does not extend beyond the possibility of real existence or perception . . . , so it is impossible for me to conceive in my thoughts any sensible thing or object distinct from the sensation or perception of it."[26] The idea of an unperceived existing object is an abstract idea to be denounced as inconceivable, granted that conceiving extends only so far as the force of imagination. Berkeley writes: "When we do our utmost to conceive the existence of external bodies, we are all the while only contemplating our own ideas."[27] A passage omitted in the second edition of the *Treatise concerning the Principles of Human Knowledge* declares even more unconditionally the identity of the idea and the object: "In truth, the object and the sensation are the same thing, and cannot therefore be abstracted from each other."[28]

The later omission of this unconditional declaration perhaps reflects the differentiation to which (even in the first edition) Berkeley's text proceeds. It is a differentiation that, despite the denial of things existing unperceived, allows the determination of ideas as imprinted to remain to an extent intact. Again it is imagination that plays a decisive, though now different,

24. George Berkeley, *A Treatise concerning the Principles of Human Knowledge*, ed. Colin M. Turbayne (New York: The Liberal Arts Press, 1957), 9f.

25. Ibid., 24f.

26. Ibid., 25.

27. Ibid., 34.

28. Ibid., 25 n. 2.

role. Berkeley differentiates between "the ideas imprinted on the senses by the Author of Nature"—these being called *"real things"*—and the ideas "excited in the imagination, being less regular, vivid, and constant," which are "more properly termed *ideas* or *images of things* which they copy and represent."[29] If there are only ideas, then what are most properly termed *ideas* are the images excited in imagination, which, even if they retain the dyadic structure of image and original, are not taken to represent things actually present but only to present something not actually present. What can be actually present as a real thing are the ideas imprinted on the senses (that is, on the mind) by the Author of Nature. These ideas, improperly so called because they lack the dyadic structure belonging to an image, are inscriptions written in the mind by the Author of Nature, who indeed authors nature precisely through these inscriptions. Once it is declared that there are only ideas and no objects beyond them, not even a corporeal substance (a "supposed I know not what") stripped both of secondary qualities and of primary qualities (as inconceivable, unimaginable, apart from secondary qualities), then the very words *idea* and *image* undergo a certain slippage as a result of the loss of the dyadic structure that would otherwise make them ideas *of* something, images *of* an original. What comes to seal the identity of perceptual ideas with their objects—hence to displace and deform them as ideas *of* objects—is the writing or the printing press of the divine author.

As the mourning sets in, calling back the spirit—but only the spirit—of this spirit, the deformation becomes unlimited: what were called *ideas* are stripped not only of their imaginal reference to an object but also of that identity with objects that, with Berkeley, still came to legitimate them. Now they are neither images of objects nor images as objects but only simulacra.

A critique that would establish the limits of the discourse of simulacra needs therefore to return to the modern philosophical theory of the image, which, in the development just traced, provides the theoretical figure that comes to be translated as the reign of simulacra. Only through a critique of this theoretical figure can the contemporary discourse of simulacra be addressed in a radical fashion. Such a critique is initiated by Kant, whose "Refutation of Idealism" is aimed explicitly at "the *problematic* idealism of Descartes" and "the *dogmatic* idealism of Berkeley." What Kant demonstrates specifically is that "the consciousness of my existence is at the same time an immediate consciousness of the existence of other things outside me," since "the determination of my existence in time is possible only through the existence of actual things that I perceive outside me."[30] In other words, consciousness of oneself, and hence of ideas in the mind, is not more certain than, nor even possible without, consciousness of things

---

29. Ibid., 38.
30. Kant, *Kritik der reinen Vernunft,* B 276f.

existing outside oneself, of the things that would be represented in ideas. Through this demonstration Kant thus shows that the identity that Berkeley posits between ideas and things, or rather, the assimilation of things to ideas, must be undone in such a way that ideas or images are reconfigured as opening onto things as such, as presenting sensible things to the mind, as the means by which the sensible becomes present to sense. One will perhaps insist that this critique has its limits, that the *Critique of Pure Reason* reencloses things transcendentally within the sphere of phenomena, so that it becomes possible for Fichte—echoing, without simply repeating, the earlier result—to say: "Everything we see, we see within ourselves. We see only ourselves."[31] Yet, whatever its limits, the Kantian project does succeed in establishing a prohibition against conflating the object of consciousness with what occurs in consciousness, whether the occurrence be called image, idea, *Vorstellung,* or whatever.

B. INDIFFERENCE

On the one hand, Kant's establishing of the difference between occurrences in consciousness and objects of consciousness prefigures the schema of intentionality: an act of consciousness is always directed at an object distinct from that act; that is, consciousness is always *of* an object. On the other hand, insistence on this differentiation can serve, instead, to lead back to a theory of consciousness in which the very discontinuity that plagued Postcartesian philosophy reemerges, as it did in its most refined guise in the Kantian problem of the thing-in-itself. In its more general form, this theory hardens the differentiation into a rigid distinction between the object and the consciousness by which it would be perceived. Especially notable is the spatial schema that here comes to determine virtually everything: outside consciousness there is the object, the thing itself, which must somehow be reached from within consciousness, the assumption being that consciousness is essentially a *within,* an interiority, that it is incapable of turning itself inside out without ceasing to be itself. Perception can occur, then, only indirectly, by way of something within consciousness that represents the thing outside. This is the point at which an inner image is posited and this formal schema of a theory begins to take the shape of those modern philosophical theories of the image that have been traced above. The inner image can represent the thing outside only if it resembles it, and perception would occur in the consciousness of this image through which, indirectly, the thing outside would be presented. Consciousness of the image would be nothing other than its presence in consciousness, its presence in

---

31. Fichte, *Wissenschaftslehre nova methodo (1796–99)* (Hallesche Nachschrift), in vol. IV 2 of *Gesamtausgabe der Bayerischen Akademie der Wissenschaft,* ed. Reinhard Lauth, Hans Jacobs, and Hans Gliwitsky (Stuttgart–Bad Cannstatt: Frommann, 1964), 49.

the inner space. Perception would occur, then, insofar as an image is present in consciousness; it would occur precisely *as* this presence of the image.

The chain of aporias with which such a theory, whatever its specific form, comes to be bound is already prefigured in the ancient debate between the Stoics and the Academics as to whether cataleptic φαντασίαι bear an idiomatic mark certifying them as such and thus guaranteeing that they are impressed in accordance with things themselves. More elaborately figured in the development of the modern philosophical theory of the image, these aporias can be given a more general formulation. If only the image is present in consciousness, how is it possible ever to effect the transition from the image to its original outside? If only the image is present in consciousness, how does it happen that it comes to be taken *as an image* and hence as representative of something else outside consciousness? Can the mere presence of the image ever effect that displacement that must be enacted within vision in order for it to extend to objects? Even if it happens somehow that the image is referred to something outside, how can there ever be even the slightest assurance that the thing outside is thus revealed as it is? Even if there is a way from the image to the thing itself, how could one ever be assured of having gone that way?

What is most remarkable is the way in which, despite all the aporetic results, the spatial schema that is so decisively operative here goes for so long virtually unquestioned. What prescribes—one must finally ask—that perception occurs in an inner space? What determines here the sense and the pertinence of the opposition between inner and outer? What requires that the opposition be construed so rigidly that all exchange between inner and outer is abolished and the two isolated spheres are allowed then to communicate, if at all, only by way of an abstract relation of resemblance? From what source could one possibly draw the assurance that the space of perception is an inviolable interiority and that any opening of that space onto the things themselves is inconceivable? A vague analogy with a bodily schema of inner and outer is perhaps in play, but, rigorously considered, such an analogy would do more to break down the opposition than to provide assurance regarding it: one touches the surface of an object, not in some inner space isolated from that surface, but at the place where the surface of one's hand comes into contact with that of the object.

One cannot but endorse therefore the disruption of this schema. In the most direct form it will be a matter, then, of opening the space of perception to the things themselves, dissolving the interiority and especially the boundary isolating this space from that of the things perceived. By the same stroke one will have disrupted the concept of consciousness—or at least *a* concept of consciousness, one that has remained dominant for a long time. Now it will be said that in perceiving something one is always there alongside the thing itself, one's hand gliding across its surface, one's vision embracing its contours as with one's other hand one gently knocks on its surface, producing a sound that draws one's listening to its hollow interior. Rather than having somehow to escape the confines of an inner space in order to perceive the thing outside, one is always already outside, already engaged there with the thing. Even the concept of subject will begin to erode, not only at the boundary where subject meets object, but, even more, in the ecstatic character that will be had by that being previously called subject.

And yet, such a move may well prove too direct, too thoroughly determined by the schema it opposes, by its very opposition to that schema. If everything is outside, if the schema is simply eliminated, then the perceiver cannot even be characterized as extending into the open space of the perceived thing; the very differentiation required by the concept of ecstasis would be lacking, or at least some other way of establishing it would have to be found, some way other than by way of the schema of inner and outer. Of still greater concern is the danger that the simple, direct disruption of the schema may leave no basis for taking into account the distinctively *presentational* character of perceptual experience and the specificity prescribed thereby. In perception things come to show themselves to a perceiver, so that to such showing, to perceptual manifestation, a certain difference belongs, a certain difference across which the showing takes place. What is specific to such showing is linked to that difference. Even if one resolutely forgoes—as is appropriate—letting that difference ossify into an impenetrable boundary between an inner and an outer space, one will still be obliged to retain and to think this difference.

Thus, instead of simply replacing the old spatial schema with its opposite, indeed with its very dissolution, the more appropriate course will be to replace it with the schema of intentionality. First of all, because the schema of intentionality marks the difference in question, marks it indeed as the primary difference: fundamental to the schema is a rigorous differentiation between the intentional act, in which, for example, one perceives an object, *and* the intentional object, the object perceived. Built upon this differentiation, the schema then construes presentation as intentional in character: the presentation that occurs in, for example, the perception of an object is a *presentation of the object,* a presentation irreducible to the mere presence of some content, some image, in consciousness. When one perceives a star shining brilliantly in the midnight sky, it is the star itself that one perceives, not an image within consciousness that would only represent the star. If it is not to be said—at least not directly—that with one's vision one is already there alongside the star shining in its remoteness, it can, on the other hand, be said that the intentional act moves always *across the difference* separating perceiver and perceived. *Intentionality* is the very name of such movement across the difference.

The initial effect of replacing the old schema with that of intentionality will be to jettison the perceptual image. If indeed perceptual presentation is intentional in character, if the intentional act is such as to move across the difference so as to present the object, then there is no need to suppose an image within consciousness that by representation would present the object that is beyond consciousness. Indeed, the very supposition of such an image would tend to obscure the force of intentionality and thus to reinstate the old isolation of perception from the object perceived.

On the other hand, if one were to suppose that perceiving involves nothing but the intentional act (correlative to the object), one would quickly come to an impasse in attempting to account for the specificity of perception. For no matter how much one might differentiate between various modes of intending, there would always remain unaccountable differences in content, diversity of sense (in the sense of *sense* determined by reference to the senses). It is not in the respective intentional acts that one could mark the difference between the respective perceptions of two qualitatively distinct but otherwise identical objects, for instance, the perceptions of a red surface and of an otherwise identical blue surface. And so, despite the expulsion of the perceptual image and even while continuing to insist on that expulsion, one would need to suppose the presence of a certain sense-content in consciousness. It would be imperative to dissociate such content from the intentional object: what one perceives is not the sense-content but the object itself, not color-sensations but colored things. Unless this distinction is rigorously maintained, the introduction of content into consciousness will have the effect of effacing the intentional character of presentation and will risk reenclosing perception within an interiority of consciousness.

Can this schema of intentionality be made to remain intact so that from this point on it would be a matter only of determining with descriptive precision the specific character of the three primary moments (intentional act, sense-content, intentional object) and of the relatedness between them? Does the schema provide a definitive framework within which to work out a phenomenology of perception without need of disturbing again or even reinterrogating the primary moments of the framework? Or, on the contrary, does the further determination of these moments and of their relatedness have the effect of exposing an instability within the schema that prevents its simply remaining intact and providing the framework and program for phenomenological research? Is there perhaps within it an instability, an indecisiveness, of such proportion as to call for a radical transformation of the schema?

Indecisiveness there is indeed. Its locus is in the moment of sense-content, and it begins to appear as soon as the determination of that moment proceeds beyond the most general description of the relation of this moment to the others. It is most obtrusive when one comes to describe the relation of the sense-content to the object. The first move will of course have been one of differentiation, and it will have been effective insofar as it merely duplicates the difference on which the entire schema is built, that between perceiving and perceived, that across which the intentional act would move. The indecisiveness begins to appear as soon as one undertakes to determine the positive relatedness, the affinity, as it were, between these moments—as one must, since the content not only is distinct from the object but also must have in any given case an appropriateness to the object. The linguistic bind is an index of the indecisiveness. When, focusing on specific kinds or even particular instances, one undertakes to say what the sense-content is, one will have no choice but to transfer to the sense-content the name of a component or property of the object. When one sees colored things, one has—or is said to have—color-sensations. When, in particular, one looks at a piece of white paper, one has the sense-content white—so one will say, identifying the content by citation, repeating the name of something about the object.

But what warrants the citation, the assumption of synonymity? One will have no choice but to say that the content *somehow presents* that quality (for example) of the object after which it is named. One might of course use different words, saying, for instance, that the content *corresponds* to the objective quality from which it borrows its name; but as soon as one sets about specifying concretely the sense of such correspondence, one will say that it lies in the appropriateness that the particular content has for belonging, as the moment of content, to the perception of that particular objective quality; and this is only to say, again, that the content somehow presents that particular quality.

Yet what sense can *presentation* have in this connection? In what sense, if any, can one say in accord with the schema of intentionality that an immanent content presents something about the intentional object? For, according to that schema, presentation is as such intentional in character; that is, it can occur only through the agency of an intentional act and never simply through the presence of a content in consciousness. Here the indecisiveness is unmistakable: the sense-content is presentative of the object, and yet, according to the schema of intentionality, it cannot as such be presentative.

There must be, then, another order of presentation, one that precedes that effected by the intentional act. But if, according to this other order of presentation, the sense-content is presentative of (something about) the object, then it too, and not just the intentional act, effects a certain movement across the difference. *Intentionality* proves not to be the only name of such movement.

But if the so-called sense-content presents (something about) the object, no name would be more fitting to it than *image*, and, despite the initial expulsion of the image, the schema of intentionality eventually leads, by its peculiar indecisiveness, back to the operation of an image in perception. At this point where the image is reintroduced and a certain recoupment of the modern philosophical theory of the image is thus prepared, everything depends on determining the image, the sense of image, outside the discourse of interiority and yet without simply effacing the difference between what belongs to the perceiver and what belongs to the perceived, between what is one's own and what is of the object. To this end, what was said at the outset about the image needs to be kept constantly in view: *image* names the occurrence, means, and locus in which sense becomes—and so is—present to sense. Or rather, more specifically—and observing that a means can easily be construed as a *tertium quid* that separates rather than presents—let it be said that an image is the occurrence and the locus in which something sensible becomes—and so is—present to sense prehension.

The image is to be determined, then, as *one's own;* one's engagement with an image is such that the image belongs to oneself. It is thus—at least on the plane of content—that perceiving is situated and differentiated from the perceived, which shows itself to the perceiving, which shines back across the difference. It is thus that a presentation (and the minimal differentiation it requires) is operative in independence of the intentional act, perhaps even prior to any active intention, in any case, from the moment one opens one's eyes upon the spectacle of the here and now, even if with the utmost receptiveness, even if remaining utterly spellbound in one's own vision.

Can it simply be said, then, that, as *one's own,* the image is an inner double of the objective quality (for example) that it presents? Can one discover even the slightest trace of a white within that would not be at all the white that one sees, a white within that would be distinct from (even if somehow presentative of) the white of the paper at which one will look as one searches within for some trace of this other, unseen white? Or is such a double not just something projected within by a certain theoretical schema? Is it not just the same sort of image that the old schema—that of the modern philosophical theory of the image—posited as inner representative, just slightly disguised now, its ghostly double?

If the inner double is dissolved, then there will be only the image as an image *of* (something about) the object—as is perhaps most manifest in the case of the images offered to one's vision by an object that is repeatedly turned and tilted before one's eyes. Images are *of the object,* and, at a certain level that will have to be analyzed later, they prove to be presentative of aspects, faces, profiles, of the thing itself. Yet even as such, images retain their delicacy and, like shadows and reflections, are not themselves cut to the measure of objectivity.[32] Failing to grant the delicacy of the image, construing the image as a quasi-thing, is the first—and indeed decisive—step on the way that leads back into the modern philosophical theory of the image and all the aporias it produces.

---

32. On the delicacy of the image, see *Delimitations,* chap. 5.

Though of the object, images are constitutively linked to the situatedness of one's perceiving: if one changes the location from which one views the object, one alters also the images that are offered, alters them no less than does the turning and tilting of the object itself. That the image is *of the object* does not rescind its being *one's own;* nor does it require positing a double within of the image that is of the object. Rather, the image is *indifferently both—both one's own and of the object.*

Thus, in one's vision, one is indeed always there alongside what is seen and does not have first to overcome, indirectly (as by attending to a representative), the confines of an inviolable interiority. And yet, one's vision is *one's own,* and in embracing things with it, one will not simply have leapt beyond oneself or turned oneself inside out.[33]

A number of metaphors, images of the image, could be proposed at this point: for example, that the image is like a leaf (either from a tree or of paper) with its two distinct but inseparable sides. But aside from the immediacy of the self-reference and the complications it would—perhaps prematurely—introduce (does this image of the image have itself two such sides?), such metaphors will almost certainly tend to efface what is most decisive in this determination of the image: that the tension is retained between the moments, the tension that metaphors such as that of the leaf would reduce to a matter of having two sides. Even to refer to tension is perhaps to risk weakening what could more appropriately be called the *duplicity* of the image, that it is indifferently both one's own and of the object. One could perhaps picture the image as a membrane separating while also connecting the sphere of one's own and that of objects; yet mere connective tissue would hardly belong itself to both spheres, would hardly extend into them as does the image. Thus also this image of the image is exceeded by the duplicitous image. The duplicitous image is both one's own and of the object, yet without being itself divided or doubled. The duplicitous image is *indifferent* in a quite precise sense: the image is in the difference in that it belongs to each sphere and is stretched, as it were, between them, and yet it is indifferent to the difference insofar as it belongs to both.

In its delicacy, in the lightness of its shining, the image is duplicitously both one's own and of the object. It is not something (a quasi-object) that

---

33. Fichte has perhaps come closest to thematizing the indifference of the image, though, as his discourse is not entirely free of the modern philosophical theory of the image, the word *image* tends to name only the moment that falls on the side of *one's own.* He writes: "Accordingly, in intuition something hovers immediately before me [*schwebt mir etwas unmittelbar vor*]. I do not ask whence it comes; the object simply happens to be there. . . . The 'something' that hovers before the intuiting subject is, in this case, neither an image nor a thing. It is there without any relation to us. Neither image nor thing, but both at once, it is subsequently divided into the image on the one hand and the thing on the other" (*Wissenschaftslehre nova methodo,* 75f.).

presents sense to sense but rather is the occurrence and the locus in which sense becomes present to sense. To be sure, philosophers have, since antiquity, observed that in such alleged presentation there can be deception, and the preoccupation with the illusions that can be induced by sense becomes indeed decisive from Descartes on. And yet—as Merleau-Ponty observes, countering the Cartesian preoccupation with illusion—even to speak of illusion presupposes that one has identified illusions; yet one identifies illusions precisely through perceptions that offer assurance that they are not illusory but genuinely present sense to sense.[34] Illusion is not something simply opposed to the image in which sense would be presented to sense but rather is a possibility interior to such presentation. One will want to say that the image can also be duplicitous in this sense—hence doubly duplicitous, duplicitously so.

Of the image one catches only a glimpse. Not that such glimpses are uncommon or even infrequent. Catching them requires neither a method of disciplined observation nor a system of reductions that would set their objectification out of action. Catching them—which involves also not failing to let them go—requires only a certain attentiveness and receptiveness. If there is a difficulty, it lies not in any lack of manifestness but rather in the tendency to impose on what becomes manifest a reifying interpretation that distorts and conceals the image to the point that it ceases to be manifest in its lightness and indifference. One must let the image be freed to its delicacy.

If attentive and receptive, one catches a glimpse of the image. Picture the scene: Under a clear Italian sky, intense sunlight making the dry, rocky ground and its sparse vegetation scintillate almost as though they were emitting flashes of dazzling light. Then, at the very moment that one turns one's glance toward it, a small lizard, almost the same color and texture as the ground, silently slips away under a rock. One is left wondering and yet also somehow assured of what one has seen. So is it also with catching a glimpse of an image.

Precisely in catching a glimpse of the image, one will enact the very duplicity that belongs to the image, redoubling it in its very apprehension. Catching a glimpse is not an inferior mode of seeing that one would wish, in this instance, to replace by another if only it were possible (for example, by a mode to which the image would be simply, enduringly present). Rather, catching a glimpse is precisely the mode of seeing appropriate to an image; it is that very mode to which an image will entrust its utmost manifestness.

---

34. See Merleau-Ponty, *Phénoménologie de la Perception*, xi.

SPACING THE IMAGE

A. THE PROVOCATION OF SPEECH

Turning to the sensible, set within its limit, one will begin doubling it by saying: there are images, sense images. There is much to be said for letting the *to be* slide into the form *there is* (*il y a*). Yet, whatever syntactical strategies may prove appropriate, the move that cannot be avoided by a discourse on the image is that by which the sense of *being* is opened and extended to the point where one could say that there are images without thereby having reified the image, construed it as a quasi-thing, cut it to the measure of objectivity, even—to take the most telling case—in the very gesture of installing it in a mind or spirit that would be set in opposition to objects. Only through such an apertural move, detaching imaginality from objectivity, can one free the image to its delicacy. In doing so, one will also have reopened the question of the sense of being. Keeping it open to the point where a new determination can begin to take shape, keeping it open despite all the forces, even within discourse, that threaten to reenclose it within objectivity, will require vigilance.

The image—the sense image—is not a quasi-object that would mediate

between subject and object; it is not a quasi-thing inserted somehow between thinking thing and extended thing. Neither is the image, strictly
speaking, something that presents sensible things to one's sense prehension. Rather, *image* names primarily the very occurrence of presentation to
sense prehension, the occurrence in which something sensible (not yet
quite a sensible thing as such) is presented to one's vision. In its delicacy
the image is the very occurrence of presentation across the difference between the things of sense and one's sense prehension. It is the very upsurge
of presence; in this sense it is the locus in which something sensible comes
to be present to one's sense prehension. But here *locus* is to be understood
neither in relation to an object (which, for instance, would confer a certain
objectivity on the locus defined by its boundaries) nor even as a region of
a preconstituted space in which things can occur. Rather, the eventuation
of an image, the upsurge of presence, is, at once, the opening of the locus
of presence. In saying that *there are images,* one will need also to say that
images are there, though—because of the duplicity of the image—the being
there of images does not coincide with that of things.

Beginning with the image, what is then required is to trace the movement through the image to the original, the movement that the Platonic
text takes to be carried out primarily by the double vision that envisions
the original in and through the image. Yet now, at the limit determined by
the turning to the sensible, the original that would be brought to presence
in and as the image can be only the sensible thing itself. In the image what
is made present to one's sense prehension is a certain aspect of the sensible
thing itself. But what is now to be understood by *thing itself*? Can there be
things themselves once the turn to the sensible is rigorously enforced?

How is it possible for something to be itself and so to be a thing itself?
For something to be itself requires that it sustain a certain relation to itself,
specifically, a relation of identity or sameness. Thus, the thing itself is the
thing as the very thing it is, the thing in its identity with precisely what is
its own; that is, the thing itself is the thing proper, the thing in its (relation
to its) propriety. Within the classical philosophical purview, things that
come to pass (sensible things, as they come to be called) are incapable
of sustaining an identity with themselves; they are always becoming other
than themselves and thus cannot be things themselves. But even in not
being themselves they betray a reference to a propriety, though one with
which they prove incapable of sustaining an identity. In the Platonic texts
this propriety is identified as the look that shows itself in and through
things that come to pass, the look that does not itself come to pass but
remains identical with itself. Because it is ever selfsame (ἀεὶ κατὰ ταὐτὰ
ὄν),[1] such a look, an εἶδος, is a thing itself. Or if, looking ahead, one would
limit the extension of *thing* to the sensible, one would say of an εἶδος that

---

1. Plato, *Timaeus* 28a.

it is a being itself (in both senses). If, now enforcing the limit, now turning to the sensible, one would redetermine, within this limit, what constitutes a thing proper, then it will be imperative to reopen the question of the self-identity of sensible things. Once the sensible is twisted free of the intelligible, once the sensible thing can no longer be referred to the ever selfsame εἶδος so as to confirm the perpetual disruption of the thing's self-identity, it is then required that, turning back to sensible things, one consider how they show themselves as themselves, that is, how in their very self-showing there is constituted a proprietal self-relation that is distinctively sensible.

One could imagine vision coming to rest in the image, engaging itself fully with the visible presence eventuating before it. And yet, it is at most only rarely that such tranquil engagement occurs. For the most part, vision responds to a provocation that drives it on beyond the image, even while it continues to embrace the image. The result is that the occurrence of presence, the presence of something sensible in and as the image, comes to open onto a showing of the thing itself as itself.

How does this provocation operate, and what is its source?

One moment lies in a certain instability that belongs to the image, a vacillation that arises from its duplicity; every determination brought forth in the image will, if posited as being a determination of *the thing,* prove to be, also and instead, a presentation that is merely *one's own.* Thus, any determination that would be attached, in whatever way, to the thing would turn out by the same stroke to be detached from it. Since no determination could be made to adhere to the thing, the image would provide no means by which a thing could itself be determined, no determination through which a sustained identity of the thing with itself could be established; nothing transposed directly from the image to the thing would serve to determine the thing as itself, as a thing itself. Vacillating between being of the thing and being one's own, the image would never yield a determination in the rigorous sense; always, at the very moment that it would be posited as determining the thing itself, it would slip away, back toward a singular sense apprehension.

This vacillation of the image, its slipping away from the thing itself, was marked from the beginning of philosophy. Thus it was observed that what appears large to one can appear small to another and that what appears circular to one can appear elliptical to another. Rather than yielding a determination of the thing itself, the image proves to be linked to the individual location (the distance) or the singular perspective from which the thing is beheld. Rather than showing itself *as itself,* the thing presents itself only in a certain aspect correlative to the sensible idiom of the one to whom it appears. Offering merely vacillating images, its appearances are multiple and conflicting.

How is it that vision does not simply come to rest in this offering and remain absorbed in the multiple, vacillating images? How is it that the multiple appearances are construed as conflictive, so that vision is driven on beyond the image?

Even while embracing the image and its offering of presence, vision is driven to exceed the image because there is always already operative another exceeding of the image, one that can exercise a certain attraction on vision precisely because it is not of the order of vision. To say that this other exceeding has *always already been executed* is to imply that it is not an act that one overtly and deliberately carries out but that it is effected by an orientation always already assumed whenever an image is there. The pertinent orientation is one that sets things themselves apart from images; it projects them in advance beyond images, projects them as so constituted that each *is itself*, projects each therefore as submitted in advance to the requirement of self-identity, requiring that of two opposed determinations it be, at most, either one or the other but not both. The orientation is thus one that posits the thing itself as submitted—in advance of its coming to presence as image—to the demand for determinateness. In the case of the most extreme opposition, that of contradictory opposites, the demand is for noncontradiction. That the orientation includes such a demand—this prohibition of a certain kind of diction—betrays its profound affiliation with language.

Thus it is that the orientation is always already assumed: from the moment one speaks, indeed in the very opening to speech, one has already exceeded that which is present to sense, has said more than one sees. This exceeding of presence assumes several different forms. It takes an extensional form, as when one says that the earth is vast while seeing only a certain expanse stretching to the distant mountains, or perhaps while seeing only a small patch of ground, or even, if one is indoors, nothing at all that could be called *earth*. The excess can also be one of articulation and connection, as when one says, "That mountain is steep and snow-covered." Even if one trains one's gaze most acutely on the mountain, one will see only the mountain, that it is steep and snow-covered. One will never see the *that,* the *is,* or the *and;* one will never see what is said in these words, will never see it as one sees what is said in *mountain.* Indeed, it is questionable whether one can see even the mountain's *being*-steep and its *being*-snow-covered, assuming that being is not a real predicate. Whereas what one sees, initially at least, as one casts one's gaze toward the distant mountain, is the more or less undifferentiated whole, speech brings forth an articulation of moments and certain connections between the articulated moments, distinguishing, for instance, the steepness from the mountain itself and connecting them through the copula.

Yet, insofar as vision is confined to presence, it is still more impoverished, still more radically exceeded by speech. For, in the strict sense, one does not even see what is said in *mountain.* No matter how acutely one trains one's gaze on the distant mountain, no matter what technical supplements one may employ, what is said in the word exceeds all that one can see, exceeds it along two different axes.

For there are other mountains too, some perhaps even on the periphery of one's vision as one looks at the mountain of which one speaks. The word can be said also in reference to these other mountains, in reference to any mountain whatsoever. What is said in the word is not, therefore, any one mountain but rather mountain as such, which is never to be seen *as such*. One sees only this mountain or that mountain; one does not see, as such, mountain as such.

And yet, in the strictest sense, one does not see any mountain; one does not see what is called *that mountain,* not even as one points directly at it, not even if one transports oneself there and scales its steep cliffs all the way up to its snow-covered peak. For one sees only what is present to sense in and as some image or other, not the mountain itself, not even determinations belonging to the thing itself (such as its steepness). What one sees are only vacillating images, in which the mountain may just as readily appear not steep as steep; whereas that mountain of which one speaks, that mountain as set out in speech, tolerates no such vacillation. On the contrary, it is determinate, that is, it is posited in speech as determinate, regardless of whether or not one has actually ascertained its particular determinations. It is set out in speech as being what it is and not being what it is not, as being one with itself such that it cannot be other than itself: if it should prove to be steep, it would not also turn out to be, in the same sense and respect, not steep. If one were to say that it is, in the same sense and respect, both steep and not steep, then one would be speaking against the very way the thing is set out in speech; such speech against speech itself, against its very way of positing things in advance, cannot but dissolve into no speaking at all—or, at best, into a mere phantom of speech. Even if the opposed determinations are not contradictory opposites—if it is a matter of the mountain being snow-covered or rain-soaked—the determinateness of the thing as posited in speech would prohibit and consign to dissolution any speech that would attribute both determinations to the thing itself.

Therefore, a certain move beyond the image, an exceeding of what is present to sense, comes into play from the moment one speaks, indeed from the moment one assumes the very opening to speech. Through this move things themselves are set out as exceeding the image, as exceeding any and every aspect of them that can come to presence in and as an image. Their excess consists in their determinateness; precisely because they are set out as being determinate (as determinate beings), they are beyond the image and its vacillation, even though the image, making the thing present to sense, remains the indispensable aperture onto the thing itself. Things themselves, self-identical in their determinateness, are set out even in advance of any coming to presence, any configuration of presence, that could serve to confirm their determinateness. When, at another level, speech comes to introduce articulation and connection into the globally apprehended thing, its operation remains basically the same: to posit a determinateness that could never simply be given to sense, even when, as at this other level, it is set forth as a determining of something that is already an object for sense apprehension.

Thus, no matter how fondly vision may embrace presence, it will always be paired with another gift that will never cease to disturb its rest. For speech is the very provocation of provocations, calling forth things themselves, things that in their determinateness *are* themselves, the same as themselves, calling them forth in advance of their presence. Speech is the advance to being.

Philosophy begins, then, by reenacting the move beyond the image to and through speech. It sets out on its second sailing (begins in beginning again) by undergoing conversion from engagement with images to the assumption of λόγοι. More precisely, philosophy turns to what is said in speech, to the things themselves set out—even though not brought to presence—through speech, laid down as the originals merely imaged by what is present to sense, as hypotheses (ὑπόθεσις in its original determination) in the form of determinate originals.

And yet, precisely in its way of surpassing the image, speech is decisively limited. This limitation is one that philosophy recognizes from the beginning, especially in the struggle against sophistry. For, while it is speech that first sets out the things themselves, projecting them beyond the image, speech *does not itself present* the things. At most, speech merely determines something already presented, as in the articulating and connecting of the distinct moments of something already presented as a whole. But, first of all, speech merely sets out the things themselves, and this is why its move beyond the image is hypothetical. Setting out the things themselves, speech only opens the expanse in which the things themselves can come to show themselves; it opens the space of self-showing without yet broaching in the least the self-showing itself.

In this regard it is imperative to maintain the difference between the image as presentation to sense and the thing itself in its self-showing—hence imperative to mark the distinction between presence and showing. Even if a moment of presence must always be installed somehow within the configuration of showing, showing is irreducible to presence. Today, at the limit, it is imperative to insist unconditionally on this irreducibility. For the limit rigorously prohibits separating the thing itself, taken *as such* (in a generality no longer merely incipient), separating it to the point of reconstituting it as an intelligible, which as a higher, nonsensible presence (εἶδος, ἰδέα) could then command all (or virtually all) showing.

If, today, one traces the configuration of showing in such a way as to constrain it to the sensible, this is not at all to exclude incipient generality nor other doublings; it is only to insist that they be traced as doublings of and yet within the sensible. Even the doubles set out from speech—for instance, the mountain as such, which is never to be seen as such—are now to be taken only as directing, attracting, sense apprehension into the field in which sensible things show themselves, not as hypothetical traces of intelligible beings beyond this field.

The irreducibility of showing to presence has a decisive recoil on the very tracing that would make this irreducibility manifest. To trace the configuration of the showing of sensible things themselves, marking the moments that belong to this showing, cannot be a matter merely of transcribing something beheld, something eventuating in its presence before one's vision. For what is to be inscribed or traced, the showing of things themselves, is not reducible to presence, does not present itself, does not offer itself to an intuition determined as such by correlation with presence. A discourse that would inscribe the showing of things themselves cannot but transgress the limits of mere explication and violate what was to have been the principle of all principles. The inception of such a discourse marks the passage of phenomenology over into monstrology. The operation by which manifestation would be brought to double back across itself may accordingly be called *remonstration,* resuming this old word, now obsolete in its pertinent sense but common in that sense in seventeenth-century English. In *remonstrate, remonstration,* one hears again the root *monstrare* (to show), and adhering to the older sense one hears in the prefix *re-* the sense of *again* or *anew.*

Therefore, in marking remonstratively certain moments and their connections to other moments within the global configuration of self-showing, it will not be simply a matter of marking something already there, already present, something that one finds displayed before one's vision; it is not a matter of re-marking something already in effect marked through its very presence, of merely marking the mark more distinctly. On the other hand, it cannot be a matter of merely imposing on the showing a configuration of moments and connections, of imposing them simply through the marking; for a configuration thus derived could have no bearing on the things themselves in their self-showing. Rather, it is—and will prove to have been—more like a tracing, as in a drawing or even as when a thin, blank sheet of paper is placed on top of another on which there is a design so that one can then trace that design on the blank paper by following with one's drawing instrument the design, which from underneath shows through the thin, semitransparent upper sheet. Yet in remonstration one traces something that, in contrast to the ordinary case, only becomes manifest through the tracing; it is as if one could come to see the design underneath the tracing paper only by first tracing it. A kind of reversal is thus operative: that which gets traced shows itself, not in advance of the tracing, but only through it, only in the trace, and yet it shows itself as having been there already, as anterior to the tracing, and hence as not having been simply produced by the tracing. It is as if tracing an original design on the blank sheet of paper had precisely the effect of exposing for the first time that very design already printed on the underlying sheet. Or as if an original drawing let one see for the first time the beautiful lines of a familiar face.

The *re-* of *remonstration* is not, then, to signify simple repetition (showing again, showing anew). Rather, the prefix's charge is to allude to the anteriority exhibited by what gets shown in remonstration: showing itself as having been there already, it shows itself as being there again, still, at the moment of its showing.

Remonstration is, on the one hand, *originary*: it neither reproduces something seen in advance nor draws out more openly and distinctly something already, if covertly, present as such. As originary, a kind of vision is operative in it, though a kind of vision that seems more akin to what Kant calls originary intuition (*intuitus originarius*)[2] than to the mere visual engagement with an image. For the vision operative in remonstration is such that through it a configuration becomes visible for the first time, as if by the very force of that vision. Yet, on the other hand, remonstration is *memorial*: once brought forth by the force of this vision, the configuration shows itself as having been there already in advance of the vision, hence as not simply imposed by an originary vision turned into mere fancy. The configuration brought to presence through the vision proves to have been there already but to have been concealed, forgotten; and therefore the vision proves also to have been a remembrance. Yet the concealment will have been such that nothing that remained present would have provided remonstrative vision with the slightest basis for an operation of mere explication, of simply uncovering further something already—if obscurely and partially—exposed to vision. No memory, however vague, will have lingered, ready to be refreshed. Thus it is that remonstrative vision must be originary precisely in order to be memorial. As, also, remonstration must be memorial in order to be originary vision of something and not a mere fancy without any bearing whatsoever on it. If, recalling the ancients as well as Kant, one were to call this originary remonstrative vision knowledge in the highest sense (ἐπιστήμη), then it could be said that such knowledge is, at once, remembrance (ἀνάμνησις).

Thus it is that one can never simply begin.

A constraining force, necessity itself (ἀνάγκη), will prove to have been at work in the originary vision. This necessity has nothing to do with so-called logical necessity, nothing except to remain withdrawn from its grasp. There is no saying definitively how it works, except that it does not operate by presenting itself but only by remaining apart from presence, even at the moment when originary vision proves to be also memorial and thereby at-

---

2. Kant, *Kritik der reinen Vernunft*, B 72.

tests to its working. One can say also that originary vision must be receptive to its working, to its solicitation, however that may come; but rather than compromising or qualifying the originary character of remonstrative vision, such receptiveness is precisely what allows it to be an originary vision of something, not mere fancy.

Remonstrative vision will not be other than imagination in its exorbitant trait of mixing presence and absence, making present something utterly absent from view and yet (only then seen to have been) already there.

With remonstrative vision it will be as with Adam's dream.

B. HORIZONALITY

If an image is there, then, with the provocation of speech, vision comes to take up things themselves as they show themselves. In setting about to trace this advance remonstratively, it is requisite to stress again that this comportment is not reducible to a sense intuition of something present, indeed that it is irreducible to seeing in the broadest sense (and not merely because there are other senses besides sight). In order to mark this differentiation terminologically, the word *apprehension* will from this point on be reserved for the comportment to things themselves, in preference to *perception* or *intuition,* also in place of *vision,* which will however be used in a less differentiated way, thus in reference both to presence and to showing, as well as to remonstration. What is called for, then, is a remonstrative tracing of the apprehension of things themselves as they show themselves.

Does apprehension itself make its way to the thing itself? One might easily suppose so, considering the schema of intentionality and the way in which it assigns the vital role to an intentional act. Taking up the sense-content, the intentional act would objectify it, effecting thereby the move to the thing itself. Even granted the redetermination of the sense-content as duplicitous image, one might still suppose that it is through the supervention of an intentional act that the duplicity of the image is surpassed and the image stabilized as definitively *of the object.*

But what would be its mode of supervening? Would such supervention suffice to constitute an apprehension of the thing itself? What would be the character of such an act? Or, more pointedly, can apprehension retain the character of an intentional act once the sense-content has been redetermined as duplicitous image?

Is apprehension a matter of an act in which one would come to grasp the thing itself as presented in the image? In a certain respect such an act would be quite superfluous, contributing nothing beyond what the preintentional presentation in and as the duplicitous image already accomplishes: for the image, even if duplicitous, is a presentation of the thing. One might, then, regard the act as extending across a series of images, for instance, those presented when something is turned and tilted before one's eyes; the act would consist in one's intending one and the same thing through these various images. Yet, such an act would have not only to traverse the particular series of images, cancelling the differences by referring them to the variety of positions assumed by the thing in relation to the one apprehending; in order to constitute a showing of the thing itself, which cannot be presented *as itself,* such an act would have also somehow at least to refer concretely to the *entire* series of images that *could* present the thing. Simply traversing and cancelling the differences between the images successively there would never suffice to set forth the thing itself, the very propriety of which is such that an inexhaustible store of images belong to it. On the other hand, one will observe that in the normal apprehension of things it is not at all necessary that one's vision traverse a series of images, that is, such grasping across the differences is not essential to apprehension of things (though its possibility is no doubt essential): as soon as one casts one's gaze upon the image (which in its duplicity belongs also to that very gaze), one's vision moves beyond the image to the thing itself, unless impeded for the sake of catching a glimpse of the image. What is it that draws forth this vision and thus makes possible an act or series of acts in which one would traverse a series of images in such a way as to refer them to the thing itself?

Is the move driven perhaps by a power of interpretation? Could one regard the intention as essentially an act of interpretation? Does the move from image to thing have the same character as the move from one meaning to another, or from a word to its meaning, or even from an image to a meaning? Is the move from image to thing essentially a transition to meaning, even granted a redetermination of meaning as such that would rigorously differentiate such a transition from the philosophical move to the intelligible? Not at all. For when one's vision moves beyond the image to the thing, it is a matter, not at all of a transition to meaning, but of an opening upon *this particular thing itself* as it displays itself before one's vision. Even though there is an incipient generality, what one sees are things themselves, not meanings.

What takes place in the transition is neither an interpretive move to meaning nor a grasping of something present, not even of a presence assembled across the differences between various images of the thing. On the contrary, when one's vision passes beyond the image to the thing itself, that which draws it forth is something more or less unseen, something at the limit of vision.

As the horizon, itself more or less unseen, draws one's vision into the distance. This seam joining earth and sky has a double character: on the one hand, the horizon recedes indefinitely, always withdrawing still farther as one moves toward it, never becoming simply determinate in its presence; on the other hand, it delineates the compass of the visible so that whatever lies beyond the horizon cannot be seen unless, moving toward the horizon, one induces it to recede. In short, the horizon lets things be seen while itself withdrawing from determinate vision. At the limit, it bounds the visible by receding from visibility.

A rigorous extension of the word is therefore possible: when *horizon* comes to designate also what bounds particular things and lets them be seen as such, this is not just a matter of remote analogy; nor does this extended sense of horizon lose its connection with the horizon joining earth and sky.

The thing itself is never present as itself. Its showing, the showing in which it comes to show itself to sensible apprehension, is not simply a matter of presence to such vision; showing is irreducible to presence. In every instance, what there is, what is there, is the image in and as which the thing is presented. Except under exceptional, more or less contrived conditions, the image displays a singularity. Furthermore, the image is there as a more or less undifferentiated whole, as, for example, with what one sees of the distant mountain before coming to determine it as steep and snow-covered. Yet, however undifferentiated it may remain, the image has a certain centeredness. In the simplest case, that of the presentation of a relatively well-defined single thing against a relatively uniform background, the image is centered in the presentation of an aspect or profile of the thing; it presents the face, as it were, that the thing turns to one's vision, that it casts frontally to one's gaze. Regarded as thus centered in such a frontal aspect, the image is a *frontal image*. Even if every image that is there is somehow frontal, not every case is so simple. The image is not in every case centered in the presentation of a single thing. If from a certain height or distance one looks out over a city or a landscape, one sees a manifold of things at the same time; or, more precisely, there is a grouping of the respective aspects that these things cast frontally to one's gaze. Furthermore, in the case of senses other than sight, the centeredness of the image may be less well-defined and somewhat differently constituted. Even if, in the interest of a certain analytic precision, the remonstrative trace will be oriented to the simpler cases and largely to the visual image, it should not be taken for granted that mere extrapolation from these cases would suffice for the others.

In order to keep open the question of the sense of being, thus sheltering the delicacy of the image, one will say: there is an image. But it is equally imperative to say the reverse: an image is there. Partly for the same purpose but also to indicate that an image, presenting a thing, making the thing present, rendering it present, is not itself present. There is no presence *of* the image, for the image is precisely the presence—the occurrence and the locus of the presence—of the thing. If the image is there, then the thing is presented, is present to one's vision; but in saying that the image *is* there, that there *is* an image, the sense of being is no longer presence. In saying that the image is there, the intent is furthermore to stress that the image is not just the occurrence of presence but also the locus of presence, its *there*. Yet in this connection the old word *locus* is to be heard in a sense anterior to that of *space* or *place*, in a sense anterior even to the strict differentiation between space and time. What *locus* names precedes any reification that would turn it into a (spatial or temporal) container; its precedence is thus akin to that of χώρα, for which *locus* was Chalcidius' Latin translation. With the occurrence of presence that eventuates in and as the image, the aspect presented is there (has a locus), though this upsurge of presence is anterior to the spacing of the image.

As things come to pass, images come and go. Even as one and the same thing is turned and tilted before one's eyes or as, looking at something stationary, one alters one's position in relation to the thing, one image comes to replace another, each passing on into another. Suppose one looks again at the steep, snow-covered mountain in the distance. One sees only one side of the mountain, the side that the mountain presents to a viewer situated over against this side. One does not see the other side of the mountain, though one could—and is well aware that one could—see the other side if one were to look at it from the other side, that is, from a position over against the other side of the mountain. Neither does one see it from above, nor from within, though perhaps one in fact could; yet even if there were no means available to convey one to a position above the snow-covered peak nor, for instance, any caves to give one an inside view of the mountain, one says—indeed with a sense of necessity—that one *could* see the mountain from above and from within, even if in fact one could not. But what is most decisive is that one could never—in fact or otherwise—see it *from nowhere*, that is, in such a way that it would present itself simply as itself, would be present as such, rather than presenting merely one side or another. It shows itself always *from somewhere*. A certain spacing belongs to its showing.

More rigorous consideration would exclude saying even that one sees some *side* or other, as if the frontal aspect were a side of the thing itself and not still centered in the duplicitous image. No doubt one could establish a certain correlation between various possible images, on the one hand, and the front, back, sides, etc., of the thing itself, on the other hand; in one image the front of the thing will be dominant and the back not presented at all, while in another, dominated by a side, both front and back may be presented, though obliquely. But, nonetheless, each image remains not only of the thing but also one's own, so that what it presents of the thing is always correlative to one's perspective on the thing. Even a particular side is seen always in a frontal image, seen from somewhere. Even if one looks at a side directly, one's gaze centered along a line that intersects the center of the side perpendicularly, the presentation will still be correlative to one's position with respect to the thing. Even if in such a case the shape of the side is presented virtually as it is in the thing itself, one will still have seen the side from a particular distance, and the appearance of the thing, its presentation in the image, will be correlative to this distance, which will determine, for example, how minutely the texture of the surface is presented in the image.

Each frontal image that is there yields, in turn, to another. One can pass through a series of frontal images of the thing, though in such passage there is no accumulation of presence; one comes to have an image before one's gaze only by giving up another, only by relinquishing all other images of the thing, even though such passage through successive images may constitute a richer apprehension of the thing than is had when only one image is there. Normally there is even a kind of continuity between successive images, which shade into one another to such an extent that one could speak even of imaging and not just of the singular image.

Yet one need not pass through a series of images; one can, on the contrary, limit one's engagement to a single glance, or, as the thing remains motionless, one can continue looking at it from the same perspective and distance. Even if as in these cases one sees only a singular image, no others coming to dislocate it, other images are nonetheless implicated in the showing of the thing broached by the singular frontal image. Even if presented solely in a singular frontal aspect, the thing shows itself as having an unlimited store of other aspects that it could present, and only because these other lateral images are implicated with the frontal image is the showing indeed a showing of the thing itself. Nothing contributes more decisively to engendering anew the sense of sensible monstration, of the self-showing of the sensible, than marking this reference of the frontal image to lateral images. To the showing of the thing itself there belongs, along with the frontal image, a horizon of other images, a lateral horizon, which bounds the frontal image and lets it be seen as an image of the thing itself. If with a single glance one moves already beyond the image that is there to the thing itself, a stretch of that way runs through the lateral horizon in which the frontal image will be installed, by which presence will be bounded.

The lateral horizon is no more present than is the frontal image it would bound. But neither is the lateral horizon there; indeed it could not be there, could never come to meet one's gaze frontally, though of course any particular lateral image could always, subsequently, be seen frontally, gaining a locus, coming to be there. Though in any instance the lateral horizon, like the lateral images that compose it, is dislocated from the there, sensible monstration requires that it come into relation with the there, with the image that is (the) there. With respect to the thing itself, this configuration is such as to mix presence and absence: it links the presented aspect of the thing to the entire series of aspects that are withheld, absent from view, not presented as such.

The sense of being that is appropriate to the image has begun to unfold, requiring now a certain development in its determination. The development hinges on the distinction between the moments of occurrence and locus, on the one side, and that of presentation, on the other. Image as such is to be determined by the latter moment alone: it is a presentation (rendering present) of a thing. A frontal image is such a presentation in its upsurgence, that is, in its occurrence and locus; whereas a lateral image is such a presentation as nonoccurring, as displaced from the there.

Granted this development in the determination of the image, a more rigorous discourse can be deployed by delimiting the lateral horizon as a *spacing* of images. The horizon is such that the various lateral images are linked to each other and set also in a certain correlation with the various perspectives on the thing that could be assumed. Yet the images are not there together; they do not constitute a common locus, not even one dislocated from the locus of the frontal image. What the horizon effects—it is both effecting and effect, as spacing is both an operation and the effect of that operation—is a spreading-out of the images, a dispersal of them that is not reducible to merely distributing them in a homogeneous space, a dissemination more abysmally resistant to any movement of assembling them before one's vision. The spacing of the lateral images, the effecting of the horizon, sets those images apart in an apartness that leaves open the differences between them, that lets those differences persist in their opposition. As, for example, something seen from such distance that its shape is indistinct may, to a closer look, appear either circular or elliptical depending on one's perspective on it; that is, it can appear *as both;* that is, it holds in its horizonal reserve both of the images, despite the difference between a circle and an ellipse. The spacing of the lateral images unfolds a figuration for apprehension, its schematism. For as the spacing of the lateral images takes place and the horizon is effected, the lateral horizon comes to bound the frontal image, comes about it, circumspaces it. With the spacing of the lateral images, the frontal image is circumspaced so as to offer to apprehension an opening onto the thing itself as itself. Thus does the delicacy of the image give way to the density of the thing itself.

When a thing is apprehended, it always shows itself from within a periphery, as set against a background. To a greater or lesser extent the background is presented in the frontal image; specifically, it is presented in and as the margin surrounding the imaginal presentation of the frontal aspect of the thing. In this respect, in being to a degree presented, the background differs from those other aspects or profiles of the thing for which the lateral images are presentative. As presented in and as the imaginal margin, the background shades off, breaks off almost imperceptively, although it is presented as having the character of not breaking off as such, of extending on beyond what is presented in and as the margin of the image. In its full structure—as rendering present the background even in its very exceeding of the presentation—the imaginal margin has the char-

acter of a peripheral horizon, which is no less determinative for the showing of the thing than is the lateral horizon. Its effect is indeed more direct:
how something shows itself, the particular guise in which it becomes manifest, will be directly codetermined by the peripheral horizon, linked constitutively to it.

Looking at the distant mountain, one sees also the other mountains
around it and is assured that the mountain chain extends on beyond what
one sees, even beyond what one could see from one's present position.
Because one looks at it across a low, flat plane and because the surrounding
mountains appear much lower, the mountain appears to tower above everything to a greater degree than it would if seen from another perspective
from which the surroundings would appear differently.

Let it suffice merely to mention the research and the conceptual reorientation that Gestalt psychology has carried out in view of this phenomenal
implication, noting Köhler's insistence that factors in the surroundings determine the local sensory phenomena and his analyses of a wide range of
figure/ground experiences.[3] This reorientation was rigorously extended in
the work of French phenomenology. Thus, Merleau-Ponty refers to Gestalt
theory, which, he says, "tells us that a figure on a ground is the simplest
sensible given [donnée] that we can obtain." In broader terms, anticipating
his philosophical appropriation of Gestalt theory, he continues: "The perceptual 'something' is always in the midst of something else [au milieu
d'autre chose]; it always forms part of a field."[4] Merleau-Ponty's entire project
of a phenomenology of perception is launched through the rigorous redetermination thus brought to bear on the phenomenal field. Both Köhler
and Merleau-Ponty refer to the much-discussed Müller-Lyer "illusion" in
order to illustrate how surroundings codetermine perception. In this example two horizontal lines of equal length, one above the other, are the
focal objects; from both ends of each primary line there extend pairs of
slanting secondary lines, which form arrowhead shapes; on one of the primary lines all secondary lines slant outward, on the other all slant inward.
What both Köhler and Merleau-Ponty put into question is the assumption
that psychologists had made that at the truly primary sensory level the two
lines are given as of equal length, this primary sensory datum being dis-
torted by the effects of the secondary lines. The assumption is, then, that
the apparent inequality of the two primary lines is not a true sensory fact,
and in support of this assumption these psychologists refer to the fact that
if one makes an effort to view the objectively equal lines in detachment
from their surroundings one will soon discover that the illusion becomes
less striking; such "analytical perception" may even eventually make the

---

3. See Wolfgang Köhler, *Gestalt Psychology* (New York: New American Library, 1947),
chap. 3. On the Müller-Lyer illusion discussed below, see pp. 47, 55f.

4. Merleau-Ponty, *Phénoménologie de la Perception,* 10.

illusion disappear entirely. Merleau-Ponty puts the question most force-fully: "The question is whether attentive perception, the subject's concentration on one point of the visual field—for example, the 'analytical perception' of the two main lines in the Müller-Lyer illusion—do not, instead of revealing 'normal sensation', substitute an artificial arrangement for the original phenomenon."[5] If one turns back to the phenomenon, Merleau-Ponty insists, one will find that apprehension is inseparably bound up with a whole perceptual context. In something like this "illusion," in which the lateral horizonality is insignificant and as a result the operation of peripheral horizonality, reduced to the simplest form by the simplicity of the drawing, stands out all the more prominently, how the focal lines come to appear, their showing, is not simply determined by their frontal presentation but depends also on the surroundings, on the peripheral horizon.

Peripheral spacing is not restricted to conditions of homogeneity: the moments belonging to the peripheral horizon need not be presentative of other things of the same order as the one that shows itself in relation to this horizon; indeed these moments need not be presentative even of another thing at all. Even if this horizon did not have its distinctive recessional character, presenting the background as extending on beyond what is presented of it, the peripheral horizon would still be irreducible to a configuration of homogeneously present things.

In this connection the example of lighting is especially pertinent. A feebly lighted white wall appears white to unhampered vision, but if looked at through a small aperture in a screen that conceals the source of light, it then appears bluish-gray. Part of what happens in such a case is that the patch of wall seen through the aperture loses its relation to the configuration of lighting that is spread over the wall. What is seen (the same patch of wall) is not the same when removed from its field; there is a connection between the color that the patch shows itself as having and the configuration of lighting by which the spectacle is illuminated. The lighting of the field, quite determinative of the showing, is not at all a matter of other things, nor even, for the most part, of something that could be said actually to be seen; the configuration of shadows and reflections is in a sense not so much itself seen as it is rather that by which the spectacle is seen. Indeed, a considerable alteration is required in order, as in the case of a painter, actually to see—in a more or less frontal way—the shadows and reflections. For the most part, the lighting remains horizonal, a kind of prearticulation of the spectacle that precisely as such is determinative of it.

This extension to the example of lighting is indicative of the fluidity that belongs to the schema of the peripheral horizon. For the lighting, the configuration of shadows and reflections, is not restricted to the periphery in the most obvious sense of the word but rather is spread across the entire

---

5. Ibid., 15.

field; shadows fall also across the thing itself in its frontal presence, and its surface catches reflections that may obscure as well as illuminate but that, along with the shadows, provide a prearticulation that, without simply surrounding the thing, nonetheless bounds it and outlines for vision the way around and into it. Thus, when Monet paints the envelope of light and atmosphere as it spreads over a winter landscape at sunset, painting it as it obscures the things on that landscape to the point of invisibility, what is painted in such a painting is the very visibility of the landscape.

The peripheral horizon can also assume other guises, and these can be operative along with the surroundings and the lighting. For example, in the case of instrumentality, where the frontally presented thing is one that serves some definite concrete purpose, there is operative horizonally an entire network of connections that extend beyond that thing and that decisively determine how it shows itself. The instrumental thing is connected with some definite kind of work, some task to be accomplished; in that work it is perhaps used along with other instruments, with which, then, a certain complex of concrete connections will be sustained. If the instrument is used in a process of production, it may be used on certain kinds of materials, which, in turn, come from nature, though perhaps by a series of other processes of production. An instrument has also its peculiar fittingness for the one who is to use it, and its shape, for example, may appear much more readily in the guise of its fittedness to the human hand than in that of mere spatial extendedness. In many cases, not only those of production but also, for example, that of a musical instrument, there is operative a connection not only to the user but also, even if often more indeterminately, to others for whose benefit the tasks are performed, to supply them with certain products or to give them enjoyment.

Instrumentality is not the only case in which something is centered in such a network. In every case in which the frontally presented thing is something more than a mere thing to be perceived, in which it orients a mode of comportment that exceeds perception, that engages the thing pragmatically, for example, or aesthetically, there will be such a network operative. It is primarily in order not to exclude such cases that *apprehension* has been given preference over *perception:* apprehension can be carried out, not only by gazing at something, but also (and in many cases more appropriately) with one's hand, as when one picks up a tool and begins using it, or through exchange between hand and ear, as when one takes up a violin and, tuning it, then begins to play for the enjoyment of those around. It is imperative in every case that the connections woven together around the focal thing not be regarded as abstract or ideal relations, even though a certain formalizing of them is inevitable for theoretical or remonstrative purposes. What is crucial is that they are not connections merely posited by thought; it is not as though things would first of all simply be perceived and only then, subsequently, have these connections posited between them, that is, imposed upon them. Rather, the connections are concrete; they belong to the very showing of those things as such, that is, as instruments, as things of pragmatic concern, etc. One of the most significant accomplishments of *Being and Time* is to have shown through its concrete hermeneutics that certain connections of this kind are constitutive of the way in which things for the most part show themselves and that mere things, things merely present (*das Vorhandene*), only emerge when a certain disregard for such connections comes into play.[6]

In many instances the concreteness of the connections obtrudes unmistakably: as with the shape of a hand tool, its being shaped to the hand and to the work in which it is used. Or in the walking stick that one may take along when one goes off to climb the steep slopes of the snow-covered mountain in the distance. The rounded, knob-like top of the walking stick is perfectly suited to user and use: the hand rests easily over it yet can also grasp it tightly should the occasion suddenly demand. Its height is tailored to the proportions of the human body, and its sharp metal point is designed for piercing hard snow and ice. When one takes such a stick and, using it, starts up the mountain, one apprehends this thing itself as it is set within its concrete network, fitted to user and use. One apprehends it as one never could merely by looking at it.

In all such cases the network of concrete connections codetermines how the thing centered in that network shows itself, indeed more decisively than in the case of mere surroundings. Such networks also extend more decisively beyond what is present in the frontal image, linking up—concretely, if indefinitely—with nature as source of materials and with others for whose sake a certain kind of work is done for which the relevant thing is instrumental. But like all peripheral horizons, they bound the frontal presence of the thing in such a way as to refer it beyond itself; once the image is thus installed in its setting, its duplicity and delicacy give way to the self-showing of the thing itself.

The delimitation of these spacings, of these lateral and peripheral horizons, can be more or less duplicated for the other sense that has access to things themselves at a distance, namely, hearing, which involves perspective and distance as well as a surrounding space that codetermines what is heard. With the other senses the distinctions are greatly reduced though not utterly effaced. For example, one touches something from somewhere and on one side or another, so that a certain lateral horizonality is operative, though in most cases it is reinforced by and fused with the corresponding visual horizon. In general, the horizonality of the other senses tends to be thus linked to that of vision.

Even if the horizons themselves are less distinct and less complex in the case of the other senses, their concreteness is perhaps more manifest than

---

6. Heidegger, *Sein und Zeit*, 66–88.

in the case of vision. This concreteness needs to be underlined especially because one could undertake to construe the complex of horizons—this figuration or schematism—as a kind of reconfiguration of the ancient determination of form, that is, to be more precise, as a kind of displaced and dispersed εἶδος. Such a reconfigured εἶδος would have to be utterly displaced from the intelligible, for otherwise the entire analysis of horizons would only have provided a detour by which again to leave the sensible rather than turning into its depth. And yet, for ancient thought, εἶδος is the word in which was declared the very sense of the intelligible—of the intelligible that would be the sense of sense, thus opposed to sense, that is, to the sensible. Furthermore, such a reconfigured εἶδος could neither be present (as an aspect of a thing can be present) nor constitute a locus of presence (as a frontal image is there as locus of presence); even if, as with a peripheral horizon, a margin of presence is there, it remains constitutively linked to what lies beyond the margin. Consequently, εἶδος could no longer name, as it once did, a higher presence that would command all showing, that would cast its radiance through sensible things so as to empower their self-showing, while surpassing absolutely the presence of which sensible things, in their perpetual passingness, are capable.

Such eidetic discourse is, then, best put aside, along with the numerous translations and derivatives that continue to enforce, if more feebly, its original direction. Let it be replaced by discourse on horizons, by a discourse of spacing. Let it be said that what draws forth one's vision into its passage beyond the image (in and as which the thing is present) to the thing itself (as itself, as it shows itself) is not the radiance of an εἶδος but rather the effecting of lateral and peripheral horizons. What makes the delicate, duplicitous image give way to the thing itself in its depth and its setting are the spacings in which, first, the lateral images are spread out in their connection among themselves and to the frontal image and in which, second, a periphery (which can be multiple and of various degrees of complexity) comes to surround and codetermine the thing, shading off at the limit and yet extending on as such. The limit can itself be extended, if, for instance, one looks at the focal thing from a greater distance or even, for the moment, ceases to focus on it and lets one's vision range around and beyond it. Yet this limit cannot be extended without limit: one's vision comes finally to the horizon, and there, at the limit of the limit, the elements that finally delimit the space of all showing are earth and sky.

By way of these spacings, by way of the circumspacing of the image that sets it within lateral and peripheral horizons, the duplicitous image gives way to the thing itself in its self-showing.

Further remonstration could no doubt render the constitution of things more distinctly and more differentiatedly. Thus, within a more developed remonstration, one could mark again the distinction between the frontal aspect in which the image is centered and the marginal moment belonging to the (usually multiple) peripheral horizon yet exceeded by it. Even further, one could mark within the peripheral horizon the operation of a secondary lateral horizonality: any thing rendered present in the margins of the frontal image would be present in a modified frontal way (as marginally frontal, one could say), and therefore lateral images, a lateral horizon of this thing, would (at this secondary level) be implicated. Not only the thing one confronts but also what one sees marginally alongside it holds in store (as a lateral horizon) the aspects that it can offer to other perspectives. Conversely, one could mark within the primary lateral horizon the operation of a secondary peripheral horizonality: from different perspectives the surroundings of one and the same thing assume very different form. In such proliferation lateral and peripheral horizons become intertwined, woven into an ever more concrete setting for the things themselves.

C. SHINING

But spacing alone does not suffice for the self-showing of the thing. Presence, too, is required—that is, the occurrence of presence, hence also its locus, hence the frontal image on which the various spacings come to bear. Indeed the frontal image is central to the self-showing of things; it is itself centered in the frontal aspect, as which the thing is present and which, in the self-showing, comes to open onto the thing itself. And yet, even before the thing itself turns out to be dispersed through its spacings—in the sense that full presence and determination are indefinitely deferred—the frontal image, even its frontal aspect, proves to have its promise of sheer presence undermined by the binary character of certain senses, not as an anatomical fact, but as it comes into play in the unfolding of apprehension. That vision is binocular, that hearing is biaural, that one touches with two hands—this already disturbs the simplicity and stability that the frontal aspect could otherwise seem to possess, especially at a level prior to the workings of horizonality. Already with the binocular image, for instance, there will have been a minute difference of perspective and a corresponding protohorizonal operation.

In this regard the opening of the image onto the thing itself is always already under way; there is no level at which the image would be the present representation of a remote, absent original. Indeed any such duality or separation is precluded by the very determination of the frontal image as the occurrence and locus in which the thing comes to be present to one's vision. As the very upsurge of the presence of the thing, the image is distinguishable from the thing only through a distinction that is itself unstable and that tends toward self-effacement. It is a distinction that borders on being no distinction at all, for the image, even if duplicitous, is nothing other than, nothing distinct from, the thing. It is precisely as image that the thing itself is present, even if duplicitously, even if not yet showing itself as itself. When one prehends a frontal image, what is present to one's vision is the thing itself in a particular aspect or profile. The image is there as the surface—the thin, almost diaphanous surface—at which the thing itself displays itself before one's vision, casts forth a certain radiance, that is—in a word in which resounds an ancient word set at the limit—*shines*.

Most directly, *shining* (*shine*) transliterates *Schein* (*scheinen*). It is to be heard in the full range of senses carried by the German: shine, look, appearance, semblance, illusion. In this range of senses it is not a matter of simple polysemy but rather of senses so interlinked and mutually dependent that they form a field or spread rather than a series of distinct senses. The word has a kind of semantic spread such that each sense is constitutively implicated in the other senses that precede it; for instance, only if something shines forth can it put forth a certain look, and only then can it appear to some vision and thus become an appearance.[7]

Yet *shining* and *Schein* translate, in turn, an ancient word, a word that, in the superlative degree, occurs in a decisive passage in Plato's *Phaedrus*. The passage is one in which Socrates is discussing sense images, specifically their capacity to image their intelligible originals. Socrates declares that in the images of justice (δικαιοσύνη), moderation (σωφροσύνη), and other such things there is no brilliance, splendor, luster (φέγγος), and, as a result, only a few (and they very imperfectly and with great difficulty) can discern the originals by means of the dull organs with which earthly beings are endowed. None of these things shine brightly enough through their earthly images to be readily apprehended. The one exception is the beautiful: "For the beautiful alone this has been ordained, to be the most shining-forth [ἐκφανέστατον] and the most lovely [ἐρασμιώτατον]."[8] The beautiful is exceptional in that it shines brightly in the earthly region, in the region of the visible. Thus it renders being accessible to those who are bound to the visible through their embodiment. The beautiful is that εἶδος that most shines forth in the midst of the visible. Or, one could say: *the beautiful* (κάλλος) names the way in which being shines forth in the midst of the visible.

All that is required in order now to resume the Platonic discourse on the shining-forth of being in the midst of the visible is the turn from intelligible to sensible, the turn by which is cancelled the remoteness and separation of being—of the thing itself—from the image where it shines forth. Indeed one could regard the drawing of the beautiful toward the visible—declaring it an exception, the most shining-forth—as broaching, if ever so slightly, this very turn.

Yet the shining of being serves preeminently to draw those burdened by

---

7. See my analysis in *Crossings: Nietzsche and the Space of Tragedy* (Chicago: University of Chicago Press, 1991), 25f.

8. Plato, *Phaedrus* 250d–e. See my discussion in *Being and Logos*, 153–59.

embodiment up into the advance from the sensible toward the intelligible; the beautiful is called the most lovely (ἐρασμιώτατον) precisely because its shining can evoke the ἔρως capable of impelling one into the advance.

For Kant, *Schein* draws one into the same advance. But the *Critique of Pure Reason* denounces such an advance beyond the knowledge of sensible things, denounces it as illusion. Such specifically transcendental *Schein*, which "leads us completely beyond the empirical employment of the categories," positively inciting us to transgress the limits of experience, Kant characterizes explicitly as illusion (*Illusion*), thus in effect narrowing the sense of *Schein* to this single signification.[9]

Hegel, on the other hand, relaxes this restriction and brings the word into its own philosophically. Shining (*Schein*) is neither denounced as simply illusion nor assigned primarily to a single essence in distinction from all others. Not even in the *Aesthetics* with its orientation to the beautiful, where, on the contrary, Hegel says: "Yet shining itself is essential to essence. Truth would not be if it did not shine and appear. . . ."[10] The systematic account given in the *Science of Logic* locates shining more precisely and explicitly. The shining that is essential to essence is not a shining of something else, not the shining of an image or of a being of whatever sort remote from essence: "The shining of essence [*im Wesen*] is not the shining of an other, but it is shining in itself, the shining of essence itself." In other words: "Essence contains shining within itself."[11] But then, essence is not something remote from its shining, not something behind or beyond its shining. Keeping intact the connection between shining and appearance (the connection explicit in the words *Schein* and *Erscheinung*), Hegel can declare that "essence is therefore not *behind* or *beyond* appearance" but rather is such that shining and appearance belong to it.[12]

Shining does not have its locus in an image removed from the original that would shine in the image, that would shine through the image in such a manner as to show itself. What shows itself is not behind or beyond—not remote from—the shining but contains the shining in itself. In other words, it is the thing itself that shines, and if one can still distinguish the image—the delicate, shining image—from the thing, it is only by way of a self-effacing distinction that leaves the image intact only as the surface of

---

9. See Kant, *Kritik der reinen Vernunft*, A 292/B 349–A 298/B 355.

10. Hegel, *Ästhetik*, ed. Friedrich Bassenge (West Berlin: Verlag das europäische Buch, 1985), 1:19. This text is based on the second edition published by Hotho in 1842. In the recently published *Nachschrift* by Hotho of Hegel's 1823 lectures, the formulation is somewhat different: "Der Schein aber ist kein Unwesentliches, sondern wesentliches Moment des Wesens selbst. Das Wahre ist im Geiste für sich, scheint in sich . . ." (G. W. F. Hegel, *Vorlesungen über die Philosophie der Kunst* [Berlin, 1823, transcribed by Heinrich Gustav Hotho], edited by Annemarie Gethmann-Siefert, in vol. 2 of *Vorlesungen* [Hamburg: Felix Meiner, 1998], 2).

11. Hegel, *Wissenschaft der Logik I (1812/1813)*, vol. 11 of *Gesammelte Werke*, 248f.

12. Hegel, *Enzyklopädie (1827)*, §131. The passage remains unchanged in the 1830 edition.

the thing. All that then remains is to enforce rigorously the turn to the sensible, so that the thing itself that shines can be nothing other than a sensible thing.

Already in *The Birth of Tragedy* Nietzsche renews the discourse on the shining of images, of beautiful images, or rather, a discourse that again determines the beautiful as shining. The images about which Nietzsche writes are those of dreams, or rather, those for which dream images provide an analogy, namely, Apollinian images. Such images—most notably, those of the Olympian gods created by Apollinian art—are not images of some beyond but rather the shining-forth of a certain perfecting of life, images that serve as transfiguring mirrors revealing life itself in its exuberance and superabundance.[13]

Yet, even if the rigorous turn to the sensible is already thoroughly prepared in *The Birth of Tragedy,* even if the discourse on Apollinian images and shining is already situated within this turn,[14] it is in Nietzsche's very late texts and notes that one finds the most radical execution of the turn and the most explicit inscription of a discourse on shining (*Schein*) within that turn. On the one hand, the turn revokes the interpretation—at least a certain interpretation—of the sensible in terms of shining: in the final episode of the story of "How the 'True World' Finally Became a Fable," having abolished the "true world," it remains only to declare: "*with the true world we have also abolished the apparent one* [die scheinbare]."[15] With the abolition of the intelligible, the sensible is no longer to be taken as apparent (*scheinbar*), that is, as mere appearance through which shines the true, intelligible world. But, on the other hand, the very abolition of such an interpretation of the sensible as the locus of such a shining prepares the way for a new interpretation of the sensible. What is remarkable is that, as Heidegger has shown, Nietzsche ventures this new interpretation by means of a rehabilitation of shining. Heidegger cites a decisive note: "'Shining,' as I understand it, is the actual and sole reality of things." Another note, also cited by Heidegger, amplifies this identification: "Hence I do not posit 'shining' in opposition to 'reality' but on the contrary take shining as the reality that resists transformation into an imaginary 'world of truth.'"[16] It is by a certain interpretation of the sensible as shining that Nietzsche would determine it in such a way as to twist it free of the intelligible, to free it from being determined by opposition to the intelligible. In a determination rigorously adherent to the sensible, set within the limit marked by the turn to the sensible, Nietzsche would determine the "reality" of the sensible as multiple

---

13. Nietzsche, *Die Geburt der Tragödie,* in vol. III 1 of *Werke,* 30–32. See also *Crossings,* 21–36.

14. Most decisive in this regard is the following note from 1870–71: "My philosophy an *inverted Platonism:* the farther removed from true being, the purer, the more beautiful, the better it is. Life in shining as goal" (in vol. III 3 of *Werke,* 207).

15. Nietzsche, *Götzen-Dämmerung,* in vol. VI 3 of *Werke,* 75.

16. Heidegger, *Nietzsche,* 1:248.

shinings, as perspectival shining. The new interpretation of the sensible would be ventured by rethinking, within the limit, the sense of perspective and of showing. Or, as one may say, by rethinking—remonstratively—the horizonality and shining of sense.

In the most rigorous sense, to say that sensible things *shine* is already to violate, with this designation, what would be—but cannot simply be—said. Shining resists designation both as such and specifically, withdrawing inevitably from whatever one might call it. On a clear, warm summer day the sky is both the very sense of blue and yet beyond the call of the word, a stranger that the word will never quite be capable of housing. It recedes beyond the distant houses and trees, withdrawing from mere sight with the same inevitability as that with which the horizon recedes as one moves toward it. What one would call the blue of the sky recedes from sense in both senses. And yet, its recession from the sense that such words would signify is at the same time a mute recession into sense in its other sense, into what would be called—even though in a designation that, again, would have to be unsaid precisely in being said—*shining.*

Things shine. Never do they show themselves, for instance, only in and through their connections with a peripheral network, for it belongs to the very sense (in the double sense) of self-showing that it proceed from the things *themselves.* No matter how thoroughly an instrument may be integrated into a network of concrete connections, it can show itself in those connections only if it also displays itself to the senses, only if it shines forth. This is not of course to say that it first of all shines and only then comes to be linked up with its horizons; even less is it to say that, in shining, the thing becomes present so as then to be capable of connections with various horizonal moments. Rather, it will always shine from out of those connections, which, in turn, come into play only in and through the shining. As one picks up a knife, which is connected to horizonal moments by virtue of its sharpness and fittedness to the hand, one will not fail to notice the gleam of its sharp blade, and in the feel of its handle as one grips it, one will sense the lightness and balance that contribute to its handiness.

Shining is perhaps more readily apparent in the case of things whose peripheral horizons are less complex or at least less determinately instrumental: the dark, billowing surface of a stormy sea, the shimmering whiteness of newly fallen snow, the silhouette of a great city seen from a distance at dusk. In many instances a certain tranquility will be sensed in the shining of such things, and it is from such tranquil shining that the most elementary sense of beauty will arise. But there are also things that can threaten, that can shine forth as overpowering by virtue of what they show themselves as holding in store, by virtue of what they conceal within their peculiar horizonality and yet betray in their way of shining. As the raging power of the stormy sea can appear overpowering or, when seen from a safe distance or from some other position of security, can appear sublime.

Shining and spacing take place together, at once, inseparably.

Shining does not take place from afar: it is the shining of the sensible and not of something else in and through the sensible, not of something belonging to an order other than the sensible. Even in saying that shining is *of the sensible,* one must insist that it is not such that the sensible is first present and then comes to shine. As with a flash of lightning, where the lightning is nothing other than the flash and certainly not something present that then flashes, so it is with shining: shining is the very way in which sensible things come to be present and can thus show themselves as themselves.

Shining does not, then, present something that could be stabilized in a certain form, eidetically determined. One would have to say, rather, that, in its shining, the sensible is senseless, that it is meaningless (at least one would have to call it meaningless as long as meaning is configured in a way that is inseparable from eidetic determination)—not in the sense of being the opposite of meaningful, which would be already to fit it to the measure of meaning, but rather in the sense of being of another order, as escaping the very opposition between meaningful and meaningless. Shining could not even be said to prefigure meaning but remains, on the contrary, abysmally untranslatable. It is like a vanishing moment, one that cannot be caught and held fast without thereby being turned into something quite other. It is like the most delicate of surfaces, the thinnest of shells, collapsing as soon as one tries to touch it, impeding all translation beyond the sensible.

Thus it is that the thing itself shows itself, shining forth from within its lateral and peripheral horizons. Showing itself as determinable in its depth and in its involvements in its setting, it is nonetheless resistant to determination, which remains indefinitely deferred. In this way the self-showing of things themselves both confirms and yet leaves open the determinateness posited in advance in the very opening to speech. If speech always exceeds what one sees, the visible resists being carried over into something said, persisting in an untranslatability that one would like to call—were it not itself untranslatable—the sense of the sensible.

5

TRACTIVE IMAGINATION

A. THE CONFIGURATION OF SHOWING

Sensible things can come to show themselves to apprehension, can become manifest for apprehension. A sensible thing can show itself *as itself,* and indeed such showing itself as itself determines the primary sense of self-showing. In showing itself as itself, a thing becomes manifest as the very thing it properly is, manifest in its propriety. It shows itself as properly self-identical, as disposed by a proprietal self-relation that is distinctively sensible. This relation of the thing to itself, which becomes manifest in its sensible monstration, is constituted by the secret strength of the thing, by its power to keep itself in reserve, unseen, in its very display of itself, by its showing itself as self-withheld.

Such self-showing requires the effecting of horizons. It requires that lateral and peripheral horizons be gathered around the image as which the thing shines forth. The installation of the thing, as it is present, within its lateral horizon bestows on it its proper density; this horizon gives it the depth that belongs to the very flesh of sensible things, in distinction from the mere shell, the shining surface, present as image. Granted the lateral horizon, the thing shows itself as self-identical in precisely the way appropriate to sensible things. It shows itself as holding in reserve other aspects in the presenting of which it would remain one and the same thing; it shows itself as something that would remain self-identical in being seen from other perspectives. Furthermore, this self-identity has a distinctively sensible character: it is reflected in the coherence of the sense variations, in the continuity with which one image would give way to another. If, on the one hand, it is a self-identity that is indefinitely deferred in the sense of never being simply displayed, it is, on the other hand, always capable of being sensibly confirmed in any particular regard. Yet the self-identity of the sensible thing is also deferred in another sense, one corresponding to its peripheral horizons. For these horizons—in the various guises they can assume (background, instrumentality, etc.)—serve to refer the self-identity of the thing beyond the confines of the thing itself. Its being the very thing it properly is (and shows itself as) is inseparable from its setting, from its being set within the various peripheral horizons.

By being installed within its horizons the self-showing thing thus acquires the density and setting proper to a self-identical sensible thing; as it comes, hence, to show itself as itself, the duplicity of the image is resolved and the adherence of the image to the thing, as the very surface of the thing, as the very shining of the thing, is established. Such is, then, the configuration of showing: shining forth from within its lateral and peripheral horizons, the thing shows itself as itself, as the very thing it properly is.

How does such a configuration come to be drawn? What kind of drawing does it require?

In being themselves spaced, the lateral and peripheral horizons must be brought to circumspace the frontal aspect in which the image is centered. The horizons must be brought to bound the upsurge of presence in and as which the thing shines forth. Such circumspatial bounding requires that the horizons be drawn toward the locus of presence, gathered around the there. And yet, though they must be drawn toward the locus of presence, the spacing of the horizons is such as to prohibit their simply being made present. The prohibition is unconditional in the case of the lateral horizon: not even the lateral images—much less the horizon in which they are gathered and spaced, gathered by being spaced—can be made present as such. The very spacing of laterality excludes presence: as soon as one turns to face a lateral image, it ceases being lateral and, in being brought to presence, becomes a frontal image, displacing the former frontal image into the lateral horizon now reconfigured around the present aspect. Gathering the lateral horizon around the frontal image cannot, then, consist in rendering it present along with the present aspect of the thing. On the other hand, a peripheral horizon can be to some extent present; for a certain peripheral presence is borne by the frontal image itself, wrought by the very upsurge of the presence of the thing. Yet this presence is peripheral, marginal, and cannot be rendered frontal. Even a singular moment of such a horizon can be rendered frontally present only at the cost of its ceasing to be horizonal: as soon as one turns to confront such a moment, it becomes detached from the horizon, which is then redeployed around it. Turning to confront the horizon itself would similarly disrupt its horizonal character: as when, focusing on the background of a figure, one finds that it ceases to function as the ground of the figure; or as when a painter paints the spread of light and atmosphere over a landscape (obscured thereby in the work), painting thus what constitutes the very visibility of the visible. Not only is a peripheral horizon limited to marginal presence—so insistently that, if rendered frontally present, it loses its horizonal character—but also, in its way of extending on beyond what is even marginally present, the peripheral horizon retreats from presence. Such retreat is unmistakably manifest in the case of peripheral horizons that are less local than, for instance, instrumental and that depend for their constitution on networks of concrete connections that are irreducible to mere presence.

Though horizons cannot, then, as such be rendered present, they must nonetheless come to bound the upsurge of presence. Though they cannot themselves be there, they must be spaced around the there, drawn toward the locus of presence. Such drawing is requisite even for the marginally present peripheral horizon: in order to bound the upsurge of the presence of the thing, the horizon must be drawn around the locus of this upsurge. Mere (marginal) presence does not suffice to make a certain visible extent into a horizon; on the contrary, it must be held in a certain orientation to the upsurge of presence that it would bound, must be gathered around it as horizon. As must be also the horizonal extensions that continue beyond the limit of marginal presence.

In being drawn around the there, the horizons must also be withdrawn from it, set apart from the locus of presence; for they cannot, while remaining horizonal, be rendered present. They must be protracted so as to bound the present aspect of the thing, and yet, for the sake of their very spacing as horizons, they must be retracted from the occurrence of presence and its locus, dislocated from the image, from the there. As soon as the horizons come to bound presence, the very line that would mark their conjunction along this boundary will have split, will have come to mark instead an interval separating the horizons from presence, separating them in a sense itself irreducible to presence. In other words, there is here a certain impossibility, which, itself irresolvable, can only be composed in a certain interplay, in an operation that circles between protraction and retraction, between drawing the horizons around the locus of presence and withdrawing them in order that they might remain horizons and so again—since shining requires them—be drawn around presence, only again—since they cannot be rendered present—to be withdrawn. Through this operation, perpetually recommencing, presence and its horizons are brought together in the same round in which they are set apart—in a togetherness and an apartness that are themselves irreducible to presence and to horizonality. Thus they are brought together in their utter opposition, without dissolution of the opposition that as such prohibits their being brought together. This round of protraction and retraction is the operation required in order that things themselves come to show themselves as themselves. This is the drawing by which is composed the configuration of showing.

Remonstratively tracing this drawing of the configuration of showing draws out, at once and in distinct lines, the exorbitant traits of imagination. For though the drawing is, to be sure, no mere making present of something absent, not even a making present that lets remain absent in another respect precisely that which it makes present, it is nonetheless that by which all coming to presence can be said to be effected, assuming that, as with Fichte, coming to presence occurs as the very coming forth of things into self-showing. The operation by which the configuration of showing is drawn brings things forth as themselves, lets them come thus to show themselves. It effects their coming to presence *as things themselves,* that is, as shining forth from within their horizons. And it does so precisely by drawing around presence horizons so spaced that they cannot but also be withdrawn from presence, granted a retreat by which they remain irrevocably absent, though in a sense that would no longer be the simple diametrical opposite of presence. Drawing the horizons toward presence only to withdraw them to their retreat of absence, from which they cannot but again be drawn forth, this operation mixes presence and absence in an exorbitant way, and through this exorbitant mixing it lets things come to their self-showing, brings them forth. Furthermore, this drawing is composed entirely within the sensible: even that which must be withdrawn into its retreat does not retreat from the sensible but rather is precisely the sensible in that retreat proper to it as such, in the retreat that is imperative in order for sensible things to be endowed with their density and setting, in order for them to acquire their proper pith. This retreat is also the retreat of possibility in several respects but most conspicuously in the case of the lateral horizon; it is the retreat in which possibility—for instance, other possible aspects of the thing—is held secure as such, in distinction from the protraction of it into relation with the thing present. Thus, this operation of drawing extends the measure of the possible, extends it in the exorbitant sense of first establishing it as such.

The drawings are congruent: the drawing of the configuration of showing is precisely what is drawn in tracing, along the edges of the old names of imagination, the exorbitant senses that take shape there. This congruence provides the basis for saying: it is by force of imagination that the configuration of showing is drawn. This drawing takes place as a circulating, a hovering, between the upsurge of presence and its bounding horizons. Hovering so as to draw forth and yet withdraw the horizons, circling perpetually between protraction and retraction, imagination deploys its force so as to let things that are present show themselves as themselves, that is, in their proper density and setting, in their proper pith. Shining from within the horizons gathered around them by force of imagination, things show themselves as determinable and to an extent determined and yet as submitted to an indefinite deferral of their determination. Hovering between protraction and retraction, imagination lets the things that are present show themselves as hovering between determination and indetermination.

B. FORCE

Discourse on imagination as impelling the self-showing of things has now been broached by putting into effect both monstrology and remembrance. In particular, several old words that remain at the limit, sheltering exorbitant senses, have begun to be woven into this discourse through resonant native words to which they may—by means of such idiomatic translation—lend their exorbitant senses. *Hovering* is such a translation of *Schweben*, signifying the operation by which imagination "endeavors to unify what is not unifiable," its hovering thus "between determination and nondetermination"[1] in such a way that one cannot but begin to wonder whether imagination, released to such hovering, could itself continue to be determined as a power or faculty of the subject. Or whether, with its wings unbound, it will not have soared off into a region where the subject could never be at home, hovering there between earth and sky. Its hovering is a gathering: it gathers the horizons around the upsurge of presence, though in a sense that yokes together the opposed drafts of bringing together and setting apart. That *gathering* translates λέγειν intimates the bearing, yet to be measured, of speech on self-showing, of λόγος on this exorbitant εἰκασία. It is, in turn, this pairing that remains conspicuous in γραφή, which signifies, on the one hand, writing and, on the other hand, drawing or even painting. Yet *drawing* and *trait* also allude to certain not so ancient names and connections: to *Ziehen* and *Zug* as they function to name the drafting of truth, the drawing of truth into a work, the *"Zug zum Werk"*;[2] and to a certain deconstructive force of drawing, linked to the "withdrawal" or "differential inappearance of the trait."[3]

---

1. Fichte, *Grundlage der gesammten Wissenschaftslehre*, 215f.

2. Heidegger, *Der Ursprung des Kunstwerkes*, in *Holzwege*, vol. 5 of *Gesamtausgabe* (Frankfurt a.M.: Vittorio Klostermann, 1977), 50.

3. Derrida writes: "I will name it the *withdrawal* [retrait] *or the eclipse, the differential inappearance of the trait.* We have been interested thus far in the act of tracing, in the tracing of the trait. What is to be thought now of the trait *once traced?* That is, not of its pathbreaking course, not of the inaugural path of the trace, but of that which remains of it? A tracing [or: outline—*tracé*] cannot be seen [*ne se voit pas*]. One should in fact not see it (let's not say however: 'One

Force, too, has its exorbitant resonance, translating *Kraft* and, more remotely, δύναμις, but idiomatically, twisting against the senses that philosophy stabilized for these words, with these words, venturing now to release with remembrance a newly engendered sense capable of remaining operative at the limit. Even if at the risk of advancing toward the limit of what can be said with *force.*

One can say: there is nothing more forceful than the force of imagination. For this force is such that it can bring together what cannot be brought together, effecting what is absolutely prohibited. Indeed it does so even without violating—without assimilating or cancelling—the force that holds apart, that enforces the prohibition; thus it brings together without simply forcing together. Bringing together what cannot be—and so, is not—brought together, the force that is of imagination is such as to exceed, even if singularly and obliquely, that of what is called the law of noncontradiction. When, by force of imagination, the horizons both are and are not there with the upsurge of presence, there is infraction of the very law of law and of discourse itself.

And yet, one can say also: there is nothing less forceful than imagination. Not only because it does not force such opposed moments together, does not turn against the force that separates them. But, above all, because imagination forces nothing, because it only lets things show themselves as what they properly are, merely lending to things present its force of protraction and retraction.

Thus coupling these extreme degrees in its very signification, replicating in itself opposites almost as extreme as those between which it would hover, this force (that is of imagination) acquires a sense that indeed extends toward the limit of what can be said with the word. At the same time, the word *force* could serve to mark and to convey (which is not to say: to signify)

---

must not see it') insofar as all the colored thickness that it retains tends to extenuate itself so as to mark the single edge of a contour: between the inside and the outside of a figure. Once this limit is reached, there is nothing more to see, not even black and white, not even figure/form, and this is the trait, this is the line itself. . . . This limit is never presently reached, but drawing always signals toward this inaccessibility, toward the threshold where only the surroundings of the trait appear—that which the trait spaces by delimiting and which thus does not belong to the trait. *Nothing belongs to the trait,* and thus, to drawing and to the thought of drawing, not even its own 'trace'" (Derrida, *Mémoires d'aveugle: L'autoportrait et autres ruines* [Paris: Éditions de la Réunion des musées nationaux, 1990], 58). Since, according to Derrida's analysis, the trait cannot be seen as such, it proves to have the capacity to make visible ("to mark the single edge of a contour") without being itself visible as such ("there is nothing more to see"). But just as it is in this sense not visible or sensible, so, Derrida insists, it is not intelligible ("The linear limit I am talking about is in no way *ideal* or *intelligible*" [ibid., 59]). Thus, the trace falls outside the classical philosophical opposition between intelligible and sensible, serving precisely to deconstruct this opposition. In order to see a drawing *as* a drawing, one is not to see the drawn line, the trait; thus it is that drawing is as such already incipiently deconstructive of philosophy.

the deconstruction of the most global philosophical determinations of imagination. In this connection *force* would be regarded as displacing *power* or *faculty* as these occur in the determinations of imagination as a power of the soul or a faculty of the subject. It would also be regarded as operating within an oblique reversal: force would be of imagination, not of the soul or of the subject; and though the philosophical determination would allow one to speak, for instance, of the power of imagination, such a formulation would still fall within a framework in which both the power and imagination would be taken to belong to the subject.

Even in everyday discourse a difference is often marked between force and power: whereas power as such precedes the directionality and application into which it may be released, force does not precede its being directed. Force is as such already directional, vectorial; from the moment of its inception, it is already deployed. In its philosophical determination, too, force proves to be vectorial. Indeed the most rigorous execution of that determination demonstrates that since force is properly vectorial there can be no force proper; that is, force proper dissolves into something quite other.

One need only recall the dialectical dissolution that results from venturing a distinction between force proper and the deployment, the expression, of force.

In the dialectic that undoes this and every other form of natural consciousness, force is engaged in two quite distinct forms and ways. On the one hand, every stage of the advance is driven by the monstrous power (*die ungeheure Macht*) of the negative, and each shape (*Gestalt*) takes shape as an advance precisely through the magical force (*Zauberkraft*) that turns negativity into being. Yet this force continuously deployed in giving shape to every shape is distinct, on the other hand, from the delimitable shape determined by the concept of force, distinct from this shape without itself being another shape, as the scepticism that submits every shape of natural consciousness to the way of despair and loss of self is distinct from the singular shape determined as scepticism.

As at every stage, the dissolution of the previous configuration is decisive in determining the concept of force and in generating the distinction to which the singular configuration gives shape. Thus, force is the truth emerging from the dissolution of the perceptual thing, of the thing having many properties. In the constitution of the perceptual thing two moments are involved: the moment of unity, of the thing's being-for-itself, and the moment of manifoldness, of its being-for-an-other. Within the configuration of perception, the constitutive move is to retain both moments within the object, even if only by recourse to a kind of sophistry, akin to common sense, that keeps both moments only by not letting them come into contact, only by keeping them apart yet (and here lies the sophistry) within one and the same object. The dialectic of perception demonstrates the futility of such a move. It is from the consequent dissolution of the shape that force then emerges as the movement between the two moments that perception has proved incapable of unifying. The first moment (that of unity, of being-for-itself) would constitute force proper, while the second (that of manifoldness, of being-for-an-other) would be the expression of force. Force would consist, then, in the movement by which force proper would unfold into the manifoldness of expression and that manifold, in turn, would withdraw into the unity of force proper. Like the perceptual thing from whose determinate negation it arises, force would be something actual, a substance capable as such of uniting what the perceptual thing proved incapable of uniting.

The dialectic in and through which this substantial force is dissolved unfolds as a doubling of force. As a substance that, moreover, is one, force is force proper; in this regard the manifold that falls outside must be something other than force. Yet force must express itself, which is to say, that this other must approach it and solicit it. But since its expression is necessary, since expression is intrinsic to force itself, this other (or rather, that which is posited as other) can only be in force itself. This entails, then, that force is not just a one that expresses itself as manifold but that it is already the manifold. Thus, force as one, as substantial, is self-superseding, a vanishing moment—which is to say: it is not substantial. Alternatively, what was supposed to be something else soliciting force (proper) turns out to be just force itself. In this regard what results are two forces, each soliciting the other to unfold (into manifoldness) and to withdraw (into oneness). But in this case each is in effect posited by the other, each *is* solely through the other. Neither is anything simply for-itself but only a vanishing moment. Consequently, force turns out not to be anything fixed and substantial subsisting behind the play of expression. There is in actuality no force proper: what is initially posited as force proper proves in the dialectic to be nothing actual but only something thought, something that is only for the understanding. Thus, it is precisely at this point, as the outcome of the dialectic of force, that the inner being of the thing (previously determined as force proper) comes to be posited as an object solely of understanding, as something beyond the sensible: "There now opens up above the *sensible world,* which is the *world of appearance,* a *supersensible* world, which henceforth is the *true* world, above the vanishing *Diesseits* an enduring *Jenseits.*"[4]

Therefore, the most rigorous philosophical determination translates force into the supersensible, opening the very distinction between sensible and supersensible, identifying force proper with what is to be determined as the supersensible. And yet, for a discourse that refuses such translation and limits itself to the sensible, the result is a determination of force as

---

4. Hegel, *Phänomenologie des Geistes,* 89.

vectorial. Within this limit it would then be possible to twist the discourse of force against the dialectical determination in a certain oblique way and so to delimit a sense of force that, in relation to the dialectical concept, would be exorbitant. What is required is that the delimitation of force be twisted loose from the perceptual thing and its dialectical dissolution. Not that force would now be determined without any reference to things and to their self-showings in what is called perception. Rather, what would now be required is that this delimitation be oriented not primarily to the thing and its moments but to its self-showings as such. What would now be required is that force be delimited in and through a turn from the thing to its self-showings, or—marking the pertinent obliqueness—that it be delimited in a move that would set apart the self-showings as such, which in the dialectical determinations remain ambivalently composed with the thing and its moments. More specifically, it would be a matter of delimiting force by regressing from the thing as something possessing a manifold of properties to the self-showing covertly taken for granted with the thing and anterior to its perceptual self-showing. For however the thing may show itself within the shape of consciousness called perception, whether as essentially constituted by the moment of unity or by the moment of manifoldness or by some conjunction of both moments, there must already be in play the self-showing that any and every determination (for instance, of a property) requires, the shining of the thing from within its horizons.

The turn back to this self-showing would produce a palimpsest: beneath the new inscriptions oriented to this self-showing there would remain a trace of the dialectical inscription. Over the almost effaced inscription of the moment of unity and being-for-itself would now be written a discourse on the frontal aspect of the thing, on the sheer upsurge of its presence; and where the moment of manifoldness and being-for-an-other was previously inscribed, there would now be written a discourse on the manifold components that are spaced in such ways as to be gathered in the horizons that bound the present aspect of the thing. In place of the configuration of exchange between the moments of unity and manifoldness, of force proper and the expression of force, there would now take shape the configuration of an interplay in which the manifold of horizons would be gathered around the singular present aspect of the thing. But in this regard the palimpsest reverses the proper antecedence: the force of the interplay must already be in play in the exchange and hence antecedes the force of the exchange. Thus distanced from the exchange and the force constituted by it, the force that is of imagination remains unassimilable to the exchange and to the dialectical dissolution to which the force of the exchange is submitted. Nonetheless, one could reconstitute—if with a higher degree of generality—the dialectic of force proper and the expression of force, reconstitute it at the level of the force of protraction and retraction, so as to confirm that even the force that is of imagination is such as not to precede its deployment. It, too, is vectorial, always already deployed in gathering the horizons around the upsurge of presence.

As impelling the self-showing of things, the force that is of imagination is perhaps more akin to the magical force that, outside all determinate shapes, turns negativity into being. As such it would be a force of monstrosity: in gathering moments not present to sense so as to bring them to bound what is present to sense, this force would expose things to a negativity unknown to dialectic, the monstrosity by which nonsense becomes interior to, rather than the opposite of, sense.

What solicits this magical force of monstrosity? In its deployment there is, to be sure, a doubling comparable to the dialectical doubling of force; in its deployment it is doubly tractive, and though, reconstituting the dialectic, one could identify protraction and retraction as mutually soliciting, one would still need to identify what it is that solicits the entire round of traction as such. How is it that gathering takes place? What solicits tractive force to a singular deployment there, at a given locus? No doubt the unconditionally required solicitor is the upsurge of presence, the shining of the thing itself, lacking which there is no locus whatsoever for the gathering. Only if solicited by the shining of sense will the force of imagination come to gather the nonsense of sense around it. Yet what prevents one from simply coming to rest in this shining? What forestalls one's remaining wholly absorbed in the presence that is sensibly displayed? The enticement is linked to speech: what solicits the gathering of horizons around any and every upsurge of presence is the opening to speech, the resumption of the move by which things themselves are hypothetically set out in advance as exceeding any present aspect, set out in their determinateness, posited as determinable.[5] It is the provocation of speech—this provocation of provocations—that, with the occurrence of presence, solicits the force of imagination to gather the horizons (the nonsense of sense) around the locus of presence. This gathering confirms the determinableness of things while, on the other hand, deferring indefinitely their determination. With the nonsense of sense that is gathered around the presence of the thing, there is sensible fulfillment—though of a distinctively horizonal kind—of what is merely set out in the opening to speech.

From the configuration of self-showing and especially from the way solicitation operates in it, the bearing of speech on self-showing becomes manifest. Between self-showing and speech there is no simple order of precedence. In particular, self-showing cannot be delimited as a prelinguistic realm in which things would simply be given or perceived and upon which speech would only subsequently and thus inconsequentially come to bear. In this sense there is no such thing as perception—that is, no pure percep-

---

5. See above, chap. 4a.

tion utterly antecedent to speech. On the other hand, things can no doubt show themselves without speech actually coming into play so as to determine them. Neither is it a matter of a single language—assuming that the sense and possibility of singularity can in this regard be determined—constituting a kind of linguistic grid through which, for one caught in that language, things must show themselves. If for no other reason than that one is never simply caught in a language but can always turn language against itself, either within a so-called single language or in the space between such languages. It is not in its alleged singularity that speech has its primary bearing on self-showing. What counts is neither that one speaks nor that one has a singular linguistic framework but rather that—whatever the language—one *can* speak, one is open to speech, that is, open to the hypothetical setting out of things themselves that belongs to speech as such, to its very possibility. In this connection a remembrance of λόγος and λέγειν is appropriate, translating these not only as *speech* and *speaking* but especially as *gathering* in the sense of setting things out in their determinateness, gathering them as a whole and gathering each hypothetically to itself so as to set it out as self-identical, as one with itself.[6] Because of the bearing of this gathering on self-showing, because its hypotheses (in the Greek sense) are in a specific way confirmed when horizons are drawn around the presence of the thing, this drawing has also itself been designated as gathering. In this way one can underline the moment of λόγος as it belongs to the configuration of self-showing.

The force that is of imagination is vectorial. It *is* only *as deployed*, only in the deployment in which it effects protraction and retraction of horizons. Yet in this case it is such as to undermine the very discourse of deployment: if it *is* only as deployed, then it will not first *be* and then get deployed, be applied to a certain effect. If it *is* only as deployed, if it is always already deployed, then the very sense of deployment begins to erode, for in this case there is nothing at one's disposal that then gets deployed. Force, thus determined, could not *be* deployed, put into effect, for it would always already be in effect.

Hence, the genitive in *force of imagination* does not signify the possession

6. An exemplary remembrance of λόγος and λέγειν is provided by Heidegger in "Logos (Heraklit, Fragment 50)," in *Vorträge und Aufsätze* (Pfullingen: Günther Neske, 1954), 207–29. One could supplement this discussion and perhaps eventually reorient it by stressing, in a rereading of Fragment 50, that λέγειν involves the hypothetical setting out of things in their determinateness. The sense of such an operation is said in the word ὁμολογεῖν: "Such λέγειν lays out one and the same, the ὁμόν. Such λέγειν is ὁμολογεῖν" (ibid., 215). In other words, λέγειν occurs as setting out things as themselves, as setting out each as being one with itself, the same as itself. Granting, too, that Ἓν Πάντα is not what the λόγος proclaims but rather that these words say the way in which λόγος operates (Heidegger writes: "Ἓν Πάντα besagt, in welcher Weise der Λόγος west" [ibid., 220]), one could construe this operation not only collectively but also distributively, hence (in the latter regard) as setting things out in such a way that each and every one of them is set out *as one*.

of one being by another: it is not that imagination possesses force—for instance, as an intrinsic capacity, held in readiness for deployment—and then on certain occasions releases, applies, deploys that force. For, strictly speaking, force is only a being-in-effect, in such a way that its determination continues to twist against the axiomatics of *being* and the *is,* which cannot but continue to imply a force in itself that is put into effect, just as the word *lightning* implies something behind the flash (lightning itself) that then comes into effect. Such implications need to be held in check in the phrase *force of imagination*: the force that is of imagination is the force with which, by which, imagination itself draws forth and withdraws the horizons. One could say that *force of imagination* names the self-deployment of imagination itself. Or that it translates *Einbildungskraft,* even if exorbitantly. It is like the force of a word, which is nothing other than the effectualness of the word itself.

Force transcribes its French cognate, which, in turn, translates *vis.* Both words become a force in Leibniz's efforts, at the turn of the eighteenth century, to submit Cartesianism to a rigorous critique centered precisely on the concept of force: over against the Cartesian determination of material substance as extension, Leibniz maintains that force belongs essentially to the constitution of things: "we must employ in addition to the notion of *extension* that of *force* [la force]."[7] In and through this critique Leibniz seeks to bring about a rehabilitation of ancient thought (even if as mediated by Scholasticism): "But after weighing the entire matter, I find that the philosophy of the ancients is solid and that it is necessary to use the philosophy of the moderns not to destroy but to enrich that of the ancients. I have had many disputes on that score with some able Cartesians, and have shown them by mathematics itself that they do not have the true laws of nature, and that to obtain them it is necessary to consider in nature not only matter but also force, and that the ancients' forms or *Entelechies* are nothing but forces."[8] Leibniz's identification of force with substantial form (a major point of rehabilitation) continues to resonate in Hegel's presentation and, as radicalized in the *Monadology,* anticipates the dissolution that substance and force proper will undergo in the *Phenomenology of Spirit.*[9]

---

7. G. W. Leibniz, *Die philosophischen Schriften,* ed. C. J. Gerhardt (Hildesheim: Georg Olms, 1965), 4:467.

8. Leibniz, "Lettre au Père Bouvet à Paris, 1697," in *Opera Philosophica quae extant Latina, Gallica, Germanica Omnia,* ed. J. E. Erdmann (Scientia Aalen, 1959—Facsimile of the 1840 Edition), 146.

9. According to Heidegger's interpretation, Leibniz not only defended his determination of substance as force against the Cartesian thesis but also "grounded it at the same time fundamentally and philosophically through the doctrine known as 'monadology.' . . . According to the principle of monadology, it is not the individual beings that are endowed with force, but rather the reverse: force is the being that first lets an individual being as such be, so that it might be endowed with something at all. . . . In principle, then, the imputation that natural things are determined by forces is only an essential consequence of the determination of

But quite beyond *la querelle des anciens et des modernes*, it is on *force* as a remote translation of δύναμις that one needs to focus. Already in Parmenides a bond is forged between δύναμις and the chiaroscuro of self-showing. Fragment 9 proclaims that all things are named light (φάος) and night (νύξ), that light and night, each according to the δύναμις belonging to it, are assigned to all things, with the result that "all is full, at once, of light and obscure night [πᾶν πλέον ἐστὶν ὁμοῦ φάεος καὶ νυκτὸς ἀφάντου]."[10] In Plato's *Sophist* δύναμις is set within a discourse on being, from which Parmenides could not but exclude discourses such as that of Fragment 9. Indeed the Eleatic Stranger extends the bond to such an extent as to delimit being as such by recourse to δύναμις. The passage occurs in the well-known battle of giants, the Stranger saying to Theaetetus: "For I set up as a limit [ὅρος] by which to delimit [ὁρίζειν] beings [τὰ ὄντα] that they are nothing but δύναμις."[11] Within the context of the *Sophist*, in which the follower of Parmenides, hailing from Elea, at the same time puts Parmenides into question,[12] the delimitation of being as δύναμις does not represent an alternative to the bond forged in Fragment 9 but, on the contrary, integrates the latter into an ontological discourse that is, at once, a discourse on the manifestation of beings.[13]

With Aristotle, long taken—short of an exorbitant sense—to have determined φαντασία as a δύναμις τῆς ψυχῆς, the ontological discourse on δύναμις is both more developed, more articulated, and, on the other hand, oriented in a particular way that proves decisive in the history of philosophy. Now δύναμις is taken up not just as such but within the context of its complex opposition to ἐνέργεια. And in place of the Platonic-Eleatic delimitation of being as δύναμις, the schema of δύναμις and ἐνέργεια is taken up and interrogated as one of the many ways in which being is said. In its usual determination, formalized as δύναμις ἐπὶ πλέον in Aristotle's debate with the Megarians, it has the character of being held in reserve, of a capability one could have without exercising it, that one could hold in readiness in such a way that the very presence of the capability would be constituted by this holding in readiness.[14]

substance as monad, *vis*" (Heidegger, *Aristoteles, Metaphysik* Θ *1–3: Von Wesen und Wirklichkeit der Kraft*, vol. 33 of *Gesamtausgabe* [Frankfurt a.M.: Vittorio Klostermann, 1981], 101f.).

10. Parmenides, Fragment 9, in Hermann Diels and Walther Kranz, *Die Fragmente der Vorsokratiker* (Dublin/Zürich: Weidmann, 1968), 1:240f.

11. Plato, *Sophist* 247e.

12. The Eleatic Stranger says, prior to the passage on δύναμις: "We shall find it necessary in self-defence to put to the question that pronouncement of father Parmenides and to contend that nonbeing in some respect is and conversely that being somehow is not" (ibid., 241d).

13. See *Being and Logos*, 495–98.

14. Aristotle insists on this character of δύναμις in his critique of the position held by the Megarians, who maintain that something can have a δύναμις only when it is actually at work (ἐνέργεια), that is, that there is no capability apart from its enactment. See *Metaphysics* Θ 3.

This articulation suffices already to suggest that it is the Aristotelian determination of δύναμις that is ultimately the origin of the concept of force proper that Hegel first of all distinguishes from, but then lets dissolve into, the expression of force; by this route Hegel returns in a certain respect to the position of the Megarians against whom Aristotle developed his determination of δύναμις. Yet if force, determined now from that dissolution, is such as to be only in its deployment, if consequently it seems virtually to have turned into the opposite of what Aristotle called δύναμις, this transformation is by no means so symmetrical as to have brought about an identification of force (as it is of imagination) with the Aristotelian opposite of δύναμις or of that opposite, ἐνέργεια, with what is effected by force of imagination. Whatever is ἐνέργεια must be ἐντελέχεια: it must have come fully into its end (τέλος) so as to be set within the limits of the εἶδος that will always have been held in view in the production of a work. Thus, ἐνέργεια has an essential reference to a work (ἔργον) made in a process of production (ποίησις) and thus to the εἶδος that governs production and coincides with its τέλος. Ἐνέργεια is preeminently (though not exclusively) a determination belonging to the work that issues from production. As such it is decisively differentiated from the force of imagination: for there is ἐνέργεια *only through* the completion of the productive movement in which the work is set forth and *only if* there belongs to the movement an eidetic orientation that releases the work into the limits of the εἶδος. Imagination, on the other hand, comes, not to a completion, but to a hovering, which, though releasing things into their self-showing, lets them be delimited horizonally rather than eidetically.

If traces of certain exorbitant senses can be drawn from Aristotle's analysis, they will lie along the edges of those senses of δύναμις and ἐνέργεια that Aristotle himself leaves largely undeveloped. For instance, in setting out on his critique of the position held by the Megarians, Aristotle presents them as saying that something has a capability (δύνασθαι) only when it is ἐνεργῇ; the subsequent examples, that, for instance, a man is capable of building only if he is building, indicate clearly that in this context ἐνέργεια refers, not to a completed work released through a process of production, but rather to being at work in the sense of enacting the capability otherwise held in reserve.[15] Though now, following the dissolution of force proper,

---

See also Heidegger's extended commentary, which shows that the debate between Aristotle and the Megarians is much more complicated and much less one-sided than it has often been taken to be. Heidegger formulates the positive outcome in this way: "Now it becomes clearer how the actuality of δύνασθαι is to be comprehended through ἔχειν, having and holding, namely, as holding oneself in readiness, holding *the capability* [Vermögen] *itself in readiness.* This being held is its actual presence [*Anwesenheit*]" (Heidegger, *Aristoteles, Metaphysik Θ 1–3*, 219).

15. See Aristotle, *Metaphysics* Θ 3, 1046b 29ff. Heidegger stresses this double sense that the word has if taken in relation to the root word ἔργον: "The Greek 'ἔργον' has the same double

the force that is of imagination is to be kept rigorously distinct from all capability, this distinction does not entirely preclude determining such force as a being at work. Such a determination is especially promising if connection is made specifically to those ways of being at work that are distinguished as producing no work other than themselves, as in the case of sight, in which what is aimed at is not the production of something but only the seeing itself in its ultimacy.[16] If, then, force of imagination is to be set rigorously apart from δύναμις in the primary sense operative in Aristotle's text (δύναμις ἐπὶ πλέον), even to such an extent that some degree of resonance becomes possible with a certain undeveloped sense of ἐνέργεια, there remains nonetheless a structural correspondence with δύναμις (specifically with what is called δύναμις μετὰ λόγου) that is not entirely inconsequential. For, as imagination engages its force in protraction and retraction, circulating, hovering, between these opposed drafts, so Aristotle ascribes to such δύναμις a directedness to contraries, by virtue of which it has the character of being doubly directed, bifurcated: as in the case of an artisan who, knowing the right way to make his product, constantly avoids—hence is aware of—other ways that would lead his work astray and result in an inferior work.[17]

C. IMAGINATION

By force of imagination the horizons are gathered around the upsurge of presence. This force is nothing other than imagination itself as effectual in the gathering. Because the horizons cannot as such be rendered present, or rather, because they could be rendered present only by violating the very spacing that constitutes them as horizons, the gathering is no mere joining or unifying, no mere setting together, but rather is bifurcated into the moments of an interplay, into the round of protraction and retraction. On the one side, the horizons are drawn forth toward the locus of presence. In this connection it is as though prior to this draft they had, in a kind of past, already been prepared, already somehow had been there, held in a certain readiness. In drawing them out of this past readiness and bringing them

---

sense in which we use the German *Arbeit* [work]: (1) work as occupation, as when we say, for example, 'He didn't make the most of his working time'; (2) work as what is diligently worked upon and gained through work, as when we say, 'He does good work.' Ἐνέργειαι are the activities, the ways of working (ἔργα in the first sense), which are occupied with a work (ἔργον in the second sense): the ways of being-at-work" (Heidegger, *Aristoteles, Metaphysik* Θ *1–3*, 50). In his interpretation of *Metaphysics* Θ 3, Heidegger characterizes such being-at-work as ἐνέργεια κατὰ κίνησιν, in distinction from the ἐνέργεια ἐπί πλέον that Aristotle addresses beginning in *Metaphysics* Θ 6 (see ibid., 168).

16. See Aristotle, *Metaphysics* Θ 8, 1050a 30–36.

17. See, for example, Aristotle, *Metaphysics* Θ 9, 1051a 6–7. Also Heidegger, *Aristoteles, Metaphysik* Θ *1–3*, 153–59.

to bound the upsurge of presence, imagination is *memorial*. And yet, the horizons cannot have been there before imagination supervened; they cannot somehow have been present in that past. Even when drawn forth by force of imagination they cannot come *to be* present but can only come to bound presence at the very moment that they come, on the other side, to be withdrawn from the locus of presence. The horizons will never as such have been present, not in the past, not even in the present. They can be said to be only if the very sense of being is extended beyond the presence of things, only if the nonsense (of sense) as it bounds sensible presence can also, in this extension of sense, be said to be. Then, adhering to this extended sense of being, one could say: in drawing the horizons forth to bound presence while withdrawing them to secure their very character as horizons, imagination brings them into being as horizons. In this respect, imagination is *originary*. And yet, as originated through the drafts of imagination, the horizons prove nonetheless not simply to have been imposed by imagination but to have enlisted a certain precedence in relation to which, again, imagination is memorial. Imagination is, at once, both originary and memorial, its delimitation requiring precisely a hovering between these opposed determinations, turning it back, in self-delimitation, upon itself.

One could be tempted to identify the originary moment as productive imagination and the memorial as reproductive. Yet even if one insisted on the opposition as such and resisted all discourse of the kind that would weaken the opposition by distinguishing various levels and configuring a certain continuity, the identification is inappropriate and misleading. The problem lies in the very determination of production, in its incongruity with the determination of imagination. According to the ancient (and still largely effective) determination, production (ποίησις) consists in bringing forth into visible presence something envisioned in advance by what is sometimes called, in a later idiom, the mind's eye. In other words, production requires a prior vision of the essential look and determining limits of that which is to be produced, a vision that is precedent to and directive for the bringing forth of something made to look like what will have been seen in advance. Within the framework of this determination, the force of imagination could lie only in this prior vision. And yet, in its primary force, imagination has proven to be other than vision: imagination is not so much the mind's eye as, rather—if one insists on retaining this metaphorical idiom— what would have to be called the mind's hand, since its operation is to draw the horizons forth, to withdraw them, and in its drafts to span the expanse of the interplay. As configuring the self-showing of things, imagination neither produces nor reproduces something seen in advance. It is neither productive nor reproductive but rather tractive. Its dexterity allows it to draw the horizons around the upsurge of presence, its lines of force constituting the field of protraction and retraction between the present aspect of the thing and the horizons that enclose it, gathering the nonsense of sense to sense.

By force of imagination the horizons are drawn around the upsurge of presence, *around* in a sense irreducible to presence as well as to proximity inasmuch as it is determined by presence. In gathering horizon to image, nonsense to sense, imagination holds together what cannot be together. In coupling such utterly opposed moments or determinations, imagination composes monstrosity.

It is in tragedy that the irreducible force of such utter oppositions is presented in its historical, political, and/or mythical concreteness. This inner connection of tragedy to monstrosity is perhaps never more sublimely displayed nor monstrosity more forcefully presented than in *Macbeth*. Some brief indications will perhaps suffice to invoke the monstrous spell of the play.

The scene in Act 1 in which the three witches appear to Macbeth and Banquo is rife with oppositions that are readily displayed as contradictory and that, as they function in the scene, turn out to be monstrous. What is said on this scene and about what appears there—especially the three witches—pulsates with such oppositions. The scene takes place on a heath. It begins, not with words, but with thunder, which announces the entry of the three witches, while also setting the tone for the entire scene: nature assumes here its more extraordinary aspect, in which the tranquil accord of the elements is disturbed. Macbeth's first words—his very first in the entire play—refer to this aspect:

So foul and fair a day I have not seen.[18]

These words echo those uttered in unison by the witches in scene 1, as they were anticipating their meeting with Macbeth. The witches say:

Fair is foul, and foul is fair.
Hover through the fog and filthy air.

(I.i.10–11)

Here, then, is the first of the oppositions, attributed by Macbeth to the day, that is, to the weather, the elements, nature. What is remarkable is that Macbeth's exclamation couples the opposed qualities rather than submitting to the so-called law of noncontradiction and declaring that a day cannot be, at once, both foul and fair. The coupling is accentuated and the flaunting of contradiction becomes flagrant in the words of the witches: fair is foul, and foul is fair. Such speeches speak against themselves—pre-

---

18. Shakespeare, *Macbeth*, I.iii.38. Citations are from the text as edited by Sylvan Barnet in *The Complete Signet Classic Shakespeare* (New York: Harcourt, Brace, Jovanovich, 1972).

sumably, in order to say what otherwise (that is, if one obeyed the alleged law) would remain unspeakable.

Banquo speaks then of the witches:

> What are these
> So withered, and so wild in their attire,
> That look not like th' inhabitants o' th' earth,
> And yet are on't?

(I.iii.39–42)

Thus, still invoking a natural element, the earth, he concentrates the opposition in the witches, in their being on the earth while, at once, seeming not to be of it.

Banquo concentrates opposition still more pointedly in the visages of the witches, concentrates it to the point of eroding their sexual identity:

> You should be women,
> And yet your beards forbid me to interpret
> That you are so.

(I.iii.45–47)

After the witches vanish, Banquo and Macbeth continue their flagrant coupling of oppositions; indeed they do so precisely as a way of saying the vanishing of the witches. Now the opposites invoked and unnaturally coupled are the natural elements themselves. Banquo begins:

> The earth hath bubbles as the water has,
> And these are of them. Whither are they vanished?

(I.iii.79–80)

Macbeth continues:

> Into the air, and what seemed corporal melted
> As breath into the wind.

(I.iii.81–82)

It is in this coupling that monstrous opposition, that is, monstrosity as such, is most purely delineated. For here Banquo and Macbeth put the natural elements together (in their speech) in the most unnatural couplings, declaring transfers and transformations that are counter to nature, picturing the earth bubbling like water and earthly bodies melting into thin air. Such a kind of occurrence is precisely monstrosity, that is, something of nature, something within nature, that is counter to nature, something that deviates from or exceeds nature within nature. By these unnatural couplings of natural elements, these monstrous couplings, Banquo and Macbeth venture to say the monstrosity that occurs in and as the vanishing of the witches.

Yet what, above all, deserves to be called monstrous, as the other couplings indicate, are the witches themselves.[19]

It is Banquo who broaches the connection between these monstrosities and imagination. His question is posed in the name of truth:

> I' th' name of truth
> Are ye fantastical, or that indeed
> Which outwardly ye show?

> (I.iii.52–54)

There is good reason for the question, reason why the question addressed in the name of truth to the monstrous witches is the question of their being fantastical. For one who is confident of the truth of nature, convinced that nature as such is true to itself, that it remains nature *as such* and does not deviate from itself—for such a one, monstrosities will always be taken as fantastical, as a matter of phantasy, of imagination.

If one takes into account the fact that Banquo's question is posed on the theatrical stage, then it will be self-evident that the answer must fall on the side of the fantastical. In the theatre everything is fantastical; nothing and no one is that which outwardly is shown. Indeed one could say that Banquo's question is precisely what must always remain suspended in the theatre, its suspension constituting the very condition of theatre.

Macbeth orders the witches to speak:

> Speak, if you can: what are you?

> (I.iii.47)

It is hardly surprising that when these monstrosities come to speak, their utterances are filled with monstrous oppositions, even though they ignore the question of what they are and speak only of what Macbeth is—or rather, of what he will be: now Thane of Glamis, he will become Thane of Cawdor, and hereafter king.

Startled, fearful, at the almost unimaginable possibility that he will become king, Macbeth begins to yield to phantasy when, as this scene continues, messengers from King Duncan arrive to inform him that he has been

---

19. One could trace a certain contagion of monstrosity as the play continues. The monstrosity of the deed of murdering King Duncan taints—hypothetically—those suspected of the deed: "Who cannot want the thought how monstrous / It was for Malcolm and for Donalbain / To kill their gracious father?" (III.vi.8–10). And yet, it is finally Macbeth who, in this connection and far beyond, proves to be utterly monstrous. When, in the final scene of the play, he is confronted by Macduff and has his final illusion of invulnerability shattered by the disclosure that "Macduff was from his mother's womb / untimely ripped—" (V.viii.15–16), Macbeth, refusing to fight, is thus addressed by Macduff: "Then yield thee, coward, / And live to be the show and gaze o' th' time. / We'll have thee, as our rarer monsters are, / Painted upon a pole, and underwrit / 'Here may you see the tyrant'" (V.viii.23–27).

declared Thane of Cawdor. Once this prediction has proven true, the other possibility—that he will be king—comes to hover before him, and, as he says, he yields

> to that suggestion
> Whose horrid image doth unfix my hair
> And make my seated heart knock at my ribs,
> Against the use of nature.

(I.iii.134–37)

The horrid image is monstrous—"against the use of nature"—these "horrible imaginings," in Macbeth's phrase, the thought, as he says,

> . . . whose murder yet is but fantastical.

(I.iii.139)

The monstrosity that hovers before him is the image, the phantasy, of a deed itself so monstrous that once it is done nature cringes in horror. Ross will say to an old man:

> Ha, good father,
> Thou see'st the heavens, as troubled with man's act,
> Threatens his bloody stage. By th' clock 'tis day,
> And yet dark night strangles the traveling lamp:
> Is't night's predominance, or the day's shame,
> That darkness does the face of the earth entomb,
> When living light should kiss it?

(II.iv.4–10)

The old man replies:

> 'Tis unnatural,
> Even like the deed that's done.

(II.iv.10–11)

Yet, the connection of imagination with monstrosity does not lie solely in its capacity to engender monstrous things—as (is always suspected) with the appearing and vanishing of witches, as with the phantasy of murder. Neither does the monstrosity of imagination consist only in its composing monstrosities, putting together, yoking together, what does not—indeed cannot—by nature go together, so that, in Hume's phrase, nature "is totally confounded" in fables about "winged horses, fiery dragons, and monstrous giants,"[20] or, recalling a previous example, in the phantasy of a being with

---

20. David Hume, *A Treatise of Human Nature* (Garden City: Doubleday, 1961), 9.

mechanics

a human body, the head of a lion, and the tail of a horse.[21] Rather, imagination is monstrous, before all else, in that it configures in a profoundly monstrous way the very field of self-showing, installing monstrosity on the scene of what one would—even nonetheless—call natural appearances. Drawing the horizons around the upsurge of presence, imagination brings nonsense to intrude upon and become interior to sense, so that from sense there issues the self-showing of things. One could hardly not suspect that imagination can bring forth the various monstrosities of which it is capable in its various differentiations only because, as tractive, it installs monstrosity—one could call it true monstrosity, that is, the monstrosity of truth—within the very self-showing of things themselves.

Even if now one will hesitate to say, even drastically reconstruing it, that imagination is "a fundamental faculty of the human soul," one would have to say that it is *blind*—"a blind but indispensable function of the soul, without which we would have no knowledge whatsoever, but of which we are only seldom conscious."[22] The discourse on imagination that one could piece together from this and other passages in the *Critique of Pure Reason* as well as other Kantian texts is remarkable for its capacity to sustain various tensions—bordering sometimes on contradiction—rather than resorting to facile resolutions. For instance, though imagination is called "a fundamental faculty of the human soul," it is (as noted above) omitted entirely from the complete list of such faculties given in the *Critique of Judgment*. And though Kant calls it blind, he also reaffirms its classical determination as a secondary mode of intuition: "Imagination is the power of representing in intuition an object that is *not itself present*."[23] To be sure, the latter tension can be weakened somewhat by distinguishing between different forms or levels of imagination or of its operation, for it is precisely in relation to the a priori synthesis and to transcendental schematism that imagination ceases to conform to the determination of it as a secondary mode of intuition. Yet, even if one grants a certain stratification of forms or operations, the threat posed by such tensions does not simply disappear, and the unity of the word and its signification remains fragile.

As configuring the self-showing of things, imagination is, as Kant says, blind; or rather, it is neither sighted nor blind, for only what can be sighted,

---

21. This example comes from Albertus Magnus. See above, chap. 2b. In drawing the connection with imagination, it is imperative to insist on the word *monstrosity*. Even if this example suggests also *monster*, it is by no means only to monsters that imagination has this kind of connection. The image of the murder of King Duncan neither is a monster nor is the image of a monster, but it is—and is the image of—something monstrous, a monstrosity. In the connection to imagination, monstrosity needs to be thought in a way that adheres rigorously to its determination as something within nature that is counter to, that deviates from, nature. Thus, a monstrosity is not necessarily something horrible, threatening, or terrifying.

22. Kant, *Kritik der reinen Vernunft*, A 124, A 78/B 103.

23. Ibid., B 151.

what is capable of sight, can be blind. Tractive imagination is not a mode of vision: it does not deploy itself in an intuition of images; its force is not one of envisioning images either in advance of their production or in what is produced. Neither can it be identified with a phantasy that would generate the very image that would, at once, be intuited, a phantasy circling, as it were, in its own interior orbit. As tractive, imagination drafts the configuration of the self-showing of things themselves, and this is why without it there would be, as Kant says, no knowledge (of things) whatsoever. Yet tractive imagination operates with such anteriority that one is, in Kant's words, only seldom conscious of it.

And yet, though tractive imagination is not deployed as vision, its drawing is precisely what lets things be seen, lets them come to show themselves to a vision. This drawing prepares a vision by tracing the invisible contours that outline the visible and give it its shape. As with the lines of any drawing, which tend toward the limit at which their disappearance would constitute the very delimiting and spacing of the figure of the drawing.

In any case, the relation of tractive imagination to the image (determined as the upsurge of the presence of the thing) is entirely different from that which is for the most part presupposed by the phenomenology of imagination and which makes possible the reduction of imagination to imagining, the latter construed as a certain kind of envisioning of images. Likewise, the other connections that go to constitute the confining tendency of the phenomenology of imagination are now breached by the monstrological analysis. In the case of tractive imagination, the connection with so-called perception can no longer be construed as one of mutual exclusion; tractive imagination is not something secondary that would be founded on a perceptual act or sphere distinct from and independent of it. If so-called perception is delimited as the self-showing of things themselves, then it will have to be said that imagination is integral to perception, that it is, again in Kant's words, a necessary ingredient of perception itself.[24] Once imagination is thus installed in perception, its impoverishment with respect to disclosure and truth disappears. As drafting the very configuration of the self-showing of things, tractive imagination is requisite for any disclosure of things themselves in their truth. There is disclosure and truth only by force of imagination.

Force of imagination names, not some capacity belonging to imagination, but rather the self-deployment of imagination itself at some site, indeed, as tractive, at some locus of presence. But what about imagination itself, assuming that, in contrast to force, it has a certain propriety, whatever may be the manner in which that propriety is constituted? Within what limits can imagination be identified—as it almost always has been from Aristotle on—as a power of the soul or, in modern idiom, as a faculty of the subject?

---

24. Ibid., A 120.

Or rather, what exorbitant sense of δύναμις can now be brought to resound in *imagination* as determined (as tractive) in the foregoing remonstrative discourse? Granted that in *force* (as it occurs in *force of imagination*) there can appropriately be brought to resonate the exorbitant sense of ἐνέργεια as a being at work that aims at no production of a work.

An indication of such an exorbitant sense in *imagination* is provided by the possibility that imagination (under the name φαντασία) may not have been simply determined as a power of the soul even in the Aristotelian text, that is, by the undecidability in this regard to which Brann most explicitly refers; a comparable undecidability with respect to imagination as a faculty of the subject is marked by Gasché in the Kantian text.[25] If, in an exorbitant sense, imagination is not a power of the soul or faculty of the subject, such divergence could result from imagination's not being a power or faculty. Or it could result from imagination's not being of the soul or the subject. In the latter case, it would not be impossible to continue to determine imagination as a power, faculty, capability—that is, as δύναμις—though, detaching it from the soul or subject, such a determination could not but carry out, at once, a deconstruction of δύναμις.

Even prior to the remonstrative discourse on imagination as such, the determination of the image put decisively in question the pertinence of such concepts as that of soul and of subject. In its duplicity the image is both *one's own* (hence, *of* the being that is called *subject*) and *of the thing*. Hence, even before the discourse on imagination is broached, the incipient determination of the being to which one would take imagination to belong begins to turn obliquely against such determinations as subject and consciousness, against the interiority constitutive for these determinations. For in the mere engagement with the image, this being already transgresses—through the circuit of the duplicity—the limit of its proper interiority.

Still more decisive in this regard is the reversal first broached—if still not radically—by Fichte. In the idiom of the remonstrative discourse, it is a matter of a reversal that results from imagination's drawing the very configuration of self-showing. For it is not only things other than oneself that show themselves; one comes also oneself to be shown to oneself, and this self-showing along with the self-relation that it makes possible are constitutive for the modern concept of the subjectivity of the subject, as for the determination of consciousness as essentially self-consciousness. But in this case—and even if self-showing to oneself should not prove to presuppose the self-showing of things other than oneself—the very constitution of the subject presupposes the drafting operation of imagination, its self-deployment into being at work in drafting the configuration of self-showing as such. The reversal would require, then, that one say: rather than imagination belonging to the subject, the subject would belong to imagination.

---

25. See above, chap. 2a.

Through this reversal one could begin to engender a sense of imagination as capability that would fall outside the orbit of subjectivity. Yet mere reversal is insufficient: both imagination and the being previously determined as subject need also to be redetermined at the limit in a way that effects the deconstruction of the very schema that, in the philosophical determination, joins imagination to the subject.

Such a deconstructive move requires suspending the possession that is decisive in this connection. For, as a capability, imagination has been construed as belonging to a certain being, one determined as subject or, in premodern philosophy, as soul. But whatever sense this belonging, this possessing, may be construed to have, imagination as now determined cannot in this sense belong to the subject, cannot be a possession of the soul; it cannot be a capability that one would possess, almost as one can possess capital that can be put to work to produce a certain return. The question is how the being that has been called soul, subject, etc. will have to be rethought now that its relation to imagination can no longer be assumed to be one of possession.

One consequence is manifest and decisive. If imagination is not a capability possessed by this being, then this capability and its self-deployment at any particular site will always *have come*. It will be a capability that one does not oneself hold in readiness. It will be like a gift—will *be* a gift, to the extent that it can be said to be—but a gift that must come ever anew, not a gift that, once it comes, is then possessed and at one's disposal. Imagination will be a pure gift, coming to draft the configuration of the self-showing of things.

6

THE ELEMENTAL

A. ELEMENTAL NATURE

Imagine the philosopher. In Greece. Under the cloudless sky the land-scape is dominated by vineyards and groves of olive trees, extending in one direction toward the distant mountains, in another direction toward the sea. There in the distance the deep blue waters of the Aegean sparkle in the brilliant sunlight. The shining is exquisite.

Hegel, too, tells how the Greek philosopher is to be imagined: "we must imagine [*vorstellen*] the ancient philosophers as human beings who stand entirely in the midst of sense intuition and presuppose nothing except the sky above and the earth beneath." What Hegel celebrates is that thought is here free ("Greek philosophy thought freely"), that, liberated from all pregiven content such as mythological representations and sacred doc-trine, thought here withdraws into itself and is purely with itself (*rein bei sich*). This being alone with oneself "belongs to the free thinking that voy-ages on the open sea, where nothing is under us and nothing above us and we are there in solitude, alone with ourselves."[1] A curious voyage indeed. It is as if this Odyssean philosopher, drunk with freedom, had sunk into an obliviousness to all surrounding things, even to the sky above and the earth beneath. It is as if, in setting out upon the open sea, in setting out into the open (*ins Freie*), the Greek philosopher could with impunity forget about the sky above and the earth beneath, as if such a one had forgotten that thought's entry into solitude is precisely a *withdrawing* from the elements. One knows at what extreme peril the philosopher-sailor, drunk with freedom, would venture such a voyage. Oblivious to all the signs visible in the sky as well as to both the threat and the haven offered by the contours of the earth, the philosopher-sailor would be defenseless against the onslaught of the elements and, with no sense of destination, could land on the most hostile shore or sail on until overtaken by death itself. For, as every other sailor knows, the sea is anything but a mere transparent medium of locomotion.

Imagine the Greek philosopher, then, as mindful—even in the solitude of free thought—of the sky above and the earth beneath. In order to sustain a trace of the withdrawal that is its very condition, proper solitude would require that the philosopher, standing in the midst of the sensible, maintain a certain comportment to these limits of the sensible. One could imagine the solitary philosopher deliberately setting his gaze on the upward limit in order to behold the orderly revolutions visible in the sky. One could even imagine that, beholding these revolutions in the cosmos above, the philosopher would then make the revolutions within, those of the soul, imitate those celestial revolutions, engaging in a mimetic reflection of the order beheld above back into the human soul so as to stabilize and set in order the revolutions that occur there within. One could imagine such vision of the sky, mimetically reflected back into oneself—or rather, one would not really need to imagine it oneself, in one's solitude, for it is precisely the upward vision that is described at the most ascendant point in the *Timaeus*. The description comes at the very end of the first of Timaeus' three discourses on the generation of the cosmos. And yet, at just the point where unimpeded ascendancy would seem to be announced, a certain dissonance begins to be heard: though the soul may be assimilable to the noetic order, there are also other kinds of things, operative even as a condition of vision, that are incapable of receiving νοῦς—for instance, says Timaeus, such visible bodies as "fire and water and earth and air."[2] Gazing upon the sky above and the earth beneath, the philosopher beholds not only the cosmic order but also fire and water and earth and air—that is,

---

1. Hegel, *Enzyklopädie der philosophischen Wissenschaften im Grundrisse (1830)* (Frankfurt a.M.: Suhrkamp, 1970), Zusatz to §31. This passage was not published by Hegel but was added by his editors on the basis of elaborations given in his lectures.

2. Plato, *Timaeus* 46d.

what we (though not Plato) call the *natural elements*. If philosophical vision were to remain reflective even in this regard, then the solitary philosopher would be brought back to a vision of self as situated amidst the elements, as engaged by force of necessity in comportment to the elements. In any case, in the *Timaeus* this point of apparent ascendancy at which the dissonance begins to sound is also the point at which Timaeus interrupts his first discourse and launches then another beginning. As he begins this other discourse, he speaks, first of all, about necessity (ἀνάγκη) and about fire and water and earth and air.

To be sure, philosophy turns away from nature and ventures the δεύτερος πλοῦς by which it would set out for the intelligible. Not that philosophy fails to return to nature: from the height of the intelligible, for a vision on high, natural things appear as eikonic doubles of the archaic intelligibles. Since in this case the very nature of nature would lie beyond nature, what is decisive is not so much that philosophy returns to nature but that nature too returns, though in another guise, having cast off the disguise that made it seem cut to the measure of the familiar, that also allowed philosophy, in returning, to rest assured that everything in nature had its nature beyond nature. The return of nature is uncanny and elusive, like that of a shade that cannot be caught and held, that withdraws from every embrace, returning always into itself.

The turn that philosophy at the limit would carry out from the intelligible back to the sensible would adhere to the return of nature. Indeed it would venture to augment the return by releasing nature from the bond by which philosophy after Plato, with remarkable consistency, kept it secured at the limit of being. The first name of the bond—a name that up to that point had signified: forest, woodland, wood, and, by extension, that from which something is made—was ὕλη. Across a vast and complex itinerary from Aristotle to Marx, this bond was ever again reconstituted; even when materialism finally became historical, it was this same bond that enforced the reduction of nature to a historical product. Because ὕλη in its primary sense names nothing capable of showing itself as such but rather only marks the limit of nature, nothing prevents construing nature as nothing but the limit up to which everything would be assimilable.[3] In this respect materialism neither releases nature into its own nor adheres to the return of nature. In standing philosophy on its head, historical materialism remains in utter solidarity with it as regards the alienation of the nature of

---

3. It is to a limit in this sense that Marx refers in his critique of Feuerbach. Instead of speaking of the human world, Feuerbach takes refuge in nature, "specifically, in the nature that has not yet been submitted to human mastery. But with every new invention, with each step forward by industry, a new piece of the terrain will be broken off, and the basis from which the examples for similar Feuerbachean propositions arise thus becomes ever smaller" (Karl Marx, *Die Deutsche Ideologie*, in *Frühe Schriften*, ed. Hans-Joachim Lieber and Peter Furth [Darmstadt: Wissenschaftliche Buchgesellschaft, 1975], 2:53).

nature. Nothing attests more directly to the reductionism than the ecological devastation left in the wake of materialist ideology. Nor to the force of nature's return.

Thus, one would need to break off materialism, to suspend the operation of ὕλη, no less than to break off the mimetic ascendancy driven by the nature of nature posited beyond nature. One would need to interrupt the very course of modern philosophy (and even of its preparation in antiquity), heeding Schelling's declaration: "The whole of modern European philosophy since its beginning (with Descartes) has this common defect [lack: *Mangel*], that nature does not exist for it and that it lacks a living ground."[4] One would need to interrupt that course, to break off the alienating of the nature of nature, in order now to begin again, to begin with the return of nature, with the sense of nature engendered by the return.

But what is the sense of nature? Can sense in this sense be determined as such otherwise than precisely in opposition to nature? The question of the sense of nature would, then, presuppose its own answer, would presuppose a prior determination of nature.[5] One hardly knows how to question about nature. One stammers, wondering what questions to address to it, hoping for questions that will open it to interrogation rather than simply being reflected back upon the questioner. In every instance it would seem that nature—what one would call the sense of nature—has already insinuated itself into the very question that would be addressed to it. As if, in questioning about nature, one could not avoid the obtrusive circularity of asking about the nature of nature.

And yet, even if not without circling and beginning thus to draw a certain configuration, one can turn to the sense of *nature*. For *nature, natura,* translates φύσις, the sense of which was rigorously determined in Greek philosophy. For Aristotle—and even more decisively for the earlier Greek thinkers—φύσις is neither a thing of a certain kind (a natural thing, as one says, in distinction from things produced by τέχνη) nor the totality of things of this kind. Rather, φύσις names the way in which things of a certain kind— τὰ φύσει ὄντα, natural beings—come manifestly to pass. Aristotle calls φύσις itself the ἀρχή of such occurrences. Since he takes such occurrences to consist primarily in movement (κίνησις), he determines φύσις as the

---

4. Schelling, *Philosophische Untersuchungen über das Wesen der menschlichen Freiheit und die damit zusammenhängenden Gegenstände,* in *Sämtliche Werke* (Stuttgart and Augsburg: J. G. Cotta'scher Verlag, 1860), Abt. I/7, p. 356.

5. A similar complexity belongs to the other oppositions in which nature is involved: nature/art, nature/grace, nature/history, nature/spirit. In all these cases, as with nature/sense, it is not a matter of mere difference or contrast between opposed terms. Rather, as Heidegger observes, it is the determination of nature that controls all the oppositions: "In all such distinctions, nature is not just an opposite but essentially holds the position of priority, inasmuch as the other terms are always and primarily differentiated by contrast with—and therefore are determined by—*nature*" (Heidegger, "Vom Wesen und Begriff der Φύσις. Aristoteles, Physik B, 1," in *Wegmarken,* vol. 9 of *Gesamtausgabe* [Frankfurt a.M.: Vittorio Klostermann, 1976], 240).

ἀρχή κινήσεως: it is that which originates and orders the movement of natural beings. What is distinctive about φύσις—in contrast to τέχνη—is that it is a kind of ἀρχή that lies within the very being whose movement it originates and orders. Far from being a whole within which all natural beings would be contained, φύσις is itself contained within natural beings as the indwelling origin of their movement. As a result a certain double directionality belongs to natural beings, as Heidegger, commenting on *Physics* B1, specifies: "Something determined by φύσις not only remains with itself in its movedness but precisely goes back into itself even as it unfolds in accordance with the movedness (of change)." Heidegger illustrates this double movement by referring to its occurrence in plants: "While the 'plant' sprouts, emerges, and extends itself into the open, it simultaneously goes back into its roots, insofar as it secures them in what is closed off and thus takes its stand. The self-unfolding emergence is inherently a going-back-into-itself. This kind of holding-sway [*Wesung*] is φύσις."[6]

Such discourse on the retreat that belongs to the very self-unfolding emergence of natural things only echoes what had been said long before Aristotle, by one whose very epithet points in the same direction. For Heraclitus, the Obscure, says: φύσις κρύπτεσθαι φιλεῖ.[7] There remains an echo, very distant, very indistinct, even in the *Critique of Pure Reason*. Over against the material concept of nature as the sum of all appearances, Kant distinguishes a formal concept of nature as "the connection of the determinations of a thing according to an inner principle [*nach einem inneren Prinzip*] of causality"[8]—*inner principle* here translating, if remotely, the indwelling ἀρχή that the Greeks called φύσις. An echo is heard again, and in a more Greek mode, when Hölderlin has Hyperion write of nature as "the changeless, quiet, and beautiful"[9]—that is, as the ἀρχή of change that is, hence, itself changeless, which brings it about that natural things emerge, unfold themselves, into the light where they can shine forth, while, at once, retreating into themselves, into the element that is closed off, quiet. It is this same quietness, this retreat, that is evoked in Shelley's song of the secret strength of things.

As indispensable as it is, remembrance of the ancient sense and of its modern traces does not suffice for carrying out the turn to nature. For what remains of it strikes little resonance with the songs of Hölderlin and Shelley: the remains are mostly lifeless phantoms pressed into the service of providing material, grist for the mills of technical production. Deprived

---

6. Ibid., 254.

7. Heraclitus, Fragment 123, in Diels-Kranz, *Die Fragmente der Vorsokratiker*, 1:178. The conventional translation is: "Nature loves to hide itself."

8. Kant, *Kritik der reinen Vernunft*, A 419/B 446 n.

9. ". . . in die Arme der Natur, der wandellosen, stillen und schönen" (Friedrich Hölderlin, *Hyperion oder der Eremit in Griechenland*, in *Sämtliche Werke und Briefe*, ed. Günter Mieth [München: Carl Hanser, 1989], 1:582).

of their quiet reserve, there is little chance of turning their retreat into a renewed turn to nature. Even beyond the cycles of technical production in the usual sense, nature—the changeless, quiet, and beautiful that was once called nature—is submitted to ever accelerating assimilation. Or rather, nature is decomposed in order that natural things, deprived of their retreat, might be assimilated to the sphere of what can be governed, controlled, and ultimately—for this is the very sense operative here—*made, produced.* Today even living things can, in an ever more decisive sense, be produced rather than generated by nature. Even where it is deemed valuable to conserve wild nature, the wilderness areas that are laid out become sites of a transformation of nature that drives out the wild, again—and now most concretely—alienating nature from itself. There remains only the abstraction: "The ideal of wilderness arose when we no longer knew how to live with the wild. From its beginning wilderness has been its own abstraction, sacrificing wildness on its altar."[10]

Even if insufficient, remembrance can serve to prepare the attentiveness and discernment that are, above all, required. Most promising are texts that in and through their very strangeness attest to a heeding of nature so discernful, so remote from all everyday comportment to these very same things of nature, that it can only be intimated by the words themselves. As with the following paragraph, taken from the letter that Hölderlin wrote to Böhlendorff after returning—struck, as he said, by Apollo—from the south of France: "The more I study it, the more powerfully indigenous nature [*die heimatliche Natur*] seizes me. The thunderstorm, not only in its highest appearance, but in precisely this respect, as power and as shape among the other forms of the sky; the light in its effect, forming nationally and as a principle and mode of destiny [*nationell und als Prinzip und Schicksalsweise bildend*], that something be sacred to us, its impulse in coming and going; that which is characteristic of the forest and the concurrence of various characters of nature in one region; that all sacred places of the earth are together around one place, and the philosophical light around my window, is now my joy; may I remember how I have come hither."[11]

One knows little about how he came hither. Only that he came back from the south, where, as he says near the beginning of the letter, he had been moved by "the powerful element, the fire of the sky." There, too, in the region bordering on Vendée, his interest had been captured by what he

---

10. Irene Klaver, "Silent Wolves: The Howl of the Implicit," in *Wild Ideas,* ed. David Rothenberg (Minneapolis: University of Minnesota Press, 1995), 120. Klaver offers the following characterization of the wild: "to be wild is to stand out *and* to disappear. . . . What constitutes the wild and the silent is this very play between appearance and disappearance, the slipping in and out of the limits of presence." She adds: "The conceptualization of wilderness goes hand in hand with a reduced capacity for living with the wild, this otherness that is not controlled by human culture" (ibid., 117, 120).

11. Hölderlin, *Sämtliche Werke und Briefe,* 2:934.

calls simply "the wild" ("*das Wilde*"). He writes also of the southern people, crediting their athletism with having made better known to him the proper essence of the Greeks. Yet from all these sights of the south he returned, and it was precisely in returning to his own region that he came hither, came to write—was enabled to write—this strange paragraph about the nature belonging to his region, to his *Heimat*. He tells not only about certain aspects of this nature but how they belong to the region, how they concur in the region, as if gathered by and around the singularity of the country. This is what Hölderlin discovered upon his return—when he had "come hither"—and what he ventured to say in the letter to his friend Böhlendorff: not various features of nature in general (irrespective of locality) but rather nature as it holds sway in his own region, indigenous nature. And yet, even within the limits of the region's nature, Hölderlin writes neither about particular natural things or kinds of natural things nor about specific features of the indigenous nature but rather about what one would perhaps most readily call—taking the word primarily in its meteorological sense—the elements. The paragraph invokes earth and sky: the earth as offering places of shelter, sacred places, to be sure, but also the forest, which shelters most living things; the sky as admitting, among the forms that take shape in it, the thunderstorm, but also, above all, the light, which in its manner of coming and going in the passing of day into night, of one season into another, of one year into the next, forms those at home in the region and provides, in an eminently concrete sense, the principle (ἀρχή) that originates and orders their lives.

Thus Hölderlin writes of nature by evoking the elements, elemental nature, as holding sway in the region, at a singular locale on the earth, one place around which, in the writing, all is gathered. As, poetically, in remembrance of sites never seen, he writes of another elemental nature—in the hymn *Griechenland,* in the lines translatable thus:

> For firmly fixed is the navel
> Of earth. For captive in banks of grass are
> The flames and the common
> Elements. But above, all reflection, lives the Aether. But silver
> On pure days
> Is light. As a sign of love
> Violet-blue the earth.[12]

Early Greek thought engages what we call—adapting the Latin translations—the natural elements. The operative word in Empedocles is ῥιζώματα: fire, water, earth, and air—or rather, the phenomena that the corresponding Greek words name (since simple translational invariance cannot be assumed)—are the roots that convey sustenance to all things, enabling

---

12. Hölderlin, "Griechenland" (Dritte Fassung), in *Sämtliche Werke und Briefe,* 1:434f.

natural things to grow, to come to light, to unfold into the open expanse bounded and configured by these very roots. To be sure, Empedocles declares that all things are from these (ἐκ τούτων),[13] from the roots; yet there are indications that this declaration pertains primarily to the *from which* of manifestation, not merely that of simple composition. As in Fragment 38: "Come, I shall tell you of the origin from which became manifest all the things we now look upon, earth and billowing sea, damp air, and Titan aither who fashions his circle around all things."[14] Also, as in the injunction: "Ponder each thing in the way by which it is manifest."[15] In the Platonic text these same four begin to be called—not without reservations and sometimes not at all—στοιχεῖα.[16] Thus extended to cover not only the constituents of λόγος (the earlier sense) but also those of natural things, the word becomes established from Aristotle on. What is most decisive in governing the force and range of this word, which the Romans will translate as *elementa*, is the way in which it comes to be differentiated from ἀρχή once the latter is restricted, at least in its primary sense, to signifying the intelligible term that orients philosophical ascendancy as such. The elements are taken to constitute, not the primary origin of things, but rather only the *from which* of composition, which as such constitutes the limitation setting things apart from the intelligible originals that command nonetheless their manifestation.

But if, now, the manifestation is no longer to be commanded from afar, the turn back to the sensible opens the way also for a turn back to the elements that would grant them the same full sway throughout nature that they were taken to have by the early Greek thinkers—or, more precisely, that would redetermine nature itself in and as the holding sway of the elements. Yet such a turn can be consequential only if it simultaneously twists free of the determination of the elements as constituting the *from which* of composition, leaving to the mathematical project of modern physics the decomposition of things into elements and indeed into subatomic components at the level of which even the differentiation between elements ceases to be primary. What is, rather, required of philosophy at the limit is that it turn back to the elements as constituting the *from which*, not of composition, but of manifestation, that it return to the elements as they bound

---

13. Empedocles, Fragment 21, in Diels-Kranz, *Die Fragmente der Vorsokratiker,* 1:320.

14. In the form handed down by Clement and reproduced in Diels-Kranz, the initial line reads: "εἰ δ' ἄγε τοι λέξω πρῶθ' ἥλιον ἀρχήν." Among the various proposals for dealing with ἥλιον ἀρχήν, Freeman's maintains that ἥλιον is a corruption (*Ancilla to the Pre-Socratic Philosophers* [Oxford: Basil Blackwell, 1956], 57). My translation omits it. Yet the sense of the passage would remain pertinent even if one adopted, for instance, the rendering proposed by Kirk and Raven: "Come, I shall tell thee first of the sun" (G. S. Kirk and J. E. Raven, *The Presocratic Philosophers* [Cambridge: Cambridge University Press, 1962], 332).

15. Empedocles, Fragment 3, in Diels-Kranz, *Die Fragmente der Vorsokratiker,* 1:310.

16. See Plato, *Theaetetus* 201e, *Timaeus* 48b–c.

and articulate the expanse of the self-showing of things themselves. In such a turn one will, then, recover an exorbitant sense of *element,* a sense that was in play in early Greek thought but that also survives in the common discourse that refers to wind, rain, snow, etc. as the elements—or, marking the difference unmistakably, as elemental nature or simply as the elemental. Beyond all that *nature* has endured since its inception as *natura,* breaking with almost everything it has been compelled to bear, another sense would now—exorbitantly—be ventured: nature as holding sway in and as the concurrences of the elemental.

One may be prompted by remembrances of nature: remembrance of its inceptional determination in Greek thought and of its return in the ascendancy of that thought; remembrance of the elemental nature poetized around the poet's *Heimat* or echoed poetically from the remote valley of the great mountain gleaming on high; remembrance of the shining manifestness of the elements in Greece. By such remembrance one can nurture solicitousness for elemental nature, can practice a kind of receptive prospection capable of opening one's vision to the rare sight of the natural elements gathered in the very retreat that impels ever again the return of nature. As in Greece, still today, there are scenes staged by nature itself that display a gathering of the elements in their utmost visible manifestness. As on an island in the Cyclades, looking out across the Aegean at sunset. In the distance and somewhat to the side another island—Delos—is silhouetted against the darkening sky. The fire of heaven has cast off its sheer brilliance and lightness to become a dense, dark-red sphere lowering itself, almost perceptively, into the sea. As the lowest point on its periphery is about to touch the horizon, the thin wisps of clouds trailing horizontally across its face catch its orange glow. Before such a scene, beholding—or catching a glimpse of—such visible gathering of sun, sky, clouds, sea, and stone, one can sense how elemental nature was once apprehended and perhaps can begin, perhaps elsewhere too, to open one's vision to the solicitation of the elemental.

The move called for at the limit is palintropic in every respect. It is a turn that recovers an exorbitant sense to be heard in *the elemental;* it is, at once, also a turn back to what has a certain anteriority with respect to natural things. It is a turn provoked, solicited, by the ever recurrent return of nature to those sites where natural things have been robbed of their quiet reserve, for the specters that return—often devastatingly—to those sites are for the most part borne by the elemental. Turning back to the elemental in the exorbitant sense, as those anterior elements from which manifestation proceeds, the turn enacts remonstratively the retreat of elemental nature.

What is called for is to begin again with sense, to begin anew by regression to a beginning anterior to the beginning previously made with the sense image. For before that beginning, before things can ever have come to shine forth in the image, the elemental will have been in place, delimiting the very expanse in which enchorial things can shine forth from within their horizons.

What is needed, then, is to begin anew, to begin palintropically, with the sense of the elemental. In this connection *sense* can assume any of its possible senses. Thus, (1) it is a question of what is to be meant by *the elemental*, of its sense in the sense of its signification and possible reference. It is a matter of recovering the exorbitant sense that sounded in early Greek thought only to be virtually silenced through the translations of ῥίζωμα into στοιχεῖον and of στοιχεῖον into *elementum*. It is a matter of letting this sense again resound, now in *the elemental*. Yet also, (2) to begin with the sense of the elemental has the sense of beginning with the domain of sense that is bounded and articulated by the elemental, that is, of beginning—as already from the beginning—with the sensible but now in such a way that it can be delimited in a more positive manner as *of* (that is, bounded and articulated by) the elemental. Such delimitation furthers the task of determining the sensible outside the oppositional relation to the intelligible, of decisively twisting it free so as to unfold a sensible interpretation of the sensible. Yet, (3) delimiting the sensible by way of the elemental and doing so in a manner that adheres to the sensible require remonstrating the sense of the elemental in the sense of drawing the sensible configuration of those elements from which the manifestation of things proceeds. Furthermore, (4) as bounding and articulating the sensible, the elemental constitutes the directionalities that hold sway within the expanse of enchorial things. Thus, exposing the elemental involves also delimiting its sense in the sense of directionality. In every regard, (5) whether it is a matter of engendering anew the sense of the elemental or of tracing its sensible configuration and directionality as these determine the sensible as such, there is required a sense of the elemental in the sense of an opening of one's vision and discourse to its solicitation—a sense, as it were, for the elemental.

Such a sense is indeed never entirely lacking. Who does not have some sense for the sea as its surface sparkles brilliantly under the intense rays of the summer sun; and for the air above (the aither, as the ancients called it) on days when it superabounds with dazzling, silver light; and for the wind as it is given voice by the swaying pines; and for the dark, rapidly approaching storm clouds and the heavy downpour they will bring; and for the clear night sky of midwinter with its splendent profusion of stars; and for the earth and the forest as once again in early spring they offer their promise of abundance to come? What is needed is that attentiveness and discernment be brought to bear on the common sense of the elemental and, above all, that the elemental not be dissolved, decomposed by way of seemingly rigorous compositional projects, that it not be thus concealed precisely in its configuration as elemental.

But how is the elemental configured as such? Or rather, how are the various elements configured as elemental? How, in particular, are the elementals to be distinguished from things, especially from natural things? In showing themselves, things stand out from a background. As it bears most directly on the self-showing of the thing, the background consists of the peripheral horizons in the various guises that can be assumed (local, instrumental, etc.). And yet, the system of peripheral horizons does not constitute the entire background as such, which, on the contrary, runs on beyond the horizons, exceeding them indefinitely yet in such a way that this indefinite excess bears back upon the horizons, enclosing the self-showing thing and its horizons. Already in the remonstrative analysis of peripheral horizonality, a certain excess was marked in the configuration of such horizons: presented to some extent in and as the imaginal margin, the peripheral horizon shades off, breaks off almost imperceptively; yet the background, visible to an extent within the compass of the peripheral horizon, is configured as extending on beyond that compass. Offering in most cases little more than marginal traces, this indefinitely extended background encloses the thing itself as well as the operative horizons. In other words, the thing shows itself not only as bound by horizons but also as encompassed, beyond its horizons, by an indefinitely extended medium or element. As the towering oak and the other trees of the grove that surround it are silhouetted against the sky, enclosed, encompassed by its indefinite extent.

Elementals are encompassing, though in different ways, each in its own way. As the thunderstorm approaches, the landscape, canopied by black clouds, becomes ever more somber, as if in preparation for those first heavy raindrops that portend the downpour soon coming to drench everything. Enclosed by the low cloud cover and pounded throughout by the driving rain, the entire valley is encompassed by the storm. Living beings may flee before the approaching storm, taking shelter from the elements; yet the very sense of their flight and of their taking shelter is linked to the inevitably encompassing character of the storm, which they endure in a certain way rather than escape. If there is also high wind, it too will sweep through the entire length of the valley, encompassing it, though in a way different from the clouds and the rain. Also encompassing, though in its own way, is the lightning flash that momentarily illuminates the entire valley, as is, too, the thunder when its rolling echo outlines the very contours of the earth as shaped around and into the valley. The storm brings these various elements together, and, as each encompasses the region in its own distinctive way, they also intersect, overlap, and envelop one another. Indeed the thunderstorm is itself nothing other than these elements, or rather, their coincidence.

The sea, even just its surface, is encompassing in still another way, as one knows who, like the Greek philosopher portrayed by Hegel, sets out on the open sea. The solitude of the philosopher-sailor will be inseparable from the sense of being encompassed, surrounded as far as the eye can see, by the broad expanse of sea. Yet there is expanse also above: the very sense of the expanse of sea is inseparable from the openness above, from the celestial vault that, arising from the horizon as if from the sea, has the effect paradoxically of opening indefinitely the region above rather than closing it off. Especially on clear days the expanse of the sky appears unlimited, while precisely as such it also encompasses, even encloses, the entire indefinitely extending expanse of the sea. On such days, too, the sun will bestow its light and warmth over this expanse, as the gentle breeze fills the sail and drives the frail bark of the philosopher-sailor on across the seemingly endless expanse.

In such connections the sense of element is determined, not by a project of decomposition, but by the configuration of showing to which such elements, the elementals, belong. At every site of manifestation, things and their horizons show themselves as encompassed in various ways by various elementals, which intersect, overlap, or envelop one another, which therefore in some manner run together, that is, are themselves configured in a certain elemental concurrence. Yet, despite their concurrences, elementals are not—do not reveal themselves as—determinately bounded in the way that things are. Even if, as with the rain and the wind brought by the storm, they are not—and do not even unqualifiedly appear to be—completely unlimited in their extent, the compass of an elemental has, whatever the site, a certain indefiniteness, indeed as constitutive of it as elemental. Not that certain meteorological measures could not be applied: yet as soon as the rain and the wind are submitted to such measure, their character as elemental will have been reduced and the difference, sustained at every site of manifestation, between elementals and things will have been leveled out. As they bear on a site of manifestation, as they come to encompass self-showing things and the horizons of such showing, elementals have an expanse that is not only indefinite but also, as such, gigantic in the sense of lacking, or exceeding, all proportionality with respect to things that show themselves and those to whom they show themselves. It is in this respect that the elementals are also monstrous: their monstrosity lies in their exceeding the things of nature while also themselves belonging to nature. As a kind of hypernature within nature, the monstrous elementals require, for their remonstration, the mutation of pragmatology into monstrology.

While, on the one hand, they are indefinite, even gigantic, in their extent, the elementals display, on the other hand, a certain peculiar one-sidedness. As the storm moves through, one feels the edge of the wind, and, looking across the valley, one observes the sheets of rain, which thoroughly drench the earth, or rather, its surface, on which the puddles barely take shape before overflowing to form an array of momentary rivulets. The one-sidedness of the elementals differs in kind from that of things. The side that an element displays is not an aspect or profile of a thing, and the depth of an elemental does not harbor a wealth of other profiles that could be offered to various perspectives. The surface of the earth is not simply one profile among many that the earth might present; rather it is in a sense the only side, which would only be replicated by any attempts, for example, by excavation, to disclose another side. To be sure, there is depth behind the side displayed by an elemental, but it is a depth of another kind than the secret strength of things. The difference is perhaps most manifest when, as in the storm, one is utterly encompassed by the elements. But even when, from the frail bark, one looks out across the surface of the sea and then through that surface into the depth, the character of surface and depth differs from that of the frontal and lateral images of a thing. To be sure, there is retreat both of elementals and of things. Yet what is held in reserve in the display of an elemental is neither a series of other profiles nor therefore a thing itself; rather, the retreat of an elemental is a withdrawal into a depth that, in its gigantic indefiniteness, borders on the fathomless.[17]

The monstrous depth that this retreat opens within elemental nature is what makes the elemental a primary site or ambiance of the mythical. Beyond the surface of the otherwise ordinary elemental phenomena, as the very depth of the elemental, there is harbored what is least ordinary, the monstrosity as which the mythical gods can—and to the Greeks did[18]—appear. From this depth they shine forth with (or in or as—none of these prepositions quite suffices) the elemental: Zeus with the thunderbolt, Poseidon with the sea.

The differentiation of elementals from things is hinted at in the so-called impersonal or agentless formulations in which the holding sway of an elemental is commonly expressed: one says "it is raining," "it is snowing," "it is windy," without any pretense that the pronoun has an unexpressed antecedent identifying an agent-thing. Even if one says "the lightning is flashing" and "the wind is blowing," the merest reflection suffices to remind one

---

17. Though the difference between the depth of a thing and that of an element is marked by Levinas, it is immediately assimilated to the global opposition between existence and existent (which translates—in a certain direction—Heidegger's distinction between *das Sein* and *das Seiende*). Thus: "What the side of the element that is turned toward me conceals is not a 'something' susceptible of being revealed, but an ever new depth of absence, existence without existent, the impersonal par excellence" (Emmanuel Levinas, *Totalité et Infini: Essai sur L'extériorité*, 4th ed. [The Hague: Martinus Nijhoff, 1984], 116). This assimilation allows Levinas, in turn, to link the recession of the elemental to the *il y a* ("L'élément se prolonge dans l'il y a" [ibid.]). The result is not only, as Levinas no doubt intends, to deprive elemental nature of the capacity for heterogeneous provocation but also to efface the specificity of the elemental. Levinas' further step, identifying the depth of the elemental with "the materiality of the elemental non-I" and with "the fathomless obscurity of matter" (ibid., 132), risks reinscribing the entire analysis of the elemental within the most classical philosophical conceptuality and effacing the very differentiations that otherwise make this analysis obliquely—and indeed effectively—resistant to such a conceptuality.

18. See Heidegger, *Heraklit,* vol. 55 of *Gesamtausgabe* (Frankfurt a.M.: Vittorio Klostermann, 1979), 8.

that the lightning is nothing other than the flash and the wind nothing other than the gale.

To the extent that one is encompassed by an elemental, one lacks the distance with respect to it that, on the other hand, can always be taken from things, at least from all things other than oneself. From within an elemental, bathed, as it were, in it, one cannot gain a perspective on it from which to let it deploy itself as a thing, that is, present itself in a frontal image shining forth from within lateral and peripheral horizons. On the other hand, there are ways in which one can limit one's immersion in an elemental and gain a certain extraterritoriality from which vantage point the elemental can be deployed in a manner approximating that of a thing. Thus the rain, the forest, even the wind and the storm can be deployed as if they were simply things or complexes of things, provided one assumes an aloof lookout; to the extent that they are thus deployed, their holding sway as elemental is effaced. Not all elementals yield equally to being redeployed as quasi-things: the forest or even perhaps the sea will yield more readily than will the wind or the light. Most resistant are those elementals to which all others, in the prolongation of their virtually fathomless depth, eventually lead back and in which they, in their depth, are in a sense finally lost— namely, earth and sky.

Both in dreams of flight and in the project of securing an Archimedean point, the aim is extraterritoriality with respect to the earth, that is, extraterrestriality as such. An elaborated, though theoretical project of extraterrestriality is put decisively into effect with the inception of modern (Galilean-Newtonian) physics, which cancels the ancient dichotomy between earth and sky in the interest of universally valid laws. As Arendt observes, modern physics "always handle[s] nature from a point in the universe outside the earth. Without actually standing where Archimedes wished to stand . . . , still bound to the earth through the human condition, we have found a way to act on the earth and within terrestrial nature as though we dispose of it from outside, from the Archimedean point."[19] But now the project is no longer only theoretical, now that the technological means of achieving actual extraterrestriality are available. Yet if such means indeed suffice to allow the earth to be sensibly deployed as a thing, the very sense of this deployment and of the unheard-of transformations it may

---

19. Hannah Arendt, *The Human Condition* (New York: Doubleday, 1959), 238. Arendt goes on to link such theoretical extraterrestriality to the role and the transformation of mathematics in modern physical science: "earth alienation became and has remained the hallmark of modern science. . . . Modern mathematics freed man from the shackles of earth-bound experience and his power of cognition from the shackles of finitude. . . . What is decisive is the entirely un-Platonic subjection of geometry to algebraic treatment, which discloses the modern ideal of reducing terrestrial sense data and movements to mathematical symbols." This "opened the way for an altogether novel mode of meeting and approaching nature in the experiment" (ibid., 240f.).

herald can be determined only through reference back to the sense of the earth as elemental.[20] The available technological means also serve, not to deploy the sky as a thing (since it utterly resists such deployment), but to dissolve the elemental sky and to replace it—extraterritorially—with the cosmos (again, if now more decisively, translating οὐρανός into κόσμος). Yet now that there are astronomical instruments capable, for instance, of taking the measure even of superclusters of galaxies (these long, thin strands can, by recent estimates, extend for hundreds of millions of light-years), it becomes ever more insistently a matter of a cosmos no longer deployable before a panoptic subject,[21] an acosmic cosmos in which vision at a distance is also vision into the remote past, in which presence is thus disseminated, indeed shattered, almost beyond the limits of recovery even by imagination.

Nonetheless, this side of extraterritoriality in all forms (theoretical, envisaged, actual), one perdures upon the earth and beneath the sky, encompassed by the elemental earth and sky and by other elementals, which in various concurrences come to hold sway there in that expanse. Encompassed by the elemental, one cannot readily take distance from it as from a thing; nor, consequently, can one deal with it as with a thing, abandoning it, appropriating it, altering it, or destroying it. Short of the extreme withdrawal that would enable one effectively to deploy it as a thing, one has no choice but to endure it, even if by taking shelter from it. Yet, for the most part, the elementals remain unobtrusive and inconspicuous, their marginal traces sufficing to let them operate as the indefinitely extended background that encloses things as well as the horizons of their self-showing. At times, though, and often through certain concurrences, elementals obtrude and their manifestation gains such force that it eclipses the mere self-showing of things. Amidst the fury of a storm, everything—all self-showings of things—becomes merely indicative of the storm itself, merely another moment in its manifestation. When an elemental obtrudes, it shows itself as prodigious, as hypernature within nature, as of extraordinary extent and/or power, as monstrous, as evoking wonder. If, as Aristotle attests, "it is through wonder that men now begin and first began to philosophize,"[22]

---

20. Baudrillard marks the extraterrestriality that is achieved by satellization: "Resist the evidence: in satellization, he who is satellized is not who one might think. Through the orbital inscription of a spatial object, it is the planet earth that becomes a satellite, it is the terrestrial principle of reality that becomes eccentric, hyperreal, and insignificant" (*Simulacra and Simulation*, 35).

21. "What is coming toward us is a universe that is unique insofar as it is open on nothing but its own distance from nothing, within nothing, its 'something' having been thrown there from nowhere to nowhere, infinitely defying all themes and schemes of 'creation'—all representations of production, engenderment, or mere origination.... [What] we need [is] an acosmic cosmology that would no longer be caught by the look of a *kosmotheoros*, of that panoptic subject of the knowledge of the world" (Nancy, *Le Sens du Monde*, 37f.).

22. Aristotle, *Metaphysics* A 2, 982b 12–13.

then it is less than surprising that the elements figured so prominently in the thought of the early Greeks and that, even now, a certain beginning of philosophy, the palintropic turn of philosophy at the limit, is directly linked to the elemental.

B. NATURE AND TRAGEDY

It is as prodigious that elemental nature comes to bear upon tragedy: in their most extreme concurrences, the elements constitute a setting that lets resound in nature the very devastation released in the tragedy set within this setting. As in the scene on the heath in which Lear, alone with his Fool in the midst of the storm, rages with the elements. Precisely through this bearing, tragedy can, in turn, contribute to engendering anew a sense of nature, to putting into play a sense of the elemental that is irreducible to the nature of nature that philosophy posits beyond nature. For at least in works in which—as in *King Lear*—it is abysmality itself that resounds, the philosophical nature of nature would be incapable of the requisite resonance, having forfeited this possibility from the outset by a series of prohibitions such as that against what is deemed contradiction.

Throughout *King Lear* nature is constantly at issue, as are also deformity of nature and excess of nature, that is, monstrosity. In the opening scene in which Lear demands from his daughters their professions of love, his expressed intention of balancing bounty with nature serves to accentuate how thoroughly he is blinded to nature—to their natural dispositions—by the flattering lies of Goneril and Regan. When Cordelia, on the other hand, will say nothing, or rather, will only renounce such profession—

> ... I cannot heave
> My heart into my mouth[23]—

Lear appeals to nature, swearing by its powers and mysteries as he wrathfully disinherits her:

> Let it be so; thy truth then be thy dower:
> For, by the sacred radiance of the sun,
> The mysteries of Hecate and the night,
> By all the operation of the orbs
> From whom we do exist and cease to be,
> Here I disclaim all my paternal care,
> Propinquity and property of blood,

---

23. Shakespeare, *King Lear*, I.i.90–91. Citations are from the Arden text edited by Kenneth Muir (London: Methuen, 1972).

And as a stranger to my heart and me
Hold thee from this for ever.

(I.i.107–15)

To her suitor France, he denounces Cordelia as one almost unnatural, as

. . . a wretch whom nature is asham'd
Almost t'acknowledge hers.

(I.i.211–12)

France's inquiry as to what this thing so monstrous is that has put her so out of favor draws the pertinent connection:

This is most strange,
That she, whom even but now was your best object,
The argument of your praise, balm of your age,
The best, the dearest, should in this trice of time
Commit a thing so monstrous, to dismantle
So many folds of favour. Sure, her offence
Must be of such unnatural degree
That monsters it. . . .

(I.i.212–19)

The overturning through which the tragedy develops and in which its very composition as tragedy is accomplished brings about a reversal so powerful that, even to the blind, nature becomes manifest as nature and monstrosity as monstrosity. Then Lear sees with utter clarity that the one whose natural devotion is unquestionable is Cordelia and that the ones who are monstrous in their bearing toward him are Goneril and Regan. At the point where Lear encounters Goneril's ill treatment of him, as she deprives him of half his troop of knights, his denunciation of her is direct:

. . . Monster Ingratitude!

(I.v.37)

Much later her husband Albany describes her with the words "proper deformity" (IV.ii.60), words that with only the slightest twist say with utter succinctness precisely what constitutes monstrosity: deformity itself, deformity of one's very form, deformity of the proper, deformity of what one properly is, of what one is by nature, deformity of such scope as to deform one's natural form so as to effect within nature a transgression of the very limits belonging by nature to nature. Regan, too, is denounced in such terms. After she has conspired in the violent act of putting out Gloucester's eyes, a servant proclaims:

> If she live long,
> And in the end meet the old course of death,
> Women will all turn monsters.

(III.vii.98–100)

There is an issue of nature also in the relation of Gloucester to his sons, which throughout the play parallels and mirrors the relation of Lear to his daughters. Edmund, the bastard son, appeals to nature in his first soliloquy:

> Thou, Nature, are my goddess; to thy law
> My services are bound.

(I.ii.1–2)

Yet, Gloucester's "natural boy" (II.i.83) reveals immediately, in the soliloquy, his treacherous intent regarding his legitimate brother Edgar. He soon puts his treachery to work. As his father approaches, Edmund pretends to conceal a letter supposedly from his brother and implicating Edgar in a plot against Gloucester. Demanding to see the letter, Gloucester is thus deceived into believing that Edgar, his legitimate son, is plotting patricide. Gloucester's words,

> He cannot be such a monster—

(I.ii.91)

still suspended, return to the father and his oath:

> —to his father, that so tenderly and entirely loves him. Heaven
> and earth!

(I.ii.93–94)

Gloucester then affirms the connection already in effect posed by his oath, setting Edgar's suspended—but already believed—monstrosity into relation with that of the elements:

> These late eclipses in the sun and moon portend no good to us:
> though the wisdom of Nature can reason it thus and thus, yet Nature finds itself scourg'd by the sequent effects. Love cools, friendship falls off, brothers divide: in cities mutinies; in countries, discord; in palaces, treason; and the bond crack'd 'twixt son and father.

(I.ii.100–106)

No less deceived by Edmund's treachery than is Lear by his two daughters' flattery (Lear later underlines the parallel by calling Goneril "Degenerate bastard" [I.iv.251]), Gloucester, like Lear, is blind as regards which of his issue is on the side of nature. In the course of the tragedy, the madness of

Lear and the blindness inflicted on Gloucester confirm by enactment the blindness to nature that sets the tragedy in motion.

Nature's resounding of tragic devastation becomes all the more powerful as it becomes manifestive; that is, its power of resonance lies precisely in its capacity to echo the devastation so as to make it manifest as such. This capacity is one that belongs primarily to elemental nature, and in its release nature is impelled toward the threshold of monstrosity. But also, in order that the resonance be distinctly manifestive, it needs to be marked as such in the work, that is, all causal connection between elemental nature and the events unfolding in the tragedy must be excluded, even openly denounced.

Such a denunciation is staged at the moment when Edmund begins to weave his treachery against his father. For Gloucester these late eclipses in the sun and moon are portentous precisely because of their sequent effects; as soon as the deception begins to work its spell on him, Gloucester's speech drifts toward attributing the alleged plotting by Edgar to some such celestial causality. But from the moment of Gloucester's exit, there commences a soliloquy in which Edmund denounces all such appeals to the elements:

> This is the excellent foppery of the world, that, when we are sick in fortune, often the surfeits of our own behaviour, we make guilty of our disasters the sun, the moon, and stars; as if we were villains on necessity, fools by heavenly compulsion, knaves, thieves, and treachers by spherical predominance, drunkards, liars, and adulterers by an enforc'd obedience of planetary influence; and all that we are evil in, by a divine thrusting on. An admirable evasion of whoremaster man, to lay his goatish disposition to the charge of a star!

> (I.ii.115–25)

Edmund's soliloquy is, as it were, his moment of truth, the moment in which his unnatural treachery against father and brother is expressed with utter self-transparency. He knows fully well and tells himself directly that it is he, not the heavens, that is responsible:

> Fut! I should have been that I am had the maidenliest star in the firmament twinkled on my bastardizing.

> (I.ii.128–30)

Denunciation of all causality between the elements and the events unfolding in the tragedy lets the connection hold sway as abysmal. In turn, the abysmality of the connection augments the abysmality of the tragedy itself, the abysmality that is tragedy itself. Tragedy is always already prepared before its beginning. It begins with blindness and folly, which release the devastation already prepared, the destruction that follows its own course beyond the control of those who nonetheless are entangled in it. It is as if

it were, in the words of the Fool, "a great wheel [that] runs down a hill."
Yet it also runs upward, and the Fool, advising loyal Kent

> Let go thy hold when a great wheel runs down a hill,

(II.iv.69–70)

adds the further advice:

> but the great one that goes upward, let him draw thee after.

(II.iv.71–72)

The devastation that unfolds in tragedy is such that it also—and this *also* is
the site of the abysmality—restores and ennobles, yet without ceasing to be
devastation. There occurs a restoring and ennobling not just through the
desolation—as if the devastation were a means finally to be surpassed and
left behind—but also in the very midst of the devastation—as if by going
ever more deeply into it.

The tragedy begins, in Kent's words,

> When majesty falls to folly.

(I.i.148)

Not that the fall has not been prepared: for, as even Regan can recall of
Lear,

> . . . he hath ever but slenderly known himself.

(I.i.292–93)

Lear's folly, erupting from his self-ignorance, is staged as blindness. When,
just after Lear has disinherited Cordelia, Kent intervenes in her behalf,
Lear's explosive words literally enact the blindness:

> Out of my sight!

(I.i.156)

Kent pleads:

> See better, Lear; and let me still remain
> The true blank of thine eye.

(I.i.157–58)

When Lear swears by the very god of light and vision,

> Now, by Apollo,—

(I.i.159)

Kent responds:

> Now, by Apollo, King,
> Thou swear'st thy Gods in vain.

(I.i.158–59)[24]

Lear's blindness and folly release the devastation, and it is not long before his anxiety before the prospect of monstrosity emerges:

> I will forget my nature.

(I.v.31)

Even if Regan's words,

> Nature in you stands on the very verge
> Of her confine[,]

(II.iv.144–45)

are meant otherwise by her, they indicate also that Lear's nature is driven to the limit of nature, to the threshold of monstrosity, which appears as the madness that he dreads almost from the moment the devastation begins to unfold:

> O! let me not be mad, not mad, sweet heaven;
> Keep me in temper; I would not be mad!

(I.v.43–44)

And yet, Lear's madness becomes, in Edgar's words,

> Reason in madness.

(IV.vi.172–73)

In the devastation there comes also—the word is Cordelia's—"restoration" (IV.vii.26). As Lear sleeps, Cordelia implores,

> O you kind Gods,
> Cure this great breach in his abused nature!

(IV.vii.14–15)

---

24. A later exchange with the Fool is equally indicative, especially of Lear's folly:

Lear. Dost thou call me fool, boy?
Fool. All thy other titles thou hast given away; that thou wast born with.
Kent. This is not altogether Fool, my Lord.

(I.iv.145–48)

The doctor soon reports,

> Be comforted, good Madam; the great rage,
> You see, is kill'd in him.

(IV.vii.78–79)

It is perhaps only at this moment, when he is ennobled in the very devastation, that he first becomes king. In any case, Lear dies a king,[25] and the play ends with Edgar speaking thus of him:

> The oldest hath borne most: we that are young
> Shall never see so much, nor live so long.

(V.iii.324–25)

Gloucester's blindness and folly release the devastation that costs him his eyes. And yet, later, Lear himself attests to the vision that Gloucester has gained in his very blindness:

> No eyes in your head, . . . yet you see how this world goes.

(IV.vi.143–45)

Near the end of the play, Edgar reports his father's death:

> . . . but his flaw'd heart,
> Alack, too weak the conflict to support!
> 'Twixt two extremes of passion, joy and grief,
> Burst smilingly.

(V.iii.195–98)

Tragedy leaves Gloucester between joy and grief, even at the cost of death—not as if he had to choose one or the other, nor as if he could only alternate between them. Rather, his is a state of being filled completely by each, full of joy and full of grief, full of joy while also being full of grief. In tragedy there occurs an abysmal yoking together of devastation and restoration, of destruction and creation. In the work of tragedy this abysmal yoking is played out from beginning to end.

Devastation drives Lear back to nature. Likewise with Edgar in his disguise as Poor Tom: what is remarkable is the way in which Lear in his madness apprehends this utterly

---

25. Near the end of the play, Albany says: " . . . for us, we will resign, / During the life of this old Majesty, / To him our absolute power" (V.iii.297–99). As a result, Lear dies a king. See Arden edition, p. 204 n. 297.

unaccommodated man [who] is no more but such a poor, bare, forked animal. . . .

(III.iv.104–106)

For Lear entreats:

First let me talk with this philosopher.

(III.iv.151)

And he goes on to call him "learned Theban," "noble philosopher," and "good Athenian" (III.iv.154, 169, 177).

At precisely the moment when Lear recognizes the cruelty of Goneril and Regan, a storm is heard at a distance. Soon thereafter Lear will endure the storm and will address his rage to the elements—to "you elements" (III.ii.16)—that rage in it. Afterwards, as he, accompanied by his Fool and Kent, approaches the hovel where they would take shelter from the storm, Lear speaks of the

. . . tempest in my mind—

(III.iv.12)

coupling the storm and his madness, the elements and himself. Accompanying him, the Fool soon declares:

This cold night will turn us all to fools and madmen.

(III.iv.77)

Thus does the tragedy turn between the raging of the elements and that of fools and madmen, coupling them disclosively, letting the tempest in Lear's mind resound from the heavens.

As the scene on the heath is about to commence, Cornwall warns those with him at Gloucester's castle:

Let us withdraw, 'twill be a storm.

(II.iv.285)

Gloucester, just returning, announces that

The King is in high rage.

(II.iv.294)

Cornwall's command ensures that the raging king will not find shelter in the castle:

Shut up your doors, my Lord; 'tis a wild night.

(II.iv.306)

On the heath, exposed to the raging elements, Lear's rage resounds. Initially the scene is only reported, as a Gentleman speaks to Kent, who has come faithfully out into the storm in search of the king. To Kent's inquiry as to where the king is, he replies:

> Contending with the fretful elements;
> Bids the wind blow the earth into the sea,
> Or swell the curled waters 'bove the main,
> That things might change or cease; tears his white hair,
> Which the impetuous blasts, with eyeless rage,
> Catch in their fury, and make nothing of;
> Strives in his little world of man to out-storm
> The to-and-fro-conflicting wind and rain.
>
> (III.i.4–11)

Then, transported to another part of the heath, just ahead of Kent, as it were, one hears the king himself as, accompanied only by his Fool, he rages:

> Blow, winds, and crack your cheeks! rage! blow!
> You cataracts and hurricanoes, spout
> Till you have drench'd our steeples, drown'd the cocks!
> You sulph'rous and thought-executing fires,
> Vaunt-couriers of oak-cleaving thunderbolts,
> Singe my white head! And thou, all-shaking thunder,
> Strike flat the thick rotundity o' th' world!
> Crack Nature's moulds, all germens spill at once
> That makes ingrateful man!
>
> (III.ii.1–9)

In his monstrous rage, in the madness that breaches his very nature, Lear calls for monstrosity as such, for the self-violation, the self-destruction, of the very self-generative power of nature itself, of the self-generative power that (at least since Aristotle) has been taken to define nature as such.

But soon his

> Oppressed nature sleeps.
>
> (III.iv.95)

And then, in the balm of nature, in the repose it offers, Lear dresses himself fantastically with wild flowers and proclaims:

> Nature's above art. . . .
>
> (IV.vi.86)

C. ELEMENTAL IMAGINATION

The resonance of tragedy in its elemental setting alludes to the profound bearing of the elemental on such beings as we ourselves are, we who call ourselves human and who, now, will need to hear this name with ears capable of not hearing what *humanitas* has conveyed to it but perhaps only the allusion to *humus* (earth, soil), hence an exorbitant sense that links the human first of all to the earth. The bearing of the elemental does not lie solely in its encompassing the manifestation of things, though even in this regard a certain human comportment to the elemental would be required. But human beings also are encompassed by the elemental, always—short of extraterritoriality—by earth and sky, also by the life-supporting air that in various guises fills the expanse between earth and sky, usually by other elements as well that run together in this expanse and in their various concurrences are spread indefinitely across it. Human beings (and indeed other living beings, in their own way) belong to the elemental to such an extent that outside such belonging they could not be the beings they are. Whatever such beings may venture, whatever means of self-extension and self-empowerment their τέχναι and eventually their technology may supply—even the means to achieve extraterritoriality as such—they will always already have felt the gentle breeze and taken refuge from the howling storm, will already have walked upon the earth, enjoyed its beauty, and suffered its desolation, will already have welcomed the warmth of the sun and gazed in wonder at the stars. The elements will always have laid out in advance—prearticulated—the ways that humans come to pass, and it is from the most elemental configurations of nature that human beings acquire their primary sense of height and ascendancy, of direction as such, and of expanse and limit. These acquisitions constitute a kind of nonsense of sense without which sense as such would be impossible. In all sense there is in play the sense of the elemental.

Even in connection with the self-showing of things, a decisive comportment to the elemental is already operative. For as things shine forth from within their horizons, the configuration of the peripheral horizon is such that, though shading off, it also extends outward indefinitely; or rather, its shading off is precisely such as to refer beyond to an encompassing elemental (or concurrence of elementals). This referral may operate on the basis of the most marginal traces or, at the other extreme, may be supported by an imaginal presence of the elemental almost comparable to that of the horizon itself. In any case, the elemental can bear upon the self-showing of things only if it is held in an orientation to the thing, only if it is drawn toward the locus of presence and yet, at once—since an elemental is even more radically irreducible to presence—withdrawn from the there. In this connection it is, if possible, even less a matter of two moments, the thing and the elemental, simply being present together. For even if in some instances there is a marginal presence of the elemental, mere presence could never suffice to make the elemental encompass the thing or to let the elemental obtrude as prodigious. Only through an exorbitant mixing of protraction and retraction can the configuration be drawn in such a way that the elemental, even in its very retreat, comes to encompass manifest things, that is, becomes the very element of their self-showing. Such drawing comes only as the gift of imagination, of tractive imagination become elemental.

Mere presence bears even less on the manifold encompassings by which humans belong to the elemental and find the very ways of their coming to pass prearticulated in and by the concurrences of the elementals. It is only through the gift of elemental imagination that humans draw around themselves the elementals that will always have encompassed them.

D. EARTH AND SKY

Peripheral horizons, though limited, are deployed as extending on beyond the limit, on beyond the periphery where their visibility shades off, on beyond into the elemental. The limit is not itself immovable: one can extend it by distancing oneself from the thing seen a moment ago at close hand or by casting one's vision around and beyond the thing on which previously one had focused. Yet the limit cannot be extended without limit: even if all other elements can in some measure be assimilated to the system of peripheral horizons, one's vision comes finally to the horizon from which is drawn the very sense of horizonality as such. At the limit of the limit are the elementals that are unassimilable and that delimit the very expanse of all self-showing: earth and sky. Even when one does not see them at all, they are elementally operative, bounding all that one does see and all else that is implicated in what one sees.

All elementals tend toward breaching the distinction posed at—as—the beginning of philosophy, the distinction posited, not by philosophy, but as its very opening. This distinction between intelligible and sensible cannot withstand the counterforce of the elemental and so remain intact except through the enforcement of a reduction of the elemental to the mere *from which* of composition, together with a displacement of the elemental, as regards manifestation, by the intelligible ἀρχή. But if now, as once among the Greeks, one insists on the elemental as determinative for the manifestation of things, the displacement will in a sense be reversed and the distinction between intelligible and sensible will be disrupted. For in their capacity as determining manifestation, elements are neither intelligible ἀρχαί nor sensible things. Even if their visibility is deployed in a unique way, they are visible, sensible, and not intelligible. If some elements—most notably, earth and sky—can still be called ἀρχαί, it is only in another—indeed an archaic—sense, as the limit of the limit. On the other hand, elementals are distinct from sensible things, even though they are in their own way sensible and can, perhaps up to the limit, be deployed as—or as if they were— things. In their indefiniteness and unboundedness, in their unique kind of one-sidedness, and in their peculiar kind of depth, they are other than things. Distinct both from intelligible ἀρχαί and from sensible things, the elementals constitute a third kind that is such as to disrupt the otherwise exclusive operation of the distinction between intelligible and sensible. At the limit where, in a certain self-abandonment, philosophy turns back to the sensible, this third kind, the elemental, comes to seal the tomb of the dead god and to resume the role usurped long ago by the precursors of the god. In the case of sky and—at least short of extraterritoriality—of earth, the breach is unconditional. In addition, its onset with philosophy at the limit, with the turn to the sensible, serves to expose and restore the locus of the primal sense of vertical directionality, on which was founded the sense of philosophical ascendancy, indeed the very metaphorics of philosophy as such. One recognizes that the Platonic image of the cave is not just one image among others; rather, in the depiction of the ascent from within the earth to its surface where it becomes possible to cast one's vision upward to the heaven, the very translation (μεταφορά) is enacted that generates the philosophical metaphorics.

Thus, the turn of philosophy at the limit, the turn to the sensible, is a turn not only to sensible things but also—and, in a sense, even first of all— to the elemental. Pragmatology as monstrology requires also elementology. But what is the sense of the turn—the return—to the elemental? In particular, what is the sense in which one turns—or returns—to the earth? For, like the prisoner in the cave, one will in a certain respect never have left the earth behind. Not even if one assumes the stance of dying away from the earth and enforces it by every means possible, even contemplating suicide or picturing to oneself one's imminent demise. On that morning when he was to die, Socrates spoke with his friends about philosophy and death, and, according to the *Phaedo,* "as he spoke he put his feet down on the earth [ἐπὶ τὴν γῆν] and remained sitting in this way through the rest of the conversation,"[26] a conversation that, in the moments just before the final preparations for his drinking the φάρμακον (as it is consistently called), concludes with a great myth of the earth in which even the destination of the purest and holiest souls is presented as the upper region of the earth.

There is a curious reference to earth in Aristotle's account of the earlier thinkers who took one or the other of the elements as the ἀρχή. To be sure, the moments reductive of the elemental not only are operative in Aris-

---

26. Plato, *Phaedo* 61c.

totle's account but are explicitly called up as he begins it. From the outset he declares that these φυσιολόγοι have erred in not recognizing the incorporeal and in not positing the being (οὐσία) or whatness (τὸ τί ἐστι) as a cause of things. Precisely as he affirms this displacement of ἀρχή (αἴτιον), he puts in place the word ὕλη, inseparable from that displacement: these earlier thinkers are said to have posited one nature—that is, one element—as ὕλη. Furthermore, he declares that "things are generated from each other by combination or by separation"—that is, origination from an element is predetermined as composition (or decomposition). With this context established, Aristotle then observes how, among the elements, earth is exceptional: among those φυσιολόγοι who posited one element (στοιχεῖον) as the element of bodies, there were none who took earth to be that element. Since he has already predetermined that an element as such is a *from which* of composition, it is evident to Aristotle why earth has never been chosen as the original element: "manifestly because of the largeness of its parts." Then Aristotle adds (and this is the curious reference): "But why do they not ever name earth, as common people do? For these say that all things are earth. Hesiod, too, says that of the bodies earth was generated first; so, this happened to be an old and demotic opinion."[27] Aristotle even considers, hypothetically, inverting the order prescribed by composition so that what is composed would be prior in nature to those things that could be separated from it. With such an inversion—with which nonetheless everything continues to be determined by reference to composition—priority over the other elements could, Aristotle notes, be accorded to earth.

Whatever Aristotle and the various φυσιολόγοι declare, the demotic opinion is that all things are earth. Whatever shape things may assume, they are of earth and originate from earth. In Hesiod's *Theogony* earth is preceded only by χάος; even sky is borne by earth, "equal to herself, to cover her on every side."[28] The Homeric Hymn, "To Earth, Mother of All," celebrates "earth allmother" as "firmgrounded nourisher of everything on earth."[29] In Homer a frequent epithet of the earth is πουλυβότειρα: much- or all-nourishing.[30]

To turn back to the earth is to rediscover this archaic earth that will always have given nourishment and support. If philosophy at the limit would carry out this turn so as now to remain true to the earth, then it must recover the earth as elemental, undoing all that would serve—and has served—to reduce the elementals to things. All would hinge on declaring: though all things are earth, earth is not a thing.

---

27. Aristotle, *Metaphysics* A 8, 988b-989a.
28. Hesiod, *Theogony* 126f.
29. *The Homeric Hymns* XXX: 1–3.
30. See, for example, *Iliad* III: 89, 195.

In various guises and disguises the demotic opinion has in some measure endured. Whatever the reservations with which one would affirm that all things are earth, they will be marginalized, if not dispelled, by the rigorous execution of the turn to the sensible. Thus, philosophy at the limit will declare at least that all things are *of the earth*. The sense of the *of* is not limited to that appropriate to things produced through τέχνη, artificial things, for the making of which there is required some material taken ultimately from nature. For there are also, indeed first of all, natural things, things that occur without being produced. One of the most decisive moments in the inception of philosophy occurred when the schema derived from artificial things, the schema of production, was extended so as to apply to all things. Then it became conceivable that natural things, even living beings, consisted of material upon which a certain look, form, or shape (εἶδος, ἰδέα, μορφή) had been imposed by a producer, who, in advance of the production, would have envisioned this look, form, or shape. Thus, in the case of natural, no less than of artificial, things, their being of the earth would consist in their being made of an earthly material, of a material originating in some sense—perhaps in various senses—from the earth.

And yet, natural things are not manifestly produced; neither, consequently, is it manifest that the schema of production is appropriate to them, nor that they are of the earth in the way prescribed by that schema. Rather, it is manifest that—whatever the case may be with their material composition—they are of the earth in other ways: as stones belong to the earth; as trees, grasses, and grains grow from seeds in the earth; as humans and certain animals, born from others of their kind, are nourished by the earth's bounty and supported and oriented by its expanse. Though production may impinge on natural things and their relation to the earth, the origination and growth of natural things is thereby only directed, assisted, or hindered; one affects nature through means taken from nature, as a physician cures an illness by intervening in such a way as to entice the body to heal itself. Only at the extreme, where natural things are, as it were, pulverized into mere material, does the ancient schema of production become fully appropriate, that is, only, it would seem, when τέχνη becomes technology.

Things of the earth are, then, *of the earth* by growing from it. Their belonging to the earth is a matter of growth: as plants grow from out of the earth, as humans grow through being nourished, supported, and oriented by the earth, even as stones, gradually exposed by erosion of soil, grow in compass, take shape, from out of the earth.

Thus do things belong to the earth. And yet, not only natural things but also water and air, wind and mist, are of the earth, as is even—as Hesiod affirms and extraterrestriality confirms—the sky. Not only things but also the other elementals are of the earth; yet the other elementals belong to the earth, not by growing from it but by running together with it, by their distinctive concurrences.

But what is the earth? Is the earth even such that it has a *what*, a τί ἐστι? Or does it have a sense only in some other sense? How is one to delimit the sense of the word? What kind of word is *earth*? Is it a proper noun, the name of a unique individual: *Earth*? Or is it a common noun, a word that signifies a universal sense but that happens to refer only to a single individual, to what is called *the earth*? Is that to which the word refers by way of its sense not also something else distinguishable from this individual? For there are occasions in which one says, not *the earth*, but simply *earth*, as one says also *water, fire*, and *air*, designating what within the schema of production would be identified as material and conceptualized philosophically as matter but, now, outside that schema, would be reconfigured monstrologically as elemental.

Thus, the word functions as index of three kinds: of the individual (Earth); of the universal and only secondarily, through this, of the individual (the earth); and a third kind that has been thought as materiality but is now, outside the schema of production, to be thought as elemental (earth).

Earth is of three kinds. Two of these, the first two, are thought together by Hegel at a point in the dialectic of observing reason where *the earth* makes a sudden and brief appearance. At this point the issue is that of the relation between the inner determination of an organism and its structured shape, its being-for-an-other, that is, the relation between the genus of the organism and the actual individual organism. What is decisive in this connection is that the actual individual falls outside the genus: "What enters into actual existence is not the genus as such."[31] Between the genus, as organic universal, and the actual individual, there comes, then, the determinate universal or species, thus resulting in the schema:

genus—species—individual

In this configuration the genus differentiates itself into species (and subspecies) that fill the gap between the genus and the individual organism. What is decisive is that this self-differentiation of the genus, "the action of the genus," is severely restricted, limited. In order to represent also this limitation, Hegel extends the schema so that it becomes:

| genus (universal) | — | species (determinate universal) | — | single individual (individuality proper) | — | earth (universal individual) |

His account: "The genus, which divides itself into species according to the *universal determinateness* of number, or which may take as its ground of divi-

---

31. Hegel, *Phänomenologie des Geistes*, 164.

sion particular determinatenesses of its existence, e.g., figure, color, etc., while engaged in this peaceful activity, suffers violence from the side of the universal individual, *the earth,* which as the universal negativity preserves the differences as it has them within itself—their nature, on account of the substance to which they belong, being other than the nature of those belonging to the systematization of the genus. This action of the genus becomes a quite restricted affair, which it may carry on only inside those powerful elements and which is interrupted, full of gaps [*lückenhaft*], and stunted on all sides by its unrestrained violence."[32] Thus, the action of the genus is severely limited by the universal individual, the earth (thought, at once, in the first two senses broached by the word itself). Instead of a systematic self-differentiation, what results is a differentiation into which the earth introduces all manner of interruption and discontinuity, dividing the genus, for instance, by way of oceans, mountains, and deserts, rather than allowing the genus to differentiate itself purely on a uniform plane, in a manner akin to the self-differentiation of consciousness itself.

But what about the third kind? What about earth? What about what is said in *earth*? How is it to be delimited outside the schema of production? How is it to be thought otherwise than as material, otherwise than as designating the material composition of things?

What is required is a decisive shift from the purview of composition to that of manifestation. What is required is that earth be thought, not as the *from which* of material composition but as a *from which* of manifestation. To say that things are of earth would be, then, to signify something about the way they show themselves. Now it would need to be said that, in their self-showing, things never come forth as a pure look that would merely have been set into some material but that would be detachable as such from its material setting. What is set forth is, rather, a visage of something, a countenance inseparable from—inconceivable apart from—the face on which it appears. It is the visage of something that withholds itself precisely in offering its physiognomy, of something that displays its secret strength but in such a way as to keep it secret in the very display. However, its secret strength does not lie solely in the horizonality that frames the visage but also—decisively and, as it were, in another dimension—in the resistance that it offers to every invasive movement, to every effort to lay it out in utter transparency before one or the other of the senses. The complement of this secret strength of resistance is the vulnerability of the thing, that it is exposed to damage, that it can be destroyed, that its coming forth is—and is continually threatened by—a coming to pass. Resistance and its complementary vulnerability belong to—and, though withdrawn, are manifest in—all things of earth.

But what about the earth as earth, in distinction from things that are

---

32. Ibid., 165.

of earth?[33] The earth is also—indeed so primordially that the formulation borders on tautology—*of earth,* and discourse on the earth as earth would mark in this phrase (*the earth as earth*), not an ascent toward the universality of an *as such,* but the descent to the earth as itself of earth. Or rather, what would be marked is the descent that encounters and recoils from the earth's resistance to all invasive movements. One could say that the resistance offered by the earth is radical, drawing thus on a rhetorical, not to say metaphorical, system in which reference to the earth plays a major role, or, as may be said, doubling the reference, a system rooted in the earth. Or one could say—anticipating in its opposite what will have to be said of the sky—that the earth (as earth) is absolutely nonrecessive. It is that which remains and supports to such an extent that—short of an extraterrestriality still unattained—all other remaining and supporting not only is measured against that of the earth but also is in a sense always borrowed from it. One builds upon the earth.

The absolutely stabilizing function of the earth is the theme of a text written by Husserl in 1934 and entitled "Foundational Investigations of the Phenomenological Origin of the Spatiality of Nature." The text is exploratory, and its loose, informal style suggests that it was written spontaneously; it is not greatly worked out in its writing and remains something of a fragment.[34] Yet it ventures onto a terrain previously uncharted, or rather, it takes as its theme terrain as such and as it had always been taken for granted. Husserl characterizes the earth as the primal ark (*Ur-Arche*). As such, the earth, posed at the horizonal limit, is declared to be the basis for all experience of things (*die Erfahrungsboden für alle Körper*). Functioning thus, the earth is not itself experienced as a thing; at least at the originary level it does not show itself as a thing, though Husserl grants that it may be so constituted at other levels (such as that corresponding to scientific theory). As basis for all experience of things, it is also the stable ground against which all movement is apprehended. Hence—and Husserl makes much, perhaps a bit too much, of the opposition to the Copernican theory—the earth itself does not move. In Husserl's words: "The earth is the ark that first makes possible the sense of all motion and all rest. But its rest is not a mode of motion." In other words: "In its originary form of representation, the earth itself does not move and is not at rest; rest and motion have sense

---

33. Held draws this distinction, referring to "the earth as earth" and characterizing it as "the dark and closed domain from which the appearing arises forth." This rich account stops just short of critically suspending the concept of material (Klaus Held, "Sky and Earth as Invariants of the Natural Life-world," in *Phenomenology of Interculturality and Life-world,* ed. Ernst Wolfgang Orth and Chan-Fai Cheung [Freiburg/Munich: Verlag Karl Alber, 1998], 25).

34. See Derrida's note on this text in his Introduction to Edmund Husserl, *L'Origine de la Géometrie,* translation and introduction by Jacques Derrida (Paris: Presses Universitaires de France, 1962), 79. See also my extended discussion of this text in *Double Truth,* chap. 3.

only in relation to it."[35] Thus, by posing the earth as the basis for all experience of things at rest or in motion, Husserl effectively displaces the opposition that governs the Copernican debate; thereby he resituates his analysis on a quite different terrain.

The earth's mode of rest—its remaining and supporting—is radical (to continue posing this figure that is itself composed by reference to the earth). Its self-withholding, its self-closure, is radical to the same degree. Precisely in supporting things, in providing the terrain on which they move and come to rest, the earth withdraws, closes itself off. In this regard, in its self-closure, the earth displays, if in a more radical mode, the same kind of resistance met with in things of earth. As, for instance, in the stone of which Heidegger writes: "The stone presses downward and manifests its heaviness. But while this heaviness presses against us, it denies us any penetration into it. If we attempt such a penetration by breaking the rock to pieces, it still does not display in its pieces anything inward and opened. The stone has instantly withdrawn again into the same dull press and bulk of its pieces." But stone—to a degree perhaps unequaled by any other kind of thing—is *of earth*. Thus does Heidegger extend his conclusion: "The earth thus shatters every attempt to penetrate into it."[36]

As it grants the very expanse of self-showing, earth remains largely hidden. For the most part, one's vision even in what is called a natural setting embraces only trees, grasses, meadows, etc. Even if a recently plowed field or the sheer stone face of a mountain affords some intimation of earth itself (and of being *of earth*), to a large degree it withdraws outside and beneath the showing of things. It remains under cover—that is, withdrawn from vision and resistant to all invasive movement, refusing to disclose itself directly even in what remains after the most explosive impact. Even in its peculiar vulnerability, it retreats, withholding itself no less in its very desolation.

As self-secluding, earth not only remains itself closed off but also offers its closure to things, grants them a retreat of self-seclusion. Things coming to pass come finally to pass back into earth, if not into the earth. The holding sway of natural things—that is, φύσις—occurs as a self-unfolding emergence that is paired with a retreat into closure; in its largest compass, these are paired as origination and end, birth and death, coming to light and passing back into the seclusion of the earth. The earth is that to which the things that arise, that come forth into the light, are brought back, sheltered, and finally entombed. For human beings entombment is precisely

---

35. Husserl, "Grundlegende Untersuchungen zum Phänomenologischen Ursprung der Räumlichkeit der Natur," in *Philosophical Essays in Memory of Edmund Husserl*, ed. Marvin Farber (Cambridge, Mass.: Harvard University Press, 1940), 324, 309.

36. Heidegger, "Der Ursprung des Kunstwerkes," in *Holzwege*, vol. 5 of *Gesamtausgabe*, 33.

the sheltering of the dead. As when, according to Hegel, the family makes the dead individual "a member of a community that overpowers and holds under control the forces of particular substances [*Stoffe*] and the lower forms of life, which sought to unloose themselves against him and to destroy him." This is accomplished by wedding the dead kinsman "to the bosom of the earth, to the elemental imperishable individuality."[37]

While being of three kinds, earth is, as elemental, a third kind—indeed, a third kind that is, in a sense, first of all. As with all elementals, it is set apart from sensible things by its indefiniteness, its one-sidedness, and its peculiar depth. Likewise it is set apart from intelligibles, from the universal as such, by its peculiarly sensible character and its intrication in the self-showing of sensible things. As unassimilably elemental, earth is a third kind set apart from both the first and the second kinds (universal and individual, intelligible and sensible). It is a third kind from which the first and the second kinds, thought together by Hegel (earth as universal individual), suffer violence, by which they are submitted to a dislocation more radical even than that marked by Hegel. As with all elementals, earth, thought thus, stakes out an ontological region that is irreducible to the sensible, to the intelligible, and even to the unity of these as universal individual. This region is therefore such that it disrupts the otherwise exclusive operation by which being as such would be partitioned without remainder into sensible and intelligible. Yet, in the case of earth, the violence and the dislocation are all the greater by virtue of the self-seclusion of earth, which sets it apart most radically from the other two kinds. Because it withdraws itself from direct disclosure and because it is resistant to penetration and vulnerably exposed to the possibility of desolation, earth as elemental can no longer be thought either as unity of the opposed terms (intelligible/sensible), nor even as a third kind located ontologically between the intelligible and the sensible. Rather, earth is now to be thought as bringing such violence, such dislocation, to bear on the ancient partition of being that a new configuration begins to take shape: its foci will be, on the one side, the elementals, linked back to earth and sky, and, on the other side, sensible things in their monstrous self-showing.

As long as it is a matter of apprehending things, earth remains unobtrusive and inconspicuous. Even in the absence of marginal traces, it continues to operate as the elemental ground encompassing things along with the horizons of their self-showing. Yet, as with all elementals, earth can obtrude in such a way as to show itself as prodigious. Not that it comes to be disclosed directly: precisely because it is, as such, self-secluding, it resists being brought to light, resists direct disclosure, resists with an insistence not characteristic of the other elementals. How, then, does it come to be disclosed as such, as prodigious earth? How does it come to show itself as elemental?

---

37. Hegel, *Phänomenologie des Geistes*, 245.

Earth is disclosed in various respects—and always only to a degree—through its concurrences with other elementals; just as, for instance, light and atmosphere run together to form what the Impressionists called the envelope and thereby come to be mutually disclosive. One could consider, then, the way in which the rolling echo of a clap of thunder discloses the expanse and contours of earth. Or one could think of the sea. In a certain respect the sea is an opposite of earth, not in a purely formal sense but in a sense at once both sensible and elemental: the sea offers no support at all, in contrast to earth, which supports all, earth from which virtually all other support is, in one way or another, borrowed. And yet, sea belongs to earth, even dividing and articulating its surface. The relation of sea to earth is like that sustained by several other elementals: sea is an elemental opposite, and yet, rather than lying outside that to which it is opposed, rather than being situated over against the opposed term, sea belongs intimately to earth. Precisely because it is, in this way, *of earth*, it has a distinctive capacity to disclose earth along those lines—coastlines—where sea and earth run together. There are other elemental opposites, too, destructive ones, for instance, such as volcanic eruptions and earthquakes, which, though of earth, suspend the support and security granted by earth. Thus opposed yet belonging to earth, these monstrous elemental occurrences serve also to disclose earth.

Yet what to the highest degree is set opposite to earth, while also, even if most remotely, belonging to it, is sky. One could say, designating both sides of the relation, that sky is—to the highest degree—the opposite of earth. It is sky, above all, that draws vision upward and instils the very sense of height, of unlimited ascent. No less than earth, sky bounds all manifestation of things; even when not itself seen, even when the most marginal traces are lacking, sky encompasses the things that are seen as well as the horizons from within which they shine forth.

One knows, of course, that there is no such thing as the sky. But only extraterrestriality (actual or theoretical) can confirm this, and, as long as one is true to the earth, one will continue to behold the heaven above. Yet still, in another sense, there is no such thing as the sky: the sky, even more radically than the earth, is not a thing but an elemental. Earth and sky are joined in such a way as to grant the expanse in which all manifestation of things takes place.

As opposed to the nonrecessive, closed bearing of earth, its self-seclusion, sky is recessive and open, indeed to such an extent that, arching over the earth, it effects the very opening of the expanse where things come to pass and come to be manifest. In the sky this arching cannot, as with, for instance, an architectural arch, be seen as such. What primarily discloses it is, rather, the joining of sky to earth, the shape, as it were, of the horizon where they meet.

A clear, daytime sky is sheer recession. Its depth is so peculiar that one

can say even that it has no depth. But this is not because it is simply surface—it is not surface at all—but because it is absolute recession, because
it has a depth so absolute that it is identical with absolution from depth
as such.[38]

All elementals display a peculiar form of one-sidedness, a form differentiated to a degree from that form of one-sidedness characteristic of things,
the one-sidedness linked to adumbration by profile or aspect. In the case
of sky this differentiation is absolute. Sky offers no profiles whatsoever; it
shows always the same face, which is, then, in a sense no face at all. One
may, of course, see only part of the sky or even none at all, depending on
one's location and on the extent of the cloud cover. But one sees the sky
always from the same perspective—or rather, so much so that the very character of perspective is effaced, and one can more readily say that vision of
the sky is nonperspectival. While opening the very expanse of all spacings,
there belongs to its self-showing no spacing at all. Sky is pure radiance,
pure shining, a shining not set within spacings, a shining that is not the
shining of anything.

Nothing is more *of the sky* than clouds, and yet clouds interrupt the shining, and thus, while belonging to the sky, they pose an opposite to the pure
radiance that sky is. Scattered clouds (cumulus ones, for instance) display
a certain depth in the form of voluminosity; as they run together with the
sky, this depth of the clouds serves to accentuate, by contrast, the absolute
depth (= absolution from depth) of the sky. If the clouds are in movement,
such movement serves to disclose, again by contrast, the utter immobility
of the sky. Indeed, sky is so absolutely immobile that one cannot even determine a sense in which one might say that sky moves. Like the earth, its
immobility is such that it hardly remains within the compass of the opposition between movement and rest. To be sure, one observes movements in
the sky, the movements of clouds but also—if less perceptibly as such—of
the sun, the moon, and the stars; but these movements occur against the
absolute immobility of the sky.

Everything about the sky has to do with light—with brightness and darkness, color and shading. All changes of the sky—though not those of things

---

38. Kandinsky touches upon the recessive and nonrecessive characters of sky and earth,
respectively, in a discussion of the colors akin to earth and sky: "*Yellow is the typically earthly color.*
Yellow cannot be pushed very far into the depths. . . . There arise colors full of a wild power
[*Kraft*], which, however, lack any gift for depth. . . . We find this gift for depth in *blue* and
likewise, first of all theoretically, in its physical movement (1) away from the spectator, and
(2) to its own center. It is likewise if one lets blue (in whatever geometrical form) affect the
mind [*auf das Gemüt wirken*]. The inclination of blue toward depth is so great that it becomes
more intense the darker the tone, and has a more characteristic inner effect. The deeper the
blue becomes, the more it calls man toward the infinite, awakening in him a longing for the
pure and, finally, for the supersensible [*Übersinnliche*]. It is the color of the sky, just as we
picture it to ourselves when we hear the sound of the word *sky*" (Wassily Kandinsky, *Über das
Geistige in der Kunst*, 10th ed. [Bern: Benteli Verlag, 1952], 91f.).

in the sky—are simply changes of light and coloring. Even what is of the sky is—with only a few elemental exceptions—manifest primarily to vision.

Nighttime sky is equally recessive, but, without the radiance that sunlight affords, there shine only those things (if they be things) that are most thoroughly of the sky. It is a shining that will perhaps never cease to be evocative. Even extraterrestriality, far from stifling or extinguishing the evocative force of the clear, star-studded night sky, has only redetermined—while also perhaps intensifying—the attunement that such a sight now evokes: the sense of elevation evoked as one reflects on the immensity of the heaven and the remoteness (both spatially and temporally) of what one sees there; and the sense of abandonment as one reflects on the way in which the abode of everything human plunges, as if astray, through such enormous emptiness.

Between earth and sky, there are concurrences, exchanges. Most notable are those that go to constitute what is called weather. These exchanges are themselves elemental, and for the most part they take place through other, less unconditional elementals. As through rain as well as the aerial return of vapor in what one readily observes as a cycle. As through lightning and its attendant thunder. As by way of aerial dust by which the sky of a certain region acquires from the earth its distinctive color. As through light, which accords growth to things of the earth and sense to those capable thereof.

Or as, on the Aegean, the color of the sea is determined by the sky: its surface almost entirely red at the approach of sunset, it remains remarkably unchanged for a long time after the sun has set, a receptacle continuing to hold the sun's color even as night falls. Or as the mountains around Sils Maria and Soglio draw the earth upward into the dimension of height determined by the sky: almost as Gothic architecture, according to Hegel, makes the stone of a cathedral seem so light as to ascend into the heavens, so these Alpine peaks are, for all their stony massiveness, absolutely ascensional, not only by virtue of being more than "6000 feet beyond man and time"[39] but also by displaying patterns of vertical striation, lines and arcs sweeping upward as if in imitation of the pillars and arches of a Gothic cathedral.

Yet all such exchanges as well as the manifestation of the things encompassed by these elementals occur within the open expanse that is delimited as such by earth and sky. This elemental spacing first opens, in its originary guise, what will come—not without reduction—to be called place or space. But also this elemental spacing bears on the constitution of time. For it is primarily the sky that gives to those whose vision is drawn upward from the earth the measure of time, if not indeed time itself.

---

39. Nietzsche, *Ecce Homo,* in vol. VI 3 of *Werke,* 333.

7

TEMPORALITIES

A. MANIFESTIVE TIME

Always already—and not only in these words—time has been implicated in the monstrological inscription of self-showing. For instance, in the beginning, in the very question of beginning, the sense of the discourse relies on reference to a certain temporality. To mark a beginning is to project a progression, to anticipate that of which it would be the beginning.

One could say, too—mixing chronology with topology—that up to this point time has been almost everywhere. And yet, the question of time has been constantly submitted to a strategic move that time itself—if there be a time itself—makes possible, namely, that of deferment. The question of time—even the question of this question, of how this question is to be posed—has been continually deferred up to the point where, now (still temporalizing the discourse), the question can take shape as that of the locus (topos) of time. Anterior to the question of the constitution of time, this question thoroughly compounds chronology and topology, or rather, submits chronology to the topological question: discourse on time would begin with the question whether time is, as such, constitutively bound to a particular topos. It is a question of where time is, or, more precisely, of where its constitutive origin is to be traced.

This question is no pure transparency free of all recoil on that which would be approached through it. It is a question that cannot be finally disentangled, detached, from that about which it asks. In its very formulation it not only takes time for granted but also releases various doublings that set time and the question of time in relation to another time. Thus, the question broaches, though in a very formal way, the further question of multiple temporalities.

The question seems direct: Where is time? At what place—where among beings as a whole—does it properly belong? Or, if multiply located, where does it most properly belong? What is its most proper topos?

Though the question may seem direct and virtually unmediated, it is of course a very old question. It is the form in which the question of time has been handed down across the expanse of time separating what is called our time from the time of late antiquity. Along with the topological question of time, there has been handed down—across this expanse of what is called historical time—an answer that has remained remarkably constant. As early as Middle Platonism, the question of time becomes more insistently a topological question and its answer a psychological one.[1] For Plotinus time is of the soul in its movement of passage from one way of life to another; time is the spreading-out of life (διάστασις . . . ζωῆς).[2] Yet it is with Augustine, who translates διάστασις into *distentio*, that the topos of time comes to be decisively established: time belongs most properly to the soul, time is of the soul, is its stretching-out, its proper extension. For Augustine the locating of time within the soul provides the only means by which to shelter time from the threat of nonbeing. Since the past is no longer and the future is not yet and the present has no extent, no space (*spatium*), time as such can *be* only if it is somewhere where these three parts of time are sheltered from nonbeing by being secured in their presence. For Augustine it is the soul that provides such a place for time, for within the soul each part of time can be made present: "Some such different times do exist in the soul [*sunt . . . in anima*], but nowhere else that I can see. The presence [or: present—*praesens*] of what is past is memory [*memoria*]; the presence of what is present is beholding [*contuitus*—or, as Augustine goes on to say: attentiveness—*attentio*]; the presence of what is future is expectation [*expectatio*]."[3] Hence, through these operations of the soul each of the parts of time is doubled by a form of presence within the soul. Only thus is time sheltered from nonbeing, for, as Augustine writes, referring to the parts of time, "Wherever

---

1. See Rémi Brague, *Du Temps chez Platon et Aristote* (Paris: Presses Universitaires de France, 1980), 13–24, 69–71.

2. Plotinus, *Enneads* III.7.11.

3. Augustine, *Confessions* XI.20.

they are and whatever they are, it is only by being present that they are."[4] This is why they must be in the soul, why time as such must be in the soul—granted this perhaps most explicit of all declarations that the sense of being is presence.

Wherever and whatever time is, it *is not* except as doubled in the soul; thus, the double, which is (present), turns out to be, not the double, but time itself. Hence, the move is one by which time is withdrawn from nature (where it could not *be*) and, in this very withdrawal, is determined by the determination of being as presence: the physics of time gives way to what could be called a metaphysics of time, taking *metaphysics* to signify nothing other than philosophy as such, but philosophy considered with respect to its founding identification of being with presence. What is remarkable is that such metaphysics of time involves the double determination expressed by the double genitive: on the one hand, time comes to be determined by metaphysics, that is, on the basis of the metaphysical predetermination of being as presence, time is determined as being of the soul; yet, on the other hand, precisely through this predetermination, through the founding reference of being to presence, metaphysics proves to have been itself determined by reference to time.

Much of the history of the concept of time remains to be told, primarily because it is not simply a history of determination and redetermination yielding a series of concepts of time but is also, indeed first of all, a movement across the interval between two temporalities, from that which determines metaphysics itself (time as the sense of being) to that which metaphysics, in turn, determines (time as belonging to the soul or subject). In order to tell this history, one would need, for instance, to mark the invariance within the Kantian transformation: when time is taken as the very form of sense, its absolute precedence as form over the sensible manifold only radicalizes the withdrawal of time from nature into the soul or subject. Both as the form of inner sense and as submitted to the a priori determination that Kant calls transcendental schematism, time belongs originarily to the subject, even though to a subject that brings objects (phenomena) forth in such a way as to bestow upon them a certain temporality. If, on the one hand, Kant adheres to the metaphysical predetermination by virtue of the priority he accords to intuition, he, on the other hand, advances toward the limit by means of the proximity that he establishes between time and imagination.

It is Heidegger who has radicalized to the limit the sheltering of time within the soul, its being *of* the soul, *of* the subject. In his 1924 lecture "The Concept of Time," in which he first outlines the project of *Being and Time*, Heidegger begins with the question "What is time?" In the course of the lecture he displaces the question, replacing it, first, with the question "Who

___

4. Ibid., XI.18.

is time?" and, then, with the question "Am I my time?" By moving through this series of questions while at the same time undoing the traditional determinations of the being that we ourselves are, redetermining this being as Dasein, Heidegger arrives at an answer to the question of time, one that radicalizes to the limit the placement of time in the soul. The questions of the *what* and *who* of time coalesce with the topological question to such an extent that Heidegger's radicalizing answer responds to the entire complex of questions. For what he writes is that "Time is Dasein."[5]

In a certain respect this answer remains intact in *Being and Time*. And yet, Heidegger also expands the mere identification so that it comes to read: time is the sense of the being of Dasein. Thus mediated, the identification becomes the site of a decisive tension: on the one hand, *Being and Time* reaffirms—indeed at its most profound level of analysis—that time is Dasein, that time, originarily understood, is precisely what Dasein most originarily *is;* while, on the other hand, mediating the identity so as to set time apart as the sense of the being of Dasein, the existential analytic declares that time is beyond being, ἐπέκεινα τῆς οὐσίας, in the Platonic phrase that Heidegger cites in precisely this connection in his lectures.[6] The tension is evident: How can time be both identical with a being, Dasein, and yet beyond being? Even if, in *Being and Time,* this tension (as well as others linked to it) is not allowed to extend to the point where it would begin to distort the very shape of the project and to broach a thorough reconfiguration, there are unmistakable indicators that a secret mutation is in preparation, as if by the very force of things themselves. One such indicator is the remarkable passage about the sun and the day. This passage occurs near the end of the Second Division ("Dasein and Temporality"), as Heidegger is engaged in setting apart other temporalities in their origination from the proper temporality of Dasein. Heidegger writes: "In its thrownness Dasein is delivered over to the change of day and night. Day with its brightness gives the possibility of sight; night takes this away." For this reason sunrise and sunset, granting and withdrawing the sight-bestowing light, demarcate, as Heidegger says, "the 'most natural' measure of time, the day."[7] He observes, too, that even the further division of the day remains, in the first instance, bound to the sunlight, to its progression and to the progression of the sun across the sky. Even if outside this immediate context Heidegger continues to gesture toward an originary time that would remain anterior, the time of which he writes in this remarkable passage is not a time buried in the depths of the soul; it is a time of light, of the sun, of the sky.

---

5. Heidegger, *Der Begriff der Zeit* (Tübingen: Max Niemeyer, 1989), 26.

6. Heidegger, *Die Grundprobleme der Phänomenologie*, vol. 24 of *Gesamtausgabe* (Frankfurt a.M.: Vittorio Klostermann, 1975), 402. This lecture course was presented in summer semester 1927, just months after the publication of *Being and Time*.

7. Heidegger, *Sein und Zeit*, 412f.

Yet, even as Heidegger insists on originary time and grants to Dasein's temporality a certain anteriority, his very determination of such temporality as the "originary 'outside-of-itself'" puts the *itself,* the would-be origin, in question, presupposing it and at once, suspending it, displacing it as simple origin.[8] To say nothing of another necessity: if Dasein is always already thrown amidst things with which it cannot but concern itself, then originary time will always already have doubled itself in what Heidegger calls the time of concern (*die besorgte Zeit*). This time other than originary time is both the time operative in Dasein's concern with innerworldly things and the time with which, in its various dealings, Dasein is concerned and reckons. Would-be originary time will always already have been contaminated by this outside, will always already have drifted into this other time, eroding the distinction between the original and its double.[9]

A comparable displacement of time will be effected if one alters the reading of the formula ever so slightly in a direction that may indeed not have been foreseen but that, nonetheless, is latent in certain of Heidegger's analyses and reflections. Now the formula "Time is Dasein" would be read, not as a formula of identification, equating time with a certain (kind of) being, but rather as a topological formula, declaring that time belongs to the *Da,* to the open expanse where things come to show themselves. The formula would thus assign time to this very place of places.

Through these moves, the ecstatic character of time itself would be doubled in an ecstasis toward the open expanse of self-showing, an ecstasis that would effectively destabilize the *itself* and install another time in the open expanse without simply submitting it to the anteriority of a would-be time itself. Dislocated from the being that has been called soul, subject, and, most openly, Dasein (the being that we ourselves are—leaving aside for the time being the question of the determinability of the *we ourselves*), time would have its proper locus there where things show themselves, there where the rising and setting sun gives the most natural measure of time, measuring out the parts of the day by progression across the sky.

Time offers itself there where things show themselves. There is time precisely at the site of manifestation. To be sure, time is not simply constituted on the basis of the manifestation of things, if for no other reason than that the self-showing of things has itself a certain temporal character. It is a matter, rather, of interlacement, of the way in which time and the self-showing

---

8. Heidegger's formula, "*Zeitlichkeit ist das ursprüngliche 'Ausser-sich' an und für sich selbst*" (ibid., 329), is a veritable thicket of burgeoning questions. What is the *itself* of something that is *outside itself?* How can what is outside itself still somehow be itself? How can what is outside-of-itself be in itself (*an sich selbst*)? How can it be outside of itself in itself? And how can it be for itself, across what kind of interval and through what kind of apprehension or presentation? What can be the sense of *for itself* once the modern metaphysics of the subject (spirit, consciousness, etc.) has fallen away?

9. See *Echoes: After Heidegger,* chap. 2, esp. p. 69.

of things are intertwined in a connection of the utmost intimacy.[10] Each is implicated in the other, yet in a way that maintains, even secures, the alterity between them. In showing itself, a thing proves to have its time; and time gives itself precisely as the time of self-showing things, not in the sense of an empty continuum that self-showing would somehow come to fill up, but rather as a time constituted (if one can continue to borrow this word from phenomenology without at least also crossing it out) in the very midst of the self-showing, a time so interlaced with manifestation that it is as if woven from the very depth of sensible things. One could say that time and self-showing come about at once, at the same time; yet this simultaneity is determined primarily by the interlacement and not simply by reference to another time posited as an anterior measure.

If a thing is to show itself as the sensible thing that it itself is, it must shine forth in and as an image. It must expose its surface to apprehension, must come to be present, must come to presence. Yet, just as this upsurge of the presence of the thing falls short of self-showing, so, too, does this presence fall short of constituting the present. Presence is not yet a present of time. Virtually everything depends on this differentiation, which the word *praesens* (as well as its modern transliterations) tends to efface. If the present is reduced to presence, to the presence of the present, then the initial—and, indeed, decisive—move has been made toward drawing time back from nature into the interiority of the soul.

A decisive countermove against this reduction is carried out in Husserl's phenomenology of time-consciousness, even though Husserl stops short of letting the move he carries out recoil upon and subvert the assimilation of time to the soul (conceived subjectively as consciousness). Beginning in fact with the oft-cited statement from Augustine about time ("I know well enough what it is, provided nobody asks me; but if I am asked what it is and try to explain, I do not know"),[11] Husserl develops a rigorous analysis of retentional consciousness and of its inherence in the consciousness of the present. He stresses the uniqueness of retention, contrasting it with sensing and with the entire sphere of reproductive acts. Husserl writes: "The retentional tone is not a present tone [*kein gegenwärtiger*] but precisely a tone 'primarily remembered' in the now: it is not really present [*nicht reell vorhanden*] in the retentional consciousness."[12] This says: what is held in reten-

---

10. Commenting on Hölderlin's expression "Alles ist innig," Heidegger writes: "Die Innigkeit meint kein Verschmelzen und Verlöschen der Unterscheidungen. Innigkeit nennt das Zusammengehören des Fremden, das Walten der Befremdung, den Anspruch der Scheu" (Heidegger, *Erläuterungen zu Hölderlins Dichtung*, vol. 4 of *Gesamtausgabe* [Frankfurt a.M.: Vittorio Klostermann, 1981], 196).

11. Augustine, *Confessions* XI.14. Cited by Husserl in *Zur Phänomenologie des Inneren Zeitbewusstseins*, vol. 10 of *Husserliana* (The Hague: Martinus Nijhoff, 1966), 3. The lectures that constitute the first (and principal) part of this text date from 1905.

12. Husserl, *Zur Phänomenologie des Inneren Zeitbewusstseins*, 31.

tion now (in the present) is not itself present (for instance, bearing some mark that would serve to indicate its pastness). In other words, in the present there is no presence of the past; rather, in the present, the past (the proximal past, as held in retention) is given *as past*: "Just as I see now-being [*das Jetztsein erschaue*] in perception . . . so I see [*erschaue*] the past in memory, insofar as it is primary memory [= retention]; the past is given therein, and the givenness of the past is memory."[13] In retention the past is given in an originary, not a representational, manner; yet it is given without being present, without being a present past, without there being a presence of the past, without presence constituting the being of the past. To apprehend a temporal object—to apprehend a thing as having its time—requires more than merely intuiting now its presence; one must also intuit now the past as past, the past of which there is now no presence.[14] This determination of retention is indeed so radical in the way it calls into question the identity of being and presence that Husserl's very language is driven to the point where it borders on incoherence: to speak of an intuition of the past as past is to subvert the very sense of intuition (as intuition *of presence*). Once the present is granted an extension beyond presence, another language is needed, one more exorbitant.

If the upsurging, shining presence of the thing is to unfold into a self-showing in which, at once, a present—and that is to say, time itself—is constituted, it is necessary that the appropriate horizons come to bound the upsurge of presence. By force of imagination, the lateral and peripheral horizons must be gathered around the image as which the thing shines forth. By being installed in these horizons, the thing acquires—that is, comes to show itself as having—the density, the depth, and the setting proper to a self-identical sensible thing.

Thereby it also comes to show itself as temporal, as having its time, which is also the very time of the self-showing. Hence, again, the interlacement.

The lateral horizon is most consequential in this connection. As coming to bound the shining, frontal image, this horizon opens the present to nonpresence. For the lateral images, spaced in and as the lateral horizon, are precisely the profiles of the thing that are not now present, the aspects of which there is now no presence as such. And yet, the very orientation of the lateral horizon to the frontal image, the very bearing of the nonpresent lateral images on the thing present in the frontal image, lies in their character as aspects that *could* come to *presence at other times*. The lateral images, which in the horizon are submitted to spacing rather than brought to presence, are precisely the faces that the thing can, in the proximal past, have

---

13. Ibid., 34.

14. "An act that claims to give a temporal object itself must contain in itself 'apprehensions of the now,' 'apprehensions of the past,' etc., specifically, as originarily constituting apprehensions" (ibid., 39).

turned to one's vision or that it can, in the proximal future, set before one's eyes. In the very sense of the lateral images, the proximal past and future are implicated. In the very sense of the horizonal nonsense that belongs to the sensible, there is implicated a temporality in which the present is opened to past and future in such a way that presence is mingled—or, from the standpoint that identifies being with presence, contaminated—with nonpresence. If, as Husserl insists, the proximal past and future are indeed given, it is in this way, for the most part, that they are given, namely, as belonging to the very sense of lateral horizonality, as borne and offered by the horizonal moments, which, therefore, like spacing as such, are neither merely spatial nor merely temporal but in a certain way are both at once.

Though more indirectly and only in certain specific configurations, peripheral horizons also contribute to the constitution of time. Perhaps the peripheral horizons that most manifestly serve to let time be given concretely are those that are specifically instrumental. For instance, in the horizonal network that links certain tools to a certain product to be made for someone or other, time is thoroughly implicated. The lines of implication could be expressed by one who, situated by such a network, interpreted a typical involvement as follows: *now that* I reach for the tool needed in order that what I am making will be finished *when later* someone comes for it, I find the tool just where it was *when formerly* I used it.[15]

As horizons come to bound presence, time comes to be given there amidst the self-showing of things themselves. Yet horizons come to bound presence only by force of imagination. Thus, it is by force of imagination that time is constituted, specifically, in the sense of coming to be borne concretely there in the self-showing of things themselves. It is in this sense—and by way of sensible nonsense—that imagination draws things into time. It is in this exorbitant sense that this trait, the relation of imagination to time, to the very constitution of time, can be redrawn in philosophy at the limit.

Drawing things into time by force of imagination does not itself occur in some other time that would be posited as simply anterior, as a kind of double of time before time. On the contrary, from the moment imagination draws things into time—always already—it is itself drawn into a singular engagement with time, with the same time as that of self-showing things. Yet its engagement with this time, indeed with any and all temporalities, is unlike that of things and their self-showing. It is precisely the engagement of imagination with time that is indicated by its character as, at once, memorial and originary.

As, at once, both memorial and originary, imagination gathers the horizons in such a way that it is, at once, as though, prior to the draft, they had

---

15. Such interpretation is what Heidegger calls *Zeitangabe*. The relational structure that it makes explicit he calls *Datierbarkeit*. See *Sein und Zeit*, §79.

already been there, in a kind of past, and as though imagination first brings them into being, originating them as one originates something that comes from the future. Yet not even that most forceful force of imagination can force together presence and its horizons. Not even this force can transform the opposition between presence and horizon into a system of uniform presence. Not even this force can stabilize as a mode of presence the being-together of frontal image and horizon. On the contrary, this force can only compose an interplay in which imagination oscillates, wavers, hovers, between protraction and retraction, drawing the horizons toward the locus of presence, spacing them around the *there*, while also, since they cannot be brought to presence, withdrawing them, setting them apart from the locus of presence. Through this hovering, presence and its horizons are drawn together in the same round in which they are set apart (in a togetherness and apartness that are themselves irreducible to presence), and it is in this hovering that imagination constitutes time, brings it to be concretely offered amidst things themselves. The round cannot but perpetually recommence, and it is precisely this perpetually recommencing that renders the form of the present ideal[16] or, as Hegel would have it, universal. One arrives always at still another present: the present is infinitely repeatable in a repetition that, rather than presupposing time (across which, then, there would be repetition), belongs to the very temporalizing of this manifestive time.

B. POLYTOPICAL TIME

Time is also elemental.
Time is, above all, elemental.
Time has this other topos, has as its topos not only the expanse of self-showing things but also the encompassing elements. Time is borne and offered not only by things but also, above all, by the elementals, by some singularly, by others in their concurrence.

That such time is borne and offered by the elementals does not prevent its being also the time of these elementals, the time in which they come to show themselves as such, either singularly or in their concurrence. As with manifestive time, so here too there is no need to posit another time, a double of time, in which (as in an empty continuum) the elemental bearing and offering of time as well as the singular or concurrent manifestation of the elementals would run its course. With elemental time, between the elements and their temporalities, there is interlacement.

Homer's "circling years"[17] belong to elemental time, for it is in the sky,

---

16. "The ideality of the form (*Form*) of presence itself implies in effect that it can repeat itself to infinity, that its re-turn, as a return of the same, is necessary to infinity and is inscribed in presence itself" (Derrida, *La Voix et le Phénomène*, 75f.).

17. "περιτροπέων ἐνιαυτός" (Homer, *Iliad* II:295).

in the declinatory cycle of the sun's course, that the circle is drawn most distinctly, traced out in an openness where any who persist will be able to follow its trace. Yet it is also traced on the earth, in the comings and goings of the seasons, in the ways in which the comings and goings of the seasons are signaled by natural, more or less elemental occurrences: in the fresh rains and the buds and blossoms of spring, in the brilliant foliage and the shortening days of fall, in the stark outlines and the desolation of winter, in the gentle warmth and the exuberant bounty of summer. It is traced in the almost naked countryside of early spring, when the green is only beginning to sprout and, to these tender buds seen by the eye, imagination adds the flowers, the fruits, and even the mysteries to come, concentrating in the present moment the times that are to come, that is, drawing itself from this moment across the expanse of the season and the seasons to come.

Days, too, are traced elementally—most distinctly, in the quotidian progression of the sun but also in the way sunlight runs together with other, more terrestrial elements, their concurrences and coincidences determining the varying quality of the light in the course of the day. As with a stone protruding from the earth into brilliant sunlight: absolutely impenetrable to the light, the stone concentrates the light precisely by limiting the illumination to the surface; it lets one almost see the light itself, and, in the brilliance of the shining as well as in the ever varying distribution and configuration with which the light is spread over the stone's surface, there is traced the time and course of the day. To say nothing of the shortening and lengthening of shadows in the course of the day: merely casting a shadow suffices to make the stone and indeed virtually anything a kind of natural clock. The day is traced, too, in the rising of the morning mist and in the chill and dampness of the night air, in the coolness of early morning and in the intense heat of a mid-summer afternoon.

In painting, certain visible traces of elemental temporalities can become the principal theme, even to such an extent that these traces may come to obscure the things that go to make up a natural landscape. Thus, a kind of reversal can occur: whereas ordinarily one sees illuminated things and only marginally the illumination itself, painting the illumination over the things can obscure them and render a new, uncommon visibility to the illumination and to the tracing of elemental time that it accomplishes. It is just such a reversal that is operative when Monet, for instance, paints the atmospheric spread of light over a landscape in which, in the painting, hardly any things remain distinctly visible as such. By painting such natural traces, by painting the atmospheric spread of light as it occurs at certain times of day and in certain seasons, Monet comes perhaps as close as one ever can to rendering time visible, to presenting, in painting, the times of day and the times of the year. The result is especially forceful when, as in the series paintings (for instance, the wheatstacks), the landscape and the focal object remain virtually the same in all the paintings, so that what distinguishes each individual painting in the series is the particular spread of light and the particular times of day and year that are traced therein.[18]

The traces determine the texture of elemental time, weaving together time and element, interlacing them so intimately that the element bears and offers the temporality, which, in turn, is the time of the element, the time of its manifestation. The interlacement of time and element even determines, though only to an extent, the temporalities borne by the natural things encompassed by the element. As one patiently watches the snowflakes gently falling (in the absence of wind), blanketing all things, quieting all sounds, making everything distant fade into invisibility and silence, a certain quiet receptiveness may come over one's vision. This gift lets one sense the singular texture of a time of snowfall, which, afterwards, in reflection, one will contrast perhaps with the frenetic pace of the everyday, but which, as one is encompassed by the element—as one stands at the edge of a field, seeing no one, hearing no one, released from everyday involvements, looking out across the snowy expanse toward the mountains beyond, hearing only the quiet sound of the snowflakes impinging on one's coat and hood, feeling them as they gently strike one's face—is a time of suspension that seems almost like a suspension of time. Under the spell of such a time, even the most familiar things assume a different tempo, the snow-laden branches of the evergreens, for instance, swaying in a way unmistakably determined by the encompassing element.

Among all the temporalities with their various topoi, there is one that has a distinctive precedence. Its precedence is not one of reducibility: this distinctive temporality is not an originary time from which all others could be shown to arise by doublings adherent to particular topoi. It is not a common root to which every other temporality could be reduced by detachment from the particular topos of that temporality. This distinctively precedent temporality is not such as to cancel the polytopical character of time; it is not such that all other temporalities can finally be gathered to its singular topos and thus submitted to it. Its precedence consists only in its giving a measure that, because it is there for all to see, can be brought to bear on—though not, finally, to determine—all other temporalities.

The precedence of this temporality derives from the distinctive openness of its topos. For this topos, the sky, is also the topos of an elemental movement, the quotidian progression of the sun across the sky. This time of the heavens is measured out by the course of the sun and, first of all, as the alternation between day and night. What is distinctive about it and gives it its precedence is that this measuring out of time, this temporality borne and offered by the sun as it traverses the uranic dome, is there for all to see, whatever their other engaging temporalities may be. One could say, as

---

18. See my discussion in *Shades — Of Painting at the Limit* (Bloomington: Indiana University Press, 1998), chap. 1.

194

does Heidegger, that this distinctive temporality has a public character and that all temporalities become public (so as to belong to what Heidegger calls world-time) only through relation to this temporality; but in this designation, *public* (öffentlich) has only the root-sense of openness (of being open [*offen*]),[19] as with a time openly measured out, open to the view of any and all. This temporality is thus assignable—for instance, within an instrumental network—in a way that all can share "under the same sky."[20] Hence, Heidegger's very remarkable declaration: "'Time' first shows itself in the sky, that is, precisely there where one comes across it in directing oneself naturally *according to it,* so that time even becomes identified with the sky."[21] Though it is unlikely that Heidegger is alluding here to Plato, recent research and interpretation have shown that in the *Timaeus* time is identified with the starry heaven (οὐρανός),[22] so that in this context the expression *uranic time* is tautological. On the other hand, in Heidegger's declaration there is a hint of reservation in the marks enclosing *time:* presumably Heidegger's intent is to avoid identifying uranic time with time as such and, hence, to retain the differentiation between uranic time and the originary temporality of Dasein. Be this as it may, the question is whether Heidegger can prevent uranic time, interpreted as world-time, from assimilating all other temporalities, thus reducing the polytopical spread of temporalities to the single differentiation between originary time and self-interpreted time (as gathered in world-time).

But what about existential temporality, even granted the complications (detailed above) that come to compromise its allegedly originary character? Does the existential analysis of time ever succeed in freeing itself completely from the time of presence and self-presence?[23] Does it not, in alleging its theme to be originary time, continue to reinscribe the withdrawal of time from nature into the soul? Does the time of the existential analysis not remain a psychic time, a time of the ψυχή, of what came to be called the soul?

Here everything depends on whether or not the existential analysis can relinquish centering (grounding) all temporalities in psychic time, whether

---

19. See Hermann Paul, *Deutsches Wörterbuch* (Tübingen: Max Niemeyer Verlag, 1966), 473.

20. Heidegger, *Sein und Zeit*, 413.

21. Ibid., 419.

22. See my discussion in *Chorology: On Beginning in Plato's "Timaeus"* (Bloomington: Indiana University Press, 1999), chap. 2.

23. Derrida poses this question most pointedly: "Thus the existential analyses of time—to the extent that they remain, as it seems to me, mute or spellbound with regard to oneiric temporality (and thus phantastic or phantasmatic temporality, festive temporality, and by that very fact the virtual temporality of the poetic or literary, and so on)—also remain surreptitiously regulated by the time of presence-to-self as wakefulness and self-consciousness, no matter how vigorous the denials. . . . It is a certain phantasticity (of which the oneiric would here be an example) that is misunderstood or reduced every time" (Derrida, "Tense," in *The Path of Archaic Thinking*, ed. Maly, 51).

it can decisively interrupt the gathering of all temporalities to that of the ψυχή, soul, subject, or even Dasein. If such an interruption were to be sustained, then there would be nothing to prevent taking the ψυχή as indeed one of the many topoi belonging to polytopical time. Then, continuing to sustain the interruption, one could begin reinscribing within philosophy at the limit the rich and highly differentiated analyses of psychic time that have been handed down, reinscribing them to the point where their exorbitant moments would take shape.

Though nothing would be gained—and indeed much lost—by merely reversing their order, now taking manifestive time to be originary and psychic time to be founded and secondary, there would be need eventually, once psychic time has been reinscribed at the limit, to interrogate the ways in which psychic time and manifestive time communicate. The question would become: To what extent does psychic time involve an instatical recoil from manifestive time? To what extent is the time of oneself, the time in which one is with oneself and, at once, the time borne and offered by this being with oneself, the time of solitude (*Einsamkeit*), deflected back from the time of the self-showing of things and of one's apprehension of them? To what extent can one—despite all differences—reaffirm what Kant wrote in refutation of idealism: "the determination of my existence in time is possible only through the existence of actual things which I perceive outside me"?[24]

To say nothing of other temporalities, of temporalities attached to other topoi such as the dream or phantasy or even certain kinds of texts. Or the temporality that, in distinction from that measured and traced by the stone protruding from the earth into brilliant sunlight, is borne by the stone itself, a time to which movement is absolutely alien, a time of utter repose, a time that is utter repose, a lithic time, a time of the earth. As long as one forgoes the move of reestablishing a temporality as originary, there will be hope of according proper differentiation to oneiric time, phantastic time, festive time, fictive time, the virtual time of poetry and literature and even of certain "theoretical" texts, as well as to psychic time, manifestive time, uranic time, and geolithic time. Translation between these, movement from one to another (yet without reduction), while it takes place constantly without being thematized as such, will always be precarious and will require hovering—as only imagination can—between different temporalities that are, nonetheless, as temporalities, most intimately connected.

---

24. Kant, *Kritik der reinen Vernunft*, B 275f.

8

PROPRIETIES

A. FROM WATCH TO ACTION

summary

As things shine forth from within their configuration of showing, one apprehends them. Drawn by force of imagination, this configuration gathers around things both their systems of lateral and peripheral horizons and the concurrent elementals that encompass them. When thus released into their depth, compacted in their density, and granted their setting not only amidst adjacent things and locally operative networks but also finally upon the earth and beneath the sky, things come to show themselves. Yet, precisely by virtue of their depth, density, and settings, they retreat in their very self-showing, withholding themselves from shameless scrutiny, secured still in their secret strength. Then it is, in this chiaroscuro of self-showing, that one apprehends them. From themselves. Also, in some measure, as themselves.

It would be difficult to find—or even to invent—any mode of human comportment to things that does not in some way rely on such apprehension. Even in comportment to oneself or to others—hence to proprieties

197

incomparable to that of things—such apprehension continues to operate, even though, alone, it is insufficient.

Yet apprehension is never simply aloof from the thing apprehended, no matter how distant it may in fact be and no matter how rigorously the objectivity of the apprehension may have been secured. On the one hand, a certain detachment is, to be sure, required: the thing must be released to its self-showing, and, depending on the horizonal constitution of the thing, this release may require anything from mere observation to active manual engagement. But, on the other hand, release and apprehension can issue only from one's belonging to the elemental configuration of the thing's self-showing. Even in the mere upsurge of the image, a certain belonging is already effective, indeed constitutive: it is what prevents the image from congealing into a quasi-thing, what gives it its delicacy, what renders it duplicitous. Yet, on the other hand, this belonging is precisely what has to be relinquished in releasing the thing to its self-showing. This release of the thing to itself takes place in the gathering of its horizons and of the concurrent elementals.

Yet, as imagination comes to gather horizons and elementals around the thing that one will have sensed in and as the shining image, one is oneself gathered to the self-showing of the thing. This being-gathered is not merely a matter of a certain comportment or bearing taken up toward the horizonal and the elemental, a comportment that presumably would be prompted or solicited by the horizonal and elemental traces borne by the image. Neither is it merely a matter, in the case of the elementals, of one's being encompassed, though indeed their very operation as elementals involves such encompassing. For, as imagination comes to gather what belongs to the thing's self-showing, a double affirmation is called for: first, a receiving and accepting of the gift, a receiving that accepts the gift as gift; and, second, offering oneself as the site of the drawing through which imagination drafts the elemental configuration of the self-showing of things. As the gift of imagination comes, coming as if from nowhere, hence as free, pure gift, one will say, letting resound an abysmal freedom that is necessity itself: yes, yes. Even as mute, this double affirmation will be almost indistinguishable from the most originary opening to speech as such, to λόγος.

To say this gathering, this belonging, of oneself to the elemental configuration of self-showing, one might recall the old word *preception,* now rare but once used to signify that which must be had in advance, a kind of pre-notion, in order that one be able to set about searching for something without straying into a maze of infinity, that is, in order that such limits come into play as first make a search possible. *Preception* could begin to engender the sense of this belonging only if, on the other hand, it were twisted free of all significations oriented—as *precept* largely is—to preconception, to a certain intelligible content. What would be decisive is the exorbitant sense of *preception* (*praeceptionem*) as taking beforehand, receiving in advance.

In this regard one could also venture a remembrance of a certain ancient discourse to which the word *reception* alludes. *Reception* is to be heard, first of all, in the sense of entertaining: not as mere amusement (as in the phenomenological caricature of imagination as the self-entertainment of conjuring up images), but as hospitably receiving others into one's home. A discourse of reception is broached in the opening words of the *Timaeus*, in which Socrates' enigmatic counting (one, two, three—) gives way to his query as to the whereabouts of the fourth of the guests of yesterday, the hosts of today. As the dialogue begins, Socrates is being received by these hosts (ἑστιατώρ); they are receiving him hospitably, as one hospitably receives (ἑστιάω) guests who have come to one's home, welcoming them and accepting, first of all, whatever gifts—for instance, gifts of discourse or of remembrance or of both—they may have brought, inviting them into one's abode, to one's very hearth (ἑστία), protected by the goddess. Hospitable reception can also be said—and will be said at the threshold of the chorology—by the word ὑποδοχή, which also signifies receptacle and is another name for the χώρα. The utterly exorbitant sense of this discourse is dyadic: receiving into one's abode that which one could perhaps only have dreamed of receiving, receiving it in such a way that this abode becomes the receptacle in which things, coming to pass, have a certain look and a name, show themselves and let themselves be said.

At the point where Timaeus would finally say the truth of reception, were truth and reception not utterly discontinuous, his discourse recoils on itself and puts itself down as a bastard discoursing, hardly trustworthy, a kind of daydream. In somewhat the same way—and indeed in the very same way that one finds in other dialogues such as the *Cratylus* and the *Republic*—one may turn to comedy in its capacity to expose the nonsense that threatens discourse, in its capacity to infuse a certain nonsense into discourse in such a way as to say—even if without saying, even if precisely by not saying—just that which otherwise remains most elusive. By turning, in particular, to a certain Shakespearean comedy of the watch, one can provide a comic supplement to the discourses of *preception* and *reception*. For, if the very context of comedy makes one hesitant simply to propose *watch* as a way of saying how one is gathered to the elemental configuration of self-showing, the play of sense and nonsense around this word exposes unmistakably its pertinence to the saying of this gathering.

Picture, then, the ludicrous scene in *Much Ado about Nothing* in which Master Constable Dogberry and his compartner Verges assemble the men who are to keep watch around Signior Leonato's door. The charge that Dogberry gives them echoes throughout with malapropisms, which have the effect of infusing a moment of nonsense into everything that he, Verges, and the men say. The entire scene consists of the charge, in which the watch is told what is required in keeping watch, what belongs to a watch, and then the watch itself, through which Borachio is exposed and then arrested.

Though Watch insists that

> we know what belongs to a watch[,][1]

the entire charge circulates around telling Watch what belongs to a watch. For instance, Watch asks about how to deal with a thief:

> If we know him to be a thief, shall we not lay hands on him?

> (III.iii.53–54)

Dogberry answers:

> Truly, by your office you may, but I think they that touch pitch will be defiled. The most peaceable way for you, if you do take a thief, is to let him show himself what he is, and steal out of your company.

> (III.iii.55–59)

A bit later Dogberry adds:

> . . . for indeed the watch ought to offend no man, and it is an offence to stay a man against his will.

> (III.iii.78–80)

Then, finally, as he is about to leave, Dogberry sums up what he has said about the watch:

> Be vigilant, I beseech you.

> (III.iii.92)

To keep watch is to be vigilant, to be on the lookout for whatever may appear, to remain wakeful to the possibility that something or someone might suddenly appear from under the cloak of darkness or in some other fashion. Keeping watch requires stillness; it requires that one forgo both speech and action, lest these warn those about to appear and allow them to elude the watch. To keep watch is to remain quietly vigilant, attentive yet

---

1. Shakespeare, *Much Ado about Nothing*, III.iii.37–38. Citations are from the Arden text edited by A. R. Humphreys (London: Methuen, 1981). While it is possible that the nonspecific designation *Watch* simply indicates that the speeches are left to be distributed at the actors' discretion, the pattern of specificity and nonspecificity is striking. At the beginning of the scene a distinction is made between *First Watch* and *Second Watch*. But then, at precisely the point where the theme becomes the watch as such, what belongs to it and what (like babbling and talking) does not, the words are put into the mouth of a character designated simply as *Watch*. Then, later in the scene, once the watch begins (or—following some editions—at the point where the watch comes to an end and the arrest is then made), the differentiation between *First Watch* and *Second Watch* reappears.

detached from (undefiled by) the scene on which therefore something or someone can come to show itself as what it is.

Precisely because the watch is thus determined, all manner of incongruities arise, as it were, around the edges of the watch. For instance, in giving the charge, warning the men especially about babbling and talking, Dogberry himself babbles on almost incoherently:

> You shall also make no noise in the streets: for, for the watch to babble and to talk is most tolerable, and not to be endured.
>
> (III.iii.33–36)

Watch's response includes the assurance about the men's knowing what belongs to a watch:

> We will rather sleep than talk; we know what belongs to a watch.
>
> (III.iii.37–38)

As Dogberry drolly inverts the sense and babbles on, the nonsense of his babbling serves to expose how ludicrously the charge (telling what belongs to a watch) violates precisely what belongs to a watch.

The nonsense fails to disappear even when, fully charged, the men set about keeping watch. In order to remain attentive to the possibility that something or someone may suddenly appear and need to be secretly observed, Watch must remain hidden and silent, standing quietly aside so as to survey and overhear whatever might come to be revealed. And yet, in putting and keeping himself on watch, Watch violates precisely this requirement. As Borachio and his confidant Conrade approach the scene of the watch, Watch[2] utters an aside:

> Peace! Stir not.
>
> (III.iii.94)

As the possibility that something is about to be revealed begins to take shape, Watch ventures another aside:

> Some treason, masters; yet stand close.
>
> (III.iii.104–105)

Then as the revelation of Borachio's villainy unfolds, Watch breaks the silence once more with an aside that almost betrays the watch:

---

2. Some editors attribute the three asides to Watch (for example, David L. Stevenson, whose edition appears in *The Complete Signet Classic Shakespeare*, general editor Sylvan Barnet [New York: Harcourt, Brace, Jovanovich, 1972]); others (for example, A. R. Humphreys in the Arden edition) attribute them to Second Watch.

I know that Deformed; a has been a vile thief this seven year; a goes
up and down like a gentleman: I remember his name.

(III.iii.122–24)

Borachio momentarily interrupts his conversation with Conrade, asking
him:

Didst thou not hear somebody?

(III.iii.125)

The asides are no mere asides: they prove to be so little aside as finally
to interrupt the very revelation for which the watch is being kept. It is as if
Watch were compelled to utter these asides in order to keep the watch
intact, to sustain it, even though they do not belong to a watch, even though
they violate the watch. It is as if otherwise the men keeping the watch would
be likely to fall asleep or to become so unalert as not to overhear the revelation of Borachio's treachery. It is as if Watch had to charge Borachio before
charging him, before the watch had ended and the time for the charging
had arrived. It is as if the pure, undefiled watch were so little under control
that it required repeated enforcement, even if by forces that violate the
watch, that break with it by breaking its requisite silence. Keeping watch
over the scene where things—be they villains or otherwise—come to show
themselves is not to be brought under control, under its own control. For,
once *watch* is ventured as a name for one's being gathered to the scene of
the elemental configuration, it can be said that one is always already engaged in keeping watch. One will never simply have begun.

Yet even if, fully charged, one could fall silent and could constrain oneself to keep watch without violating what belongs to a watch, there would
remain discontinuity between the watch (what belongs to a watch) and any
action whatsoever. To keep watch is precisely to inhibit action:

The most peaceable way for you, if you do take a thief, is to let him
show himself what he is, and steal out of your company.

(III.iii.56–59)

In particular, then, a ludicrous incongruity arises between the watch and
the accomplishment of that to which the watch is directed, its end, for instance, to catch the thief, to arrest and charge him.

Keeping watch over the scene of their self-showing, one apprehends
things. In keeping watch, one inhibits or at least defers action, not only
because of the detachment of the watch but also because deliberation and
action arise only on the basis of the self-showing of things to the apprehending watch.

To keep watch is to be on the lookout for possibilities, to be attentive to
the possibility that at any moment something may appear that needs to be

apprehended. To keep watch is to have an eye and an ear for possibilities, to be on the watch for them, to be wakeful to the perpetual possibility of a possible self-showing.

Though possibilities may appear suddenly on the scene, they will never be entirely unexpected, for they are always predelineated horizonally. Indeed the character of possibility is so integral to horizonality that the very spacing of the horizons suffices, provided one is gathered to the spacing, to put one on the watch for possibilities.

The very constitution of lateral horizonality broaches possibility. Each of the lateral images that together, in their appropriate spacing, constitute the lateral horizon corresponds to a possible view that the thing could offer upon itself, to another aspect that could become frontal. Each lateral image holds out the promise of another possible aspect with which the thing itself could become further manifest. Predelineated in the horizon itself, these possibilities are neither imposed on sense nor posited (merely entertained, as it were) over against what is present to sense. Rather, they are possibilities concretely implicated in the very scene of self-showing, possibilities that pertain to the very possibility of sensible manifestation, possibilities that belong to the very flesh of the sensible.

Peripheral horizonality is more differentiated in its ways of broaching possibility. A peripheral horizon that operates primarily as background holds in store a range of images any of which *can* become frontal, throwing the previous scene out of joint by becoming the focus around which the horizons are newly gathered. These concrete possibilities inhabit the scene; they are implicated there as possibilities that can suddenly come to command the scene. The range of such possibilities includes even those implicated by the character of the horizon as not breaking off as such, those possibilities that fall beyond even the marginal traces still offered to vision. They, too, even offering nothing to sense, haunt the scene.

In the case of peripheral horizons that are specifically instrumental, the thing is apprehended precisely as something with which one *can* carry out some definite kind of work, as an implement with which a certain task *can* be accomplished. In apprehending the implement as such, one is already oriented to the work for which it is designed. Especially if it is familiar work, then as one reaches for the implement and sets about using it, one's attention is focused on the setting, for instance, the material on which the implement is to be used in order to achieve a certain result. It is not as if the result were a possibility merely pictured in advance; rather it is a possibility that concretely orients one's very engagement with the implement in the work. One sets out driving on an accustomed route, engaging the possibility offered of reaching a certain destination, yet without—or only incidentally—picturing to oneself one's future arrival at that destination.

Yet such possibilities can be freed, can be released as possibilities. They can be set forth as possibilities by being drawn out as such from the horizons in which they were previously embedded, in which they remained merely tacit and barely differentiated from the manifold of other possibilities also implicated in those horizons. Drawing them out does not consist, however, in setting them forth as an intuitive or meant content; it does not consist in making what previously was implicated only horizonally become the correlate of an intuitive or intentive act. Freeing such possibilities requires, rather, that they be set forth into a hovering, that they be lifted out of the horizon, differentiated as such, and yet held in suspension in such a way as to inhibit, for the moment at least, engagement in bringing about that of which they are the possibility. Drawn forth from the horizon, a possibility is precisely the possibility of something, that is, its character as possibility orients it to something that could be brought to pass, something that one could indeed picture to oneself in advance. And yet, set forth from the horizon, it can remain a possibility only by being also withdrawn from that—and from the bringing about of that—of which it is the possibility. Drawn forth from the horizon, a possibility must—in order to be a possibility, if and in whatever sense a possibility can be said to be—also be withdrawn even from the merely virtual coming to pass that can be pictured in advance but that, precisely in being pictured, forfeits the character of possibility as such, closing off (through determination) that which possibility as such leaves open. For it to remain as possibility, it is imperative that it not coalesce with a phantasy image of that of which it is the possibility. What is required, rather, is that tractive imagination—in a guise to be differentiated from that in which it draws the configuration of showing as such— draw the possibility into the hovering by which it is freed as possibility. In this sense and starting always from the scene of self-showing, imagination would bring about possibility as such. Yet, precisely because it starts always from the scene of self-showing, imagination's deployment of possibilities is never simply spontaneous, never just originative.

The freeing of possibilities as such opens the field of deliberation. Drawn out from the scene of self-showing, a possibility remains oriented to that scene, even though suspended, indeed precisely in its suspension. It is the possibility of something coming to pass that would be pertinent precisely to that scene to which one belongs and from which the possibility has been freed. Once a possibility is thus suspended, one can deliberate about it, weighing (*libare*) its pros and cons. With the freeing of other possibilities, one can oneself remain suspended between alternatives, hovering between various possibilities in such a way as to weigh them against one another, that is, to deliberate about them, between them.

With the advent of deliberation, there opens also the field of deliberative action, in which one enacts a possibility that one has weighed either by itself or in relation to alternatives. In deliberative action one sets about bringing to pass in its concrete determinateness that of which the possibility is the possibility. Thus, by freeing possibilities so as to open the field of deliberation, imagination opens, too, the theatre of action.[3]

In this connection *action* has the broad sense of a deliberate carrying out of a deed (ἔργον) by which something comes to pass. One could then distinguish between those actions through which what is brought about is something made, an artifact, and those that bring about, for instance, a political result, or those that bring it about that something previously hidden comes to be manifest. Not that one could now simply leave intact the articulations that the Greeks designated by the determinations ποίησις, πρᾶξις, and θεωρία. Heidegger and Arendt have effectively put these determinations in question, even in cases in which, as with Arendt's discussion of πρᾶξις (which she translates as *action*), the guiding interest is in reinstituting the articulation by setting it apart from the erosion that seems already to have set in with Greek philosophy. Even if from quite different directions, both Heidegger and Arendt show that in the classical schema πρᾶξις and θεωρία are determined, not in and of themselves, but primarily by reference to ποίησις, which thus proves to orient the entire schema of the determinations. According to Arendt's analysis, the decisive shift occurred when the Greeks came to delimit θεωρία as a knowledge distinct from πρᾶξις; as a knowledge that would precede and direct πρᾶξις in advance, θεωρία thus came to displace and to replace the knowledge that would, on the other hand, be operative within πρᾶξις, the knowledge that would belong to πρᾶξις itself. Thus impoverished, πρᾶξις comes, then, according to Arendt, to be referred to the structure of ποίησις, understood as a making in which a certain knowledge, a vision of what is to be made, always precedes and directs the actual fabrication. Πρᾶξις can easily come to be regarded, then, as merely a phase or kind of ποίησις, that is, as governed by a prior vision of a paradigm.[4] Yet it is not only πρᾶξις that is reduced by submission to the structure of ποίησις. Heidegger's analysis shows that θεωρία, too, is determined in reference to this structure, specifically, as the mere vision of a paradigm, as a vision that, in distinction from ποίησις in the full sense, stops short of the phase of fabrication by which an image of the paradigm would be produced. It is in this regard that Heidegger refers the determination of knowing as θεωρία to what he calls the technical interpretation of thinking. Completely controlled by the reference to

---

3. Thus is the connection on which Epictetus insists between action (πρᾶξις) and φαντασία to be exorbitantly reinscribed.

4. Hannah Arendt, *The Human Condition,* 197–206. According to Arendt, it is primarily in Plato's thought that the reduction of πρᾶξις and its submission to ποίησις take place. She does not note, however, that to certain Platonic discourses on ποίησις (for instance, those of the *Republic* and the *Timaeus*) there is conjoined a thoroughgoing critique of ποίησις, a limiting of the hegemony of ποίησις. See my discussion in "The Politics of the Χώρα," in *The Ancients and the Moderns,* ed. Reginald Lilly (Bloomington: Indiana University Press, 1996), 59–71.

the structure of τέχνη, that is, of ποίησις, this determination becomes then "a reactive attempt to rescue thinking and preserve its autonomy over against acting and doing."[5]

Two moves would thus now be required. The first would consist in releasing θεωρία and πρᾶξις from the hegemony of ποίησις, in reclaiming them, even if in a manner that could not but erode the determinations as such and expose them to deformation. The second move would consist in redetermining ποίησις itself in a way that would break with the hegemony of the kind of making carried out by artisans, that would bring into the determination both the character of technological production (for which the classical determination is insufficient) and that of artistic production (in which the work produced is rarely, if ever, merely the fabricated image of a paradigm envisioned in advance). Furthermore, the very unity of the determination would be put in question the moment production is referred back to apprehension, to the character that apprehension assumes within the horizonal configuration of showing. For, when governed by, for instance, a peripheral horizon that is specifically instrumental, apprehension may display an orientation that, in contrast to mere perception, engages it already in a comportment that is decidedly productive. It would not be a matter, then, of distinguishing a level of mere perception, upon which would then be founded such deliberative action as that of production. Rather, within certain kinds of horizonal configurations, production would come into play—even if incompletely—at a level prior to deliberation and deliberative action—that is, the very determination of production would cut across the differentiation between apprehension and deliberative action. As the watch is violated by the deliberative asides that serve precisely to enforce it.

In every case, action and its articulations would need to be determined in reference back to the scene of self-showing and its elemental and horizonal configuration. Since it is to this scene that one belongs—with a belonging sayable as preception, reception, and watch—it can be called also one's abode, one's accustomed place (ἦθος).[6] Thus could a discreet allusion to ethics—to a no doubt exorbitant ethics—be ventured within—rather than in opposition to—the turn to the sensible and to elemental nature.

B. PROPRIETARY MANIFESTATION

From within their elemental-horizonal configuration, things show themselves, become manifest as they properly are. Yet such things, those called

---

5. Heidegger, *Brief über den Humanismus*, in *Wegmarken*, vol. 9 of *Gesamtausgabe* (Frankfurt a.M.: Vittorio Klostermann, 1976), 314.

6. See, for example, Plato, *Laws* 865e, where ἦθος not only has the sense of usual abode or accustomed place but also is affiliated with, set in a certain proximity to, χώρα.

natural things or artifacts (in the broad sense), are not the only beings that can become manifest; neither is it only their self-showing that will have come remonstratively to double back upon itself, for, even in their self-showing, other manifestations are already implicated. There can take place—and will always already have taken place—manifestations of oneself and of others (of those whom one can address, by common words or in other ways that simulate words). One can come oneself to be shown to oneself. Others, too, can come to be shown to oneself. And others attest that one can come oneself to be shown also to them and they also to themselves. Such self-showings of oneself and of others are irreducible to self-showings of things: the mere apprehension of the sensible figure of another will no more suffice to make that other manifest as such than the apprehension of one's own trunk and limbs will suffice to manifest one to oneself. For those beings that one calls oneself and others are proprieties in a way that quite exceeds the proper being of things: they not only become themselves manifest but become manifest to themselves, each to itself and to others. Their propriety, their ownness, is such that they not only are themselves—as are things—but also are manifest to themselves. Their very coming to pass is a coming to pass for themselves, each becoming manifest to itself and to others. In order to designate the manifestations unique to those of such propriety—while relinquishing the modern philosophical designations—the adjectival form of *proprietary* will be intensified so as to signify having to do, not with what is owned or with ownership, but with ownness as such, with this distinctive propriety. *Proprietary manifestation* will thus signify self-showing that is determined by such distinctive propriety, by the doubling of the proper such that what is shown doubles back so as to be also either the one to whom it is shown or one—an other—to whom it could be shown.

Proprietary manifestation does not take place apart from other manifestative moments. On the one side, it proves to be intimately linked to self-showings in which things or thing-like constituents shine forth. On the other side—or rather, before all else—proprietary manifestation is bound—as is all manifestation—to an anterior gift and can never simply—of itself—have begun. Only as imagination comes and as one, accepting the gift and offering oneself, silently utters this double affirmative—only beginning from such antecedent responsiveness can proprietary manifestation come to take place. Thus, in proprietary manifestation something anterior will always already have been granted. Before ever coming before oneself (in self-showing), one will always have given oneself up preceptionally. No matter how profoundly proprietary manifestation may be developed, it will never enable one to recover what will always have been relinquished, to retrieve the beginning that, like birth itself, will have been anterior to one's very propriety; one will never be able to appropriate to such doubled self-showing the expropriation that is its very condition.

Hence, the limit—the limitation—of proprietary manifestation consists not only in the opaqueness that continues to haunt both oneself and the other, not only in the retreat of both into a depth even more securely closed off than that of things, but also, first of all and most unconditionally, in the expropriation of origin, in one's always already having been granted a beginning as if from nowhere.

Yet, short of such limits, what possibilities are open to proprietary manifestation? How, in particular, does one come to be shown to oneself? What is required in order for a self-showing of oneself to take place?

It is imperative from the outset to distinguish such manifestation from an interior reflection through which one would allegedly come to be present to oneself, to be given intuitively to oneself this side of all engagement with things and with others. In this connection, even less than in reference to things, mere presence does not suffice to constitute self-showing; in this case the difference is indeed accentuated by virtue of the enormous gap between the poverty of the relevant presentation and the depth of the proprieties that become manifest. This poverty, the poverty of allegedly inner intuition, has been attested within various contexts and nowhere more strikingly than around the pivot on which modern philosophy as such turns.

Hume, for example, attests that scanning one's interiority in search of oneself as something proper, something self-identical, reveals nothing of the sort: "For my part, when I enter most intimately into what I call *myself*, I always stumble on some particular perception or other, of heat or cold, light or shade, love or hatred, pain or pleasure. I never can catch *myself* at any time without a perception, and never can observe anything but the perception." Hume proposes, therefore, an analogy: the interiority to which one would turn in search of oneself—what Hume calls *the mind*—is "a kind of theatre, where several perceptions successively make their appearance; pass, repass, glide away, and mingle in an infinite variety of postures and situations." Yet Hume warns that even the analogy with the theatre goes too far, that it could be misleading, since we have not even "the most distant notion of the place where these scenes are represented, or of the materials of which it is composed."[7] Only the slightest radicalization would be required in order to conclude that the very interiority that one calls *oneself* and to which one takes oneself to be turning in the allegedly inward turn is not itself given and that consequently the very directionality of the turn to what one calls *oneself* would be disrupted. *Oneself* would not necessarily signify anything like an interiority; nor would the turn to oneself—that is, attentiveness to the self-showing of oneself—be anything inward. The very spacing of oneself and of one's self-showing would thus come into question.

---

7. David Hume, *A Treatise of Human Nature*, 228f.

Kant, too, underlines the poverty of the inner intuition of oneself: one is given to oneself only in inner sense and hence in conformity with the form of inner sense, therefore, only as appearance, not as one is in oneself. This limitation to givenness in inner sense is virtually tantamount to a denial that one is given to oneself: "Consciousness of self according to the determinations of our state in inner perception is merely empirical, always changeable; no fixed and abiding self [*kein stehendes oder bleibendes Selbst*] can be given in this flux of inner appearances."[8] And yet, *oneself*—the *I* of *I think*—signifies beyond this limitation; it expresses the thought in which "I am conscious of myself, not as I appear to myself, nor as I am in myself, but only that I am."[9] This thought without intuition can yield no knowledge of oneself—no self-showing of oneself. Hegel calls it "the motionless tautology of: I am I."[10] At most, it can perform a kind of indexical function for and within a self-showing sustained in some other way.[11] And yet, as indexical it does not necessarily refer self-showing to an interiority, to an inner theatre. While indicative of oneself, it leaves open the spacing of oneself.

It is remarkable how various intuitions of oneself come to be simulated, intuitions that would inform the mere thought of oneself, that would fulfill the mere signifying, the indexical operation, of *oneself*. As when, standing before a mirror, one not only sees oneself but also comes ever so close to seeing oneself seeing, to catching one's own glance while it is still a living glance. Or, as when one attempts to touch oneself touching, only to discover that the coincidence dissolves at the very moment it is achieved. Yet the most effective and consequential simulation of self-presence is that of which only the voice is capable—most effective because most interiorizing, most consequential because it includes speech, and not just intuition, in the circuit of simulated self-presence. This simulation exploits the connection between speaking and hearing: when one speaks, one at the same time hears oneself speaking. What allows this circuit to simulate self-presence is the absolute proximity that the signifier seems to have to the voice, the meaning intention, that animates it: in the voice, not as it sounds forth beyond oneself, but rather as it is spiritualized in the breath of an almost soundless speech withheld from the world, one hears oneself in a manner that simulates immediate presence to oneself this side of visibility, spatiality, the world of things, this side even of audition as it occurs empirically.[12] In the voice, in this spiritualized hearing-oneself-speak, there is simulated a presence to oneself, not just as a visible, tangible, or even audible being,

---

8. Kant, *Kritik der reinen Vernunft*, A 107.

9. Ibid., B157.

10. Hegel, *Phänomenologie des Geistes*, 104.

11. See my discussion in *The Gathering of Reason*, 69–76.

12. See Derrida, *La Voix et le Phénomène*, 87; also Merleau-Ponty, *Le Visible et L'invisible* (Paris: Gallimard, 1964), 299f.

not even just as a seeing, touching, or hearing being, but as one open to speech and engaged in signification.

These simulations of self-intuition need not be denounced except insofar as their character as simulations goes unrecognized. What is needed is only that the impossibility of completing the circuit be acknowledged and that the would-be presence to oneself be recognized as, rather, a self-showing of oneself in which the truncated intuition functions as only a moment. For, standing before the mirror, one is indeed shown to oneself, and one's inevitable failure to catch the living glance is not just a breakdown in the intuition of oneself but also the correlate of a withdrawal that belongs decisively to such proprietary manifestation.

Yet one will ask: Is it indeed oneself that comes to be shown in these simulations? Is what comes to be shown the same as the *I* of the *I think,* the I regarding which, on the basis of the mere consciousness that I am (transcendental apperception), Kant declares: "I exist as an intelligence [*Intelligenz*]"?[13] Or is what is shown not almost entirely something of one's body rather than of oneself as such, of oneself as something like an intelligence? When one sees one's body reflected in the mirror, does one see anything of oneself beyond that which the eye, the window of the soul,[14] renders visible?

If, now, at the limit, it is imperative to relinquish not only what is called *the intelligible* (translating τὸ νοητόν) but also its correlate, namely, what is called *intellectus, Intelligenz, intelligence* (translating νόησις), then with regard to what is called *the body* the consequence will be the same as with *the sensible.* Rarely, if ever, has what is called *the body* been determined otherwise than through its opposition to a determination of oneself as being apart— either as such or in a primary respect—from the sensible. The body is, as it were, the sensible remains of oneself; it is utterly determined by the opposition in which it is, at the same time, subordinated to what is called (among many names) *mind, soul, subjectivity, consciousness.* Indeed the very ease with which one uses the definite article with it betokens this subordinating opposition by posing one's own body as deprived precisely of all ownness, as *the* body. Now, at the limit, it will have to be asked: What can remain of (the) body once it becomes imperative to suspend the determinations in opposition to which its very sense—the very sense of such sensible remains—has been determined? Will the remains be such as even to warrant still a discourse on embodiment, which cannot but imply that something, not itself of the body, comes to be *in* the body, as the soul was

---

13. Kant, *Kritik der reinen Vernunft,* B 158.

14. "But if we ask in which particular organ the whole soul appears as soul, we will at once name the eye; for in the eye the soul is concentrated, and the soul does not merely see through it but is also seen in it" (Hegel, *Ästhetik,* ed. Friedrich Bassange [West Berlin: Verlag das Europäische Buch, 1985], 1:155).

taken to inform, enliven—or to be imprisoned in—the body? Will a discourse on the body even be warranted once the conclusion of Nietzsche's story ("*With the true world we have also abolished the apparent one*")[15] is brought to bear specifically on what is called *the body*? With the abolition of the soul, will one not also have abolished the body? Will one not need to say now— even if not without a bit of hyperbole—that there is no such thing as the body? Or can one, as with the sensible, redetermine the very sense of *body,* detaching it from the previously determining opposition in order now to redetermine it as it shows itself from itself? But does something show itself with a distinctness sufficient to warrant calling it *the body*? Or is the body not always only the remains of a *oneself* that is itself constituted apart from the body? Would the discourse not need to become at least oriented to *one's own body*—indeed, not as something owned, possessed, by oneself, but rather as belonging to one's ownness as such? But then, one's own body would belong as a moment—a moment of shining presence—to the proprietary manifestation in which one would come to show oneself.

It is decisive for such manifestation that, at least in all but the most impoverished guises, it takes place by way of a certain reflection of oneself back from something else. It is for this reason that the various simulations, especially that which relies on a mirror, have a certain paradigmatic status.

Yet any thing, even as a mere thing, casts a certain disclosive reflection back upon the one who sees it. As Merleau-Ponty observes, "The vision that he [the seer] exercises, he also undergoes from the things, such that, as many painters have said, I feel myself looked at by the things."[16] But what do things reflect back to oneself? How do they contribute to the showing of oneself to oneself? What do they show about oneself? They show one where one is: they cast their quasi-vision in such a way as to designate the very place to which it is cast, the place from which one sees them, the place of the seer amidst things. Thus Merleau-Ponty writes of "this phantom of ourselves that they [the things seen] evoke by designating a place among themselves whence we see them."[17] Yet the mere self-showing of things could never evoke such a phantom, and if there is indeed "a fundamental narcissism of all vision,"[18] it is only because imagination comes to draw back toward oneself the gaze one has cast toward the thing.

It is not only from mere things that reflection back upon oneself takes place. Indeed, the reflection is likely to be considerably richer and less extrinsic in cases where the primarily effective horizons are peripheral, especially in cases of instrumentality. For in such cases the appropriate comportment is one in which one assumes a certain role predelineated by the

---

15. Nietzsche, *Götzen-Dämmerung,* in *Werke,* VI 3: 75.
16. Merleau-Ponty, *Le Visible et L'invisible,* 183.
17. Ibid., 188.
18. Ibid., 183.

relevant horizon. One puts oneself into a connection and orientation already prepared by the spacing of the horizon. As one does so, one is reflected back to oneself from the instrumental network and the things oriented by it; one is shown to oneself precisely as one assuming—hence, also, as one capable of assuming—the predelineated role. One does not simply use a tool or an instrument; rather, in using it, one becomes manifest to oneself as user, as one who is using it, also as one who has the capability of using it. Thus imagination, drawing around certain things the instrumental horizon determining their utility, also draws this complex back toward the one engaged by it, makes it function as if it were a mirror, though one reflecting moments that could never be seen in an ordinary mirror. A capability, for instance, could never be seen as such in the movement of one's hands, in what one's moving hands would present to intuition. A capability is to these visible movements as depth is to surface, and, in letting it be reflected, imagination lets one be shown (to oneself) in a certain depth, discloses an invisible of oneself—not an invisible that, like the intelligible, would be the opposite of the visible, but rather an invisible belonging to the visible, an invisible, as it were, lining the visible, as if it were the very flesh of the visible.

Beyond the sphere of mere tools, the network and the reflection from it may be more complex. From the moment he reaches for his violin, the violinist is reflectively manifested to himself as such, reflection doubling in the imaginal reversal his comportment to his instrument. If it should turn out that he plays exceptionally well and that the music produced is beautiful, then a reflective disclosure that is of an entirely different order may come into play both for the violinist himself and for his audience. For Kant has shown that beauty is not simply something to behold but rather is such that, when it is beheld, a reflection back upon the beholder comes into play, a reflection that issues in a certain disclosive feeling of oneself.[19]

The advent of speech enhances reflection, even if—indeed because—in the preceding silence an opening to speech is already operative. Speech can lay out more distinctly the course of reflection, marking its directionalities more explicitly. One need only say of something seen that it is *there:* the *there* suffices to imply, in an eminently concrete sense, a *here* from which the thing is seen, thus intensifying the reflection from the thing seen back to the place from which it is seen.

And yet, it is not from things of any sort, not even when one's comportment to them is supplemented by speech, that the primary manifestations of oneself proceed. Rather, it is from the elementals and from others that one learns what and who one is.

From the elementals, especially from earth and sky, one is not separated by the kind of distance that separates one from things, the distance that

---

19. See my discussion in *Spacings—Of Reason and Imagination,* chap. 4.

must be spanned, as it were, by reflection. For one is encompassed by the elementals, indeed in such a way that one's self-disclosure from them is more enfolding than reflective. It is not as though earth and sky provide mirrors in which, as with things, one can catch a glimpse of oneself. Rather, encompassed by the elements, one is manifest in one's exposure to them and in one's extreme need for shelter against these forces that one cannot escape. Encompassed by the sky, standing upright in the openness that it grants, one is manifest in one's reliance on its gift of light and in the necessity that one submit to regulation by the circlings that take place in the sky. Encompassed by the earth, one is manifest in one's belonging to it, in one's being *of* the earth, in the need that, like all who could call themselves human, one has to build upon the earth and to bring forth or take from the earth what is required for human life itself.

And yet, one is on the earth with others and in such a way that one's comings and goings as well as those of others (and in relation to those of others) are governed, above all, by the sun's daily course across the sky. All humans share the earth, living from the earth, from the things that come from or are brought forth from the earth. And the lives of all continue— despite the most extravagant technological supplements—to be regulated by the alternation of day and night and by the cycle of the seasons. Yet what assures that one finds no human being to be absolutely foreign is that all share the opening to speech, that to all one can address either common words or at least gestures that simulate words. Even if one's words or gestures are misunderstood, such misunderstanding attests to the possibility of understanding.

Merleau-Ponty writes that "through other eyes we are fully visible to ourselves"[20]—one reason being, no doubt, that the other is of one's kind, capable of providing the most perfect mirror in which to see oneself. In the eyes of the other, one apprehends the same fire that burns within oneself, even though the strangeness of the other's eyes, even thus apprehended, always invites the speech that can mitigate that strangeness and dissipate its reserve. Yet always the proprietary manifestation of the other to oneself will require that imagination come to install the reserve, the depth, by which the other, no less than oneself, exceeds the visible figure offered to one's vision.[21]

But one comes to be manifested to oneself from the other, not primarily

---

20. Merleau-Ponty, *Le Visible et L'invisible,* 188.

21. This is one connection in which Levinas' discourse of the face could appropriately be taken up, even if not necessarily under this specific title. Whatever reservations one might maintain, especially regarding the discourse of absolute alterity, the following could certainly be underwritten: "the face of the Other [*Le visage d'Autrui*] at each moment destroys and overflows the plastic image it leaves me. . . . It does not manifest itself by these qualities, but καθ᾽ αὐτό. It *expresses itself*" (Emmanuel Levinas, *Totalité et Infini* [The Hague: Martinus Nijhoff, 1961], 21).

in the order of vision and mirrors, but in the order of speech. In speech one hears the appeal of the other. In speech the other places upon one a claim or a demand or a request; the other makes a promise or asks of one that one make a promise. When one is thus addressed, one becomes manifest to oneself as being not merely capable of vision; the appeal of the other discloses one to oneself as a being upon whom such things as claims, demands, and requests can be placed, as a being that can make promises and that can invite promises from others. Thus, also, as one who opens the possibility of keeping a promise.

9

POETIC IMAGINATION

A. REDRAFT

Imagination comes always as poietic. It comes to bring something forth, grants a bringing-forth (ποίησις). Such bringing-forth is to be distinguished from both production and reproduction, even in cases such as that of an artwork, where something is composed that otherwise would never come to pass. In such bringing-forth it is not (as in production in the classical sense) a matter of fabricating a concrete image of something seen in advance, of something already imagined, one will perhaps say.[1] In imaginal bringing-forth there is no anterior paradigm directive of the process, no *look* to which one would look almost constantly in fabricating something to look like the paradigmatic *look*. Neither is imaginal bringing-forth a matter of copying, of replicating—that is, of reproducing—something actually seen, something concretely manifest in advance of the process. For imagination sees nothing in advance, if indeed it sees anything at all. As tractive, its force is solely one of drawing, and it is only by drawing that it can bring

---

1. See Heidegger, *Grundprobleme der Phänomenologie*, vol. 24 of *Gesamtausgabe*, 150.

something forth. Whatever it brings forth will always prove also to have a certain precedence with respect to the bringing-forth—or rather, such precedence belongs to the very determination of imaginal bringing-forth, which is thus both originary and memorial.

It is a matter, then, of detaching the poietic from the productive and the reproductive, of reorienting it to a more exorbitant sense: that of bringing-forth by the force of drawing.

It is in this sense that imagination can be said to bring forth each thing as such: it lets the image shine forth from within the complex of horizons and elementals and in this way brings the thing as such forth into manifestness. It is also in this sense that imagination can be said to draw back toward oneself the gaze cast toward a thing or the instrumental complex that is thus made to function as an unseen mirror.

Imagination is no less tractive when, through doubling, it assumes the guise of poetic imagination. It is for this reason, because it comes still as a bringing-forth, that imagination in this guise is called *poetic* and not, as would otherwise be appropriate, simply *artistic*. What it brings forth are indeed artworks, and yet everything depends on determining the poetic moment of such works, on delimiting the poetic in art. Such a determining delimitation has nothing to do with privileging a particular art, poetry, over the others; rather, it is a matter of determining, precisely and specifically, the bringing-forth that belongs to all arts as such.

In poetic imagination there occurs a doubling of imagination as it comes to bring things forth into manifestness. As this doubling, poetic imagination is a redraft of imagination in the guise in which it will always already have been operative in the apprehension of things.

Such doubling of imagination is precisely the theme of the celebrated passage from Coleridge's *Biographia Literaria* in which the distinctions are drawn between the primary and the secondary imagination and between the secondary imagination and the fancy.[2] In Coleridge's idiom, the primary imagination is "the living Power and prime Agent of all human Perception." Reconstrued outside this idiom, *primary imagination* could be said to name the force that brings things forth to human apprehension, that lets them show themselves to sense. The secondary imagination is a doubling—an echo, says Coleridge—of the primary imagination; as such it is genuine poetic or artistic imagination, in distinction from the fancy, which is, at best, a kind of rigid, lifeless double of the secondary imagination.

The difficulty is that the moment Coleridge begins to elaborate this dyadic schema he falls back upon a very classical conceptuality, even if in its modern metaphysical guise. Thus, the primary imagination, "the living Power and prime Agent of all human Perception," is characterized "as a repetition in the finite mind of the eternal act of creation in the infinite I

---

2. Coleridge, *Biographia Literaria*, vol. 7 of *The Collected Works*, 1:304f.

AM." Aside from the massive enclosure within the metaphysics of the infinite subject, this move has the effect of orienting imagination to production as the finite analogue of creation. This effect is carried over from the primary to the secondary imagination, which, though twice removed, is also a finite repetition of the creative act of the infinite subject. Coleridge's metaphorizing of doubling as echo exemplifies what also it says: taken as an echo of the primary imagination, the secondary imagination is characterized as "co-existing with the conscious will, yet still as identical with the primary in the *kind* of its agency, and differing only in *degree,* and in the *mode* of its operation." In kind, it remains creative, a repetition of the repetition of divine creation. It differs only in degree and mode. Less creative, repetitive in its creativity, it re-creates what it has, first of all, destroyed: "It dissolves, diffuses, dissipates, in order to re-create." In the event that re-creation is impossible, it can be repetitive of the divine act of creation only by sustaining the ideal operative in such creation: "or where this process is rendered impossible, yet still at all events it struggles to idealize and to unify." In its repetition the secondary imagination remains to this extent creative, "essentially *vital,*" over against the objects created, which are "essentially fixed and dead."

The fancy is rather like these objects: it "has no other counters to play with, but fixities and definites." Like ordinary memory—and it is little more than a mode of memory—the fancy "must receive all its materials ready made from the law of association." Its creativity is limited to what can be exercised in ready-made materials, limited presumably to mere reconfigurations, as when one pictures a being with a human body, the head of a lion, and the tail of a horse. Such is the impoverishment of a repetition thrice removed from the eternal act of creation.

Thus reconstituting and compounding the ancient distinction (elaborated, most notably, by Albertus Magnus as that between *imaginatio* and *phantasia*), Coleridge's account remains largely enclosed in the classical conceptuality. The question is whether Coleridge's adumbration of poetic imagination as doubling the imaginal force that brings things forth can be paired with other indications in his text that run counter to, or at least begin to unsettle, the massive enclosure within the metaphysics of the infinite subject. Perhaps most suggestive in this regard—if less than definitive—are some remarks from a lecture on *Romeo and Juliet* antedating by a few years the writing of *Biographia Literaria.* What is striking in the lecture is that Coleridge deals with poetic imagination, not as an agent of synthesis and unity, but rather as "hovering between images": "As soon as it [the mind] is fixed on one image, it becomes understanding; but while it is unfixed and wavering between them, attaching itself permanently to none, it is imagination." Furthermore: "The grandest efforts of poetry are where the imagination is called forth, not to produce a distinct form, but a strong working of the mind, still offering what is still repelled, and again creating what is again rejected."[3] Even if the vocabulary of creation is not thoroughly suppressed, the mutation suggested is that of imagination as creative (as repetition of divine creativity) into imagination as hovering between opposites in such a way as to bring something forth. Though there are perhaps resonances, even in *Biographia Literaria*,[4] the mutation suggested by these remarks seems not to have been systematically followed up.[5]

Along with the doubling that issues in poetic imagination, there is another doubling, a doubling within poetic imagination itself—hence, two moments, two ways in which it brings something forth. In the first place, the artwork is itself brought forth in the sense that it is composed; only through being composed does it come to pass at all. One will say, therefore, that the artwork is dependent on the artist. In order to be at all, the work must be composed by the artist, not as a creator capable of finite repetition of divine *creatio ex nihilo*, not as a producer (as a δημιουργός or τεχνίτης) who would make the work under the guidance of an anterior vision, but rather, as submitted to the coming of imagination, as a site offered for its drawing. Thus, it is not surprising that artists are proverbially incapable of saying how they compose their works. Even when, as in the case of Kandinsky, the artist is also a theoretician of art, one finds still an insistence that art always outruns theory, that artistic composition is irreducible to what can be formulated in a theory. In the words and the idiom of *On the Spiritual in Art:* "The true work of art comes about in a mysterious way. No, if the soul of the artist is alive, then one does not need to bolster it with ideas and theories. It will find something to say of its own accord, something that may, at that moment, remain quite unclear to the artist himself."[6] In composing the work, as composer of the work, the artist undergoes a certain self-expropriation. It is not simply *as oneself* that one composes an artwork, but only through an excess of oneself, an excess that comes to be operative without ever becoming simply one's own, without ever being appropriated to one's ownness, to one's propriety. It is by this excess that artistic composition exceeds mere production (in the sense of τέχνη), and

---

3. "Collier Report of a Lecture on *Romeo and Juliet* (9 December 1811)," in *Imagination in Coleridge,* ed. Hill, 81.

4. For example, in the depiction of the imagination as "that synthetic and magical power [that] reveals itself in the balance or reconciliation of opposite or discordant qualities" (Coleridge, *Biographia Literaria,* 2:16).

5. Another indication would be provided if it could be definitively established that Coleridge later deleted the characterization of primary imagination "as a repetition in the finite mind of the eternal act of creation in the infinite I AM." This possibility is suggested by Sara Coleridge's testimony that this clause was "stroked out" in a copy of *Biographia Literaria* containing a few marginal notes by Coleridge himself. See ibid., 1:304 n.3, as well as the critical remarks by Hill in *Imagination in Coleridge,* 127 n.2. For the full reiteratively dyadic schema elaborated by Coleridge, nothing would be more decisive than such a deletion, since it would interrupt the entire schema as a schema determined by repetition of divine creation.

6. Kandinsky, *Über das Geistige in der Kunst,* 135f. n. 5.

it is on account of it that the pertinence of technique or technicity to art is limited. Though, to be sure, one knows that eminent artists pride themselves on their technical mastery, composition remains in excess of τέχνη.

It is this excess and expropriation that is addressed by traditional discourses on inspiration and on genius. Thus Kant, construing genius as a talent or natural gift (*Naturgabe*), as given by nature to the artist, defines genius as that "*through which* nature gives the rule to art."[7] In this regard the artist is merely the passageway of the gift, that through which the gift passes from nature to art.[8] It is for this reason that, as Kant notes, "genius itself cannot describe or indicate scientifically" how it brings the artwork about: "Thus it is that, if an author owes a product to his genius, he himself does not know how he came by the ideas for it; nor is it within his power to devise such products at his pleasure or by following a plan and to communicate [his procedure] to others in prescriptions that would enable them to bring forth like products."[9]

There is something monstrous about genius. It is the site where—the passageway through which—nature, by giving the rule to art, gives rise to something that, though born from and set within nature, nonetheless exceeds nature. Not only the passage through the site but also the site itself displays monstrosity: in bringing forth the artwork, the genius exceeds all that could be achieved by self-possessed, deliberate activity, that is, precisely through the gift of nature, he exceeds all that he could achieve as a merely natural being. Is it not because of this monstrosity—because he caught at least a glimpse of it—that Kant insists on the requirement of taste, that taste is required to discipline genius, to clip its wings, to make it civilized or polished, to provide it with guidance, to introduce clarity and order?

One could compare the monstrosity of poetic genius with that to which Plato's *Theaetetus* alludes at the most decisive moment of the dialogue, the moment when Socrates comes to identify wonder as the beginning (ἀρχή) of philosophy. Just prior to this moment, he has been discussing with Theaetetus some problems concerning opposites, among them the following: Given six dice, if one compares four with them, they are more than the four, but if one compares twelve with them, they are less. The problem is that the six dice have opposite determinations: they are both more and less. Hence, the single set of six dice conjoins, couples, opposed determinations. The problem already borders therefore on monstrosity, foreshadowing the confession that immediately precedes and sets the stage for Socra-

---

7. Kant, *Kritik der Urteilskraft*, in vol. 5 of *Werke: Akademie Textausgabe* (Berlin: Walter de Gruyter, 1968), 307.

8. Associating the discourse of genius with that of inspiration, Kant insists on the limit, on the insufficiency of genius with respect to fine art: "Now insofar as art shows genius it does indeed deserve to be called inspired [*geistreich*], but it deserves to be called *fine* art [schöne Kunst] only insofar as it shows taste" (ibid., 319).

9. Ibid., 308.

tes' identification of wonder as the beginning of philosophy. In view of the unresolved problem of opposed determinations, Theaetetus confesses: "By the gods, Socrates, I wonder excessively."[10] Here everything depends on the word translated *excessively*. The word ὑπερφυῶς means literally: in a manner beyond (ὑπέρ) nature (φυή or φύσις), beyond the natural course of things, hence, marvellously, strangely. Theaetetus, in the full bloom that nature bestows upon youth, wonders in excess of the natural course of things. The beginning philosopher—and presumably this beginning is something the philosopher never leaves behind, not even (perhaps least of all) when at the limit—is something of a monstrosity. Not, then, entirely unlike the poetic genius.

So then, of the two ways in which poetic imagination comes to bring something forth, the first is that by which the artwork is composed. Yet, as brought forth through genial, even monstrous composition, the artwork itself, in turn, brings something forth, draws something into manifestness. This is, then, the second of the two ways in which poetic imagination comes to bring something forth: by way of the work itself, by way of the bringing-forth that belongs to the work as work. Poetic imagination comes to bring the work forth by composing it in such a way that it itself brings something forth.

There is, then, a double bringing-forth of the artwork: the artwork is brought forth through composition in such a way that it itself brings something to manifestness. Such is the doubly poetic character of art. As poetic, the artwork is neither product nor reproduction: on both sides, in the composition of the artwork and in the disclosiveness thus engendered in it, the bringing-forth of the artwork falls quite outside production and reproduction.

What does the artwork itself bring forth into manifestness? What is it that by way of the composition comes to be shown? What is it that the artwork lets show itself? And how does the artwork accomplish such showing? Is the artwork an imitation, a portrayal, a representation, of that which comes to be shown? Does an artwork, in being set before one's vision, let something else become manifest by virtue of its resemblance to that something, through the artwork's imitative or representational character? But then, what kind of things can an artwork imitate or represent? And is it to the self-showing of such things that art is devoted? Whatever representational features an artwork may involve, does it ever simply let some singular being—a thing, a human, an animal, etc.—be manifest? Or do artworks reproduce—and so make manifest—not singular beings but rather so-called general ideas such as those definitive of kinds? The case of architecture is a notorious exception: the Greek temple at Sounion is manifestly not an imitation or representation of some other thing; nor does it merely portray

---

10. Plato, *Theaetetus* 155c.

some general idea of temple above and beyond the singular configuration of its stone. Even in the case of a work that most conspicuously presents an individual, one cannot for long—in view of the work—rest content with reducing it to a representational function: Michelangelo's *David* presents— lets show itself—something more (even something other) than just the obscure historical, singular person named David and than just the general idea of hero above and beyond the singularities and engagements of this individual. Whatever may be the representational features of an artwork, what the artwork lets show itself is neither a being nor a general idea of certain beings. Neither is the showing accomplished simply by means of imitation, portrayal, representation—that is, by what has usually been designated by the word *mimesis*. Indeed the construal of art as mimetic has been submitted to the most severe and decisive critique, especially since Kant. None is more caustic than Hegel, who observes that imitation of things is entirely superfluous labor, since whatever might be displayed by such imitation (flowers, landscapes, animals) is already there before us in our gardens or in the countryside beyond, already there in an original form that will always be superior to the one-sided depictions brought forth by an allegedly mimetic art. Hegel mentions, with utter scorn, Zeuxis' painting of grapes, which was proclaimed a triumph of art because doves pecked at them as though they were actual.[11] Yet what is especially noteworthy is that such critiques of mimesis are invariably doubled by an affirmative redetermination of it as a *Darstellung* (presentation, showing) of something that, irreducible to a mere singular or an abstract universal, pertains in an originary way to the manifestation of singulars and even of general representations.[12]

What the artwork brings forth into manifestness is neither a being nor a general idea of beings but rather a moment of the expanse of self-showing with its elemental-horizonal configuration. Consider, for instance, how a painting can render visible the almost invisible spread of light through a certain atmosphere, the envelope (as the Impressionists called it) that makes things visible, that lets them shine forth. Such painting can, as in the case of Monet, become so thoroughly oriented toward painting the atmospheric spread of light as it occurs at various times of day and in various seasons that the object represented may remain the same in painting after painting, its identity serving to render all the more conspicuous that what is being painted—that is, made manifest—in the painting is the envelope. Such progression is what determines the very sense of Monet's series paintings, for instance, the *Wheatstacks* and the *Poplars*. As orientation to the envelope intensifies, the object can virtually disappear, the envelope being painted over everything that in ordinary sense apprehension it

---

11. See Hegel, *Ästhetik*, 1:51.

12. On the history, critique, and redetermination of mimesis, see *Double Truth*, chap. 10.

makes visible, the invisible and the visible being reversed in the painting. Most notable in this regard are Monet's very late paintings of the gardens and house at Giverny, in which the profusion of flowering as a profusion of color virtually conceals all objects.[13] In these paintings the virtual disappearance of natural (as well as fabricated) objects lets nature itself appear as the holding sway of elemental profusion. In the series entitled *The Path of Roses*, there is virtually no longer even any object to disappear: there are only the trellises on which the roses (themselves exploded into color) grow, though in such profusion that they cover the trellises, this concealment enacting what also is painted in the paintings: the eclipse of objects by the profusion of flowering nature. In certain of the paintings in this series there opens, under the covered trellises, under the cover of the trellises, a kind of space around which the flowering is gathered in its profusion. If imagination comes to one's vision of these paintings, one will perhaps say that here Monet paints pure nature, not in the sense of a pristine nature untouched by human deeds, but rather a nature that, while nurtured by human care, nonetheless holds sway in elemental profusion.

Such painting brings forth into manifestness certain elemental moments as well as the shining as such in and through which things become present. Such painting brings forth the elementals into a manifestness with regard to their bearing on the expanse of self-showing, a manifestness beyond any they would ever display within the mere apprehension of the self-showing things. To this extent painting inaugurates a doubling back of manifestation upon itself. This is furthered also by the way in which painting can bring shining to a manifestation that it never has in mere apprehension, elevating it, as Hegel says, from mere sensible presence to the level of pure shining.[14]

---

13. The series *The Japanese Bridge* (W 1911–1933), *The Path of Roses* (W 1934–1940), and *The House Seen from the Rose Garden* (W 1944–1951). These series date from the period 1918–1924.

14. Hegel explains: what spirit "wants is sensible presence, which indeed should remain sensible, but liberated from the scaffolding of its pure materiality. Thereby that which is sensible [*das Sinnliche*] in the artwork, in comparison with the immediate existence of natural things, is elevated to a pure *shining* [*zum blossen* Schein], and the artwork stands in the middle between immediate sensibility [*Sinnlichkeit*] and ideal thought" (Hegel, *Ästhetik*, 1:48).

Without explicitly referring to Hegel or to pure shining, Nancy indicates a way in which this theme could be elaborated outside the Hegelian context and in specific connection to the question of the plurality of the arts, of what Nancy calls the singular plural of art: This plurality "decomposes the living unity of perception or action, but it does so in a way opposite to the abstract decomposition into sensations. . . . It isolates what we call a 'sense,' or a part or feature of this sense; it isolates it so as to force it to be only what it is outside of signifying and useful perception. Art forces a sense to touch itself, to be this sense that it is. But in this way, it does not become simply what we call 'a sense,' for example, sight or hearing: by leaving behind the integration of the 'lived,' it also becomes something else, another instance of unity, which exposes another world, not a 'visual' or 'sonorous' world but a 'pictorial' or 'musical' one" (Nancy, *Les Muses* [Paris: Galilée, 1994], 42).

To say that the artwork inaugurates a turning of self-showing back upon itself is not to exclude the human from what can be artistically disclosed. It is only to say that the human can be artistically disclosed neither as a singular human being nor as a general idea but rather only in its preceptive, receptive, watchful belonging to the expanse of self-showing and its elemental-horizonal configuration.

Thus, through the double bringing-forth of the artwork, the expanse of self-showing is itself disclosed, its moments coming—in various ways and connections in the various arts—to be sensibly manifest. Yet such disclosure—turning self-showing upon itself—is possible only because this double bringing-forth is itself a double of the bringing-forth of things at the level of apprehension. Because imagination is what comes to draw the configuration of self-showing from within which things can shine forth, it is possible for imagination to come—even if inconstantly—to compose the artwork in such a way that it brings forth into manifestness the moments belonging to precisely that configuration. Because imagination will always already have drawn the lines of this expanse, it can come again, in an oblique repetition, to draw a figure in which these lines, which otherwise remain at the margin of visibililty, become manifest as such.

B. ARTS OF IMAGINATION

In a sense the title is redundant, for all arts—all fine art, as one says—are arts of imagination. Regardless of whether the work is one of painting, of sculpture, of poetry, of music, of architecture, of dance, or of some other art (in this strange plurality, this singular plural of art, as Nancy calls it),[15] imagination will always have come to compose the work, to bring it forth in such a way that it itself brings forth into manifestness certain moments belonging to the expanse of self-showing. Yet the title could also be construed otherwise, the genitive reversed, so that what is designated is not only imagination as bringing forth arts (that is, artworks) but also ways in which imagination could be taken up or deployed, ways not necessarily restricted to the fine arts, even if never without a certain intrinsic connection to the arts.

But suppose that, for the moment, consideration is restricted to the fine arts in order to remonstrate more precisely the character of the artwork as a composition. What is it, then, that is composed, what are the moments that are put together, so as to bring forth an artwork? And how are these moments put together, by what kind of bond, through what kind of operation? As an operation into which imagination enters, as an operation that is primarily *of* imagination, it can be nothing other than a drawing. In the composing of the artwork, the force of imagination comes to draw the lines

---

15. See Nancy, *Les Muses,* 13.

and figure of the work, the lines and figure that belong to its very constitution as a work. It is especially in coming to draw the lines and figure of the work that imagination is poetic.

Yet the lines and figure—the very kind of lines and figure—differ enormously from one art to another. For the lines and figure must be drawn on some surface or in some medium and with a stylus appropriate to that surface or medium. And yet, to designate merely as *surface* or *medium* that on or in which the lines and figure are drawn does not suffice to delimit this moment of the artwork. Thus, a sense needs to be engendered that exceeds that of surface or medium, a sense appropriate to the imaginal drawing that is to be traced on it and secured in it. This exorbitant sense can perhaps begin to be heard in the word *matrix*, oriented to signify a place where something is brought forth or developed but also protected, held, sheltered, a place like the womb (*matrix*, linked to *mater*, also means *womb*). Or rather, only something like place, if anything can be like place. Even if in calling it place—or something like place—one would not be speaking falsely, that which *matrix* would signify is unlike what has, since Aristotle, been called place (τόπος), to say nothing of the even more remote isotropic space of modern thought; of a matrix the most secure way of speaking would perhaps lie in saying that it is a kind of place before place. Yet this is not to say—not quite—that it coincides with (a moment of) the open expanse of self-showing, of which one also will say that it is a kind of place before place. Indeed it is precisely within the difference thus marked— across this difference—that the manifestation effected by the artwork operates.

Let it be said, then, that imagination comes to draw in a certain matrix the lines and figure of the artwork. Thus it is that imagination composes the artwork, brings it forth.

And yet, can it be said that imagination composes the artwork? For surely when a painter or sculptor goes about composing a work, it is necessary not only to call upon imagination and to let it come into play but also to have and to put to use skilled hands and trained eyes. In bringing forth a work of sculpture from a block of marble, the sculptor must use hammer and chisel with the utmost dexterity and constantly in conjunction with a visual surveillance on the lookout for the sculpture as it emerges from— yet as—the marble. And yet, it is not as though the artistic imagination were some pure subjective vision above and beyond the visual-tactile-motor operation by which the artist brings forth the work. It is not a matter of a prior imaginal vision of the work that is then merely expressed, duplicated, imaged, in marble. It is not as though the artist first has in view, in the so-called mind's eye, the work itself and has then only to set it into a matrix. In that case, the *look* presented to this prior vision would have absolute priority, and one could say that this *look* is already virtually the work itself, its realization in the marble being no more than, at best, a kind of translation.

However, the artist does not bring forth the work either by imaginally envisioning it in advance or by translating into the appropriate matrix what he has already envisioned through imagination. To bring forth an artwork is neither to produce it nor to bring it about by reproducing something else already seen. Rather, the work is brought about by hands so skilled as to be capable, under the surveillance of trained and perceptive eyes, of drawing the lines and figure in the matrix, that is, of actually composing the work. When imagination comes, it does not assume the guise of a power belonging to a subject or a consciousness to be kept distinct from what has been called the body. Rather, when imagination comes, it enters precisely into the visual-tactile-motor circuit that is activated as the sculptor draws the work out from—and, hence, in—the marble. When imagination comes to the artist, it enters primarily into the hands and eyes as they are employed in bringing the work forth. If one would observe imagination itself, imagination in operation, imagination in its propriety, one could do no better than to watch the hands of a sculptor as he fashions the work.

It is distinctive of every artwork that it exhibits a certain repose. In one respect, this is a feature that it shares with everything that is made (in the broadest sense, hence including both artworks and products). Once something has been made, it is released by its maker, released from its maker, into its own self-subsistence.[16] But there is another kind of repose that is characteristic of the artwork but never displayed by mere products. The distinctive repose of an artwork lies in its spacing: an artwork does not belong to the immediate environment in which it is set, but rather it is set apart from all the ordinary things that may surround it. It is spaced in such a way that all the things that would ordinarily comprise the peripheral horizon of its apprehension are cancelled as such, though of course it is always possible to reactivate them as horizonal by adopting a stance in which one regards the work merely as a thing. To be sure, when one attends to the artwork as such, for instance, to a painting hung in a museum, one will retain one's marginal vision of the wall surrounding the painting, but at the same time the painting will be spaced in such a way as to be itself utterly apart from the surrounding wall, cancelling all pertinence that the surroundings might otherwise have to it. It is this repose, this peculiar spacing, this apartness, that is confirmed and marked when one places a painting in a frame or performs a drama on stage.

One could say that the artwork bears its own locus. It is not a matter of

16. Even at this level, Kandinsky traces out significant consequences: "In a mysterious, puzzling, mystical way, the true work of art arises 'from out of the artist.' Once released from him, it assumes an independent life, takes on a personality, and becomes an independent, spiritually breathing subject, which also leads a real material life, which is a *being* [*ein* Wesen]" (Kandinsky, *Über das Geistige in der Kunst*, 132). Kandinsky repeatedly stresses the necessity of attending to the independent, inner life of the painting itself, the life lived out, as it were, in and through the colors and forms.

setting it into a place that would then be its own, but rather it is its own place, no matter where it is set. Even in the case of an architectural work, for instance, a building (an ancient temple or a modern skyscraper) that gives orientation, directionality, and specific significance to the entire region around it, such spacing, such repose, remains in force: only because the building is set apart from all the things around it can it give orientation, directionality, and significance to those things and to the entire region.

In the artwork the matrix does not disappear, as the material of a piece of equipment, for instance, disappears by being assimilated to the equipment's use-function.[17] It is thus that equipment must be given its place, assigned a place, whereas, at the moment it is released or performed, the artwork is its own place. Indeed it is precisely because a matrix is a kind of place before place that the artwork, arising through drawing in a matrix, bears its own place.

It would be tempting to suppose that the matrix consists of what could be called material, even, in some cases, at least, of earthly material. This supposition can be sustained only within limits, only if supplemented in a way that cannot but lead to its utter mutation; for it is manifest that, within the work itself, the spacing of repose effects a mutation of the "material" that renders it otherwise than mere material—assuming that one could determine with precision what constitutes material, what material is as such, that one could determine it otherwise than by recourse to some reductive concept of ὕλη. But if one begins with the supposition merely as an opening toward the eventual mutation, then one will say that the sculptor takes as matrix such "materials" as stone, wood, steel, etc. These and others will be taken as matrix by the architect. In both cases, though in very different ways, the imagination of the artist (that is, the imagination that comes to inhabit the eyes, hands, etc. of the artist) draws in the matrix certain lines and figures, shaping and assembling the "material" in the appropriate way. Correspondingly, one will say perhaps that the painter takes the canvas, this "material," as matrix, though one will at once need also to distinguish from the mere canvas, which could not constitute a matrix for painting, the canvas as a surface of/for color, as a surface of/for shades (in the very broadest sense).[18] At the very least, one would, then, have granted that the matrix is both material and spacing, though such simple conjunction remains inadequate. In the reference to color and shades, one would also have intimated how the very constitution of the matrix already orients it to a certain way of drawing; it is this orientation that is confirmed in deed by the artist's first draft, which always consists in drawing forth the matrix. In the case of some arts, one will be less tempted to suppose that the matrix consists of some material: consider how dance draws its lines and figures in

---

17. See Heidegger, "Der Ursprung des Kunstwerkes," in *Holzwege*, vol. 5 of *Gesamtausgabe*, 32.
18. See my discussion in *Shades — Of Painting at the Limit*, 1–21.

the human itself as a mobile, gestural being. One will say that the matrix of music is sound, though it is never just sound as such, but the sound of the human voice or of certain instruments or even so-called electronic sounds; for there is no sound as such, no mere acoustical material, but—except perhaps to an extremely abstract disposition—only the sound of something or other. Poetry requires not just vocal sound but articulable vocal sound in which can be figured what is called sense—figured in such a way that there is balance between sound and sense. In the (translated) words of the poet Paul Valéry: "You will find that with each verse the signification produced within you, far from destroying the musical form communicated to you, calls this form back again. The living pendulum that has swung from *sound* to *sense* swings back to its sensible point of departure, as though the very sense offered to your spirit can find no other outlet or expression, no other response, than the very music that gave it birth."[19] In general, it is not because artworks are composed of earthly material that they can be disclosive of the elemental earth but rather because they are so composed as to bring to manifestness the expanse of self-showing to which the earth elementally belongs. This is why things as remote from earth as the steel, glass, and concrete of a modern skyscraper or the sounds of Mahler's *Das Lied von der Erde* can nonetheless disclose the elemental earth.

Just as the matrix exceeds and even diverges from what is called material, likewise the drawing of lines and figures in the matrix exceeds and even diverges from drawing in the ordinary sense, which, though indeed itself an art, is limited to drawing lines and figures of a certain kind on a surface. It is primarily from the indefinite plurality of matrices that the question of the plurality of arts would need to be developed, though one could not for long avoid reference also to the peculiar drawing appropriate to each matrix and implicated in it as matrix. Because there is no matrix as such but only the matrix of this art or that art, there is no art as such but only various arts, a singular plural of art. This singular plural is peculiarly indefinite. Because there are various matrices, there are various arts; and though these matrices (and, hence, the corresponding arts) are for the most part heterogeneous with respect to each other, there are various arts that can nonetheless be mixed with others, as poetry and pictorial presentation are mixed in theatre or, for example—since here one is "most in need of examples"[20]—as Mendelssohn's exquisite music is mixed with Shakespeare's *A Midsummer Night's Dream*.[21] There is also variation among possible matrices: some prove more suited to an imaginal drawing from which issue art-

---

19. Paul Valéry, "Poésie et Pensée Abstraite," in *Oeuvres* (Pléiade) (Paris: Gallimard, 1957), 1:1332. An aphorism from the Notebooks (16:908) reads: "*The sound of a meaning and the meaning of a sound. Poetry!*"

20. Kant, *Kritik der Urteilskraft*, 283.

21. See my "Mixed Arts," in *Proceedings of the Eighth International Kant Congress,* ed. Hoke Robinson (Milwaukee: Marquette University Press, 1995), 1.3:1093–1104.

works that either more expansively or with greater intensity turn manifestation upon itself and its very space. On this basis a differentiation becomes possible between major arts and minor arts.

One could also resume the classical determination of beauty as the most shining (τὸ ἐκφανέστατον), since in the drafted matrix the merely sensible would be transfigured into sheer shining, a shining that would no longer be the shining of some thing, hence, in this sense, the most shining. In the character of the artwork as apart from the ordinary, as in repose, one could sense a certain resonance with the other character that the Platonic determination attributes to the beautiful: as most lovely (ἐρασμιώτατον),[22] the artwork is enrapturing. It transports one beyond the ordinary and to that extent beyond oneself—precisely through the captivating charm of its shining.

But how is it that the artwork, issuing from a drawing in a matrix, discloses the open expanse of self-showing? To be sure, it is decisive in this connection that imagination comes, as poetic, to redraft—but now in a matrix and through oblique repetition—the lines and figures that, as tractive, it will always already have drawn in opening the expanse. But it is equally decisive that these lines and figures are drawn *in a matrix*, which is not just material but also—in a way that makes it quite other than so-called material—a kind of place before place. As such, the matrix replicates what could perhaps best be called a kind of nature before nature, a kind of holding sway of the elemental antecedent to its coming to hold sway through the advent of elemental imagination. Such replication cannot be a matter of mimesis, for in this case what is replicated is not a being, not something that could be represented. Except perhaps in a dream, perhaps in a daydream of it as the place of all places, still, then, not as truly underlying nature. But in composing the artwork, in drawing lines and figure in the matrix, the artist—if not just as himself—reenacts the drawing of nature from which issues the open expanse of all self-showing.

Imagination can be otherwise deployed. Or rather, a certain impoverishment of imagination can come about, and the result can even be mistaken for imagination itself in its highest possibilities. When poetic imagination ceases to be poetic, it becomes mere imagining. This occurs, specifically, when the drawing is withdrawn from every matrix, when it ceases to bring about a draft in stone, on the shadable surface of a canvas, or in the sound of a voice. It becomes what one might call, in a very restricted sense of the word, a free drawing: lacking a matrix in which figuration could bring to manifestness some moment of the expanse of manifestation, imagining loses all connection with self-showing as such. In contrast

---

22. "Now for the beautiful alone this has been ordained, to be most shining forth and most lovely [νῦν δὲ κάλλος μόνον ταύτην ἔσχε μοῖραν, ὥστ᾽ ἐκφανέστατον εἶναι καὶ ἐρασμιώτατον]" (Plato, *Phaedrus* 250d–e).

to the disclosive artwork, it can only summon up mere phantoms (φάν-τασμα), capable, at the most, of functioning only as pale images of things, images that do not shine, images in which nothing present shines forth, images sustained by little more than the spacing that keeps them apart from the expanses of self-showing things.[23] It is hardly surprising that the disclosive force that imagination brought to phenomenology proved para-doxical insofar as the phenomenology of imagination remained a phenom-enology of imagining.

One will need, instead, to offer—to have offered—a site to poetic imagi-nation and to venture a response, engendering whatever sense one can, now, at the limit. The affinity with art should further rather than hinder the venture, though, despite all the possibilities opened for engendering sense through recourse to the arts, especially to poetry, it is an affinity from a distance that must always also be secured. But, like the poet, one who would philosophize at the limit must always hope—since one cannot simply begin—that imagination will have come. And seek to attest to its coming.

---

23. See *Double Truth*, 123.

ENGLISH INDEX

GREEK INDEX

JOHN SALLIS

is Edwin Erle Sparks Professor of Philosophy at The Pennsylvania State University. His previous books include *Phenomenology and the Return to Beginnings; Being and Logos: Reading the Platonic Dialogues; The Gathering of Reason; Delimitations: Phenomenology and the End of Metaphysics; Spacings — Of Reason and Imagination; Echoes: After Heidegger; Crossings: Nietzsche and the Space of Tragedy; Stone; Double Truth; Shades — Of Painting at the Limit;* and *Chorology: On Beginning in Plato's "Timaeus."*